CW01084118

The Fall of the Seleukid Empire 187–75 BC

The Fall of the Seleukid Empire 187–75 BC

John D. Grainger

Pen & Sword
MILITARY

First published in Great Britain in 2015 and reprinted in 2021 by
Pen & Sword Military
an imprint of
Pen & Sword Books Ltd
47 Church Street
Barnsley
South Yorkshire
S70 2AS

ISBN 978 1 78303 030 9

Typeset in Ehrhardt by
Mac Style Ltd, Bridlington, East Yorkshire

Printed and bound in the UK by CPI Group (UK) Ltd,
Croydon, CRO 4YY

Pen & Sword Books Ltd incorporates the imprints of Pen & Sword
Archaeology, Atlas, Aviation, Battleground, Discovery, Family
History, History, Maritime, Military, Naval, Politics, Railways,
Select, Transport, True Crime, and Fiction, Frontline Books, Leo
Cooper, Praetorian Press, Seaforth Publishing and Wharncliffe.

For a complete list of Pen & Sword titles please contact
PEN & SWORD BOOKS LIMITED
47 Church Street, Barnsley, South Yorkshire, S70 2AS, England
E-mail: enquiries@pen-and-sword.co.uk
Website: www.pen-and-sword.co.uk

Contents

Maps and Tables		vi
Introduction		x
Chapter 1	The Beginning of the End (187–170 BC)	1
Chapter 2	The Wars of Antiochos Epiphanes (170–164 BC)	16
Chapter 3	The Advent of Demetrios I (164–159 BC)	36
Chapter 4	The Problems of Demetrios I (160–150 BC)	50
Chapter 5	The Destruction of Alexander Balas (150–145 BC)	66
Chapter 6	The Travails of Demetrios II (145–138 BC)	77
Chapter 7	The New Seleukid Kingdom (139–131 BC)	88
Chapter 8	Defeat (131–129 BC)	106
Chapter 9	Dynastic Conflict (129–121 BC)	116
Chapter 10	The Kingdom Failing (121–108 BC)	136
Chapter 11	Destruction in the South (108–96 BC)	151
Chapter 12	Survival in the North (103–88 BC)	166
Chapter 13	The End of the Seleukids (88–75 BC)	181
Conclusion – The Seleukid Legacy		200
Notes and References		208
Abbreviations		227
Bibliography		228
Index		232

Maps and Tables

Maps

Syria and Palestine   vii

The Seleukid Regions   viii

Table

The Later Seleukid Dynasty   ix

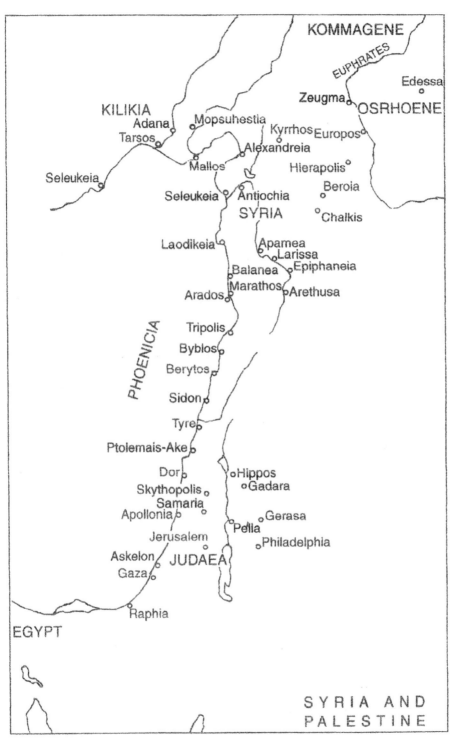

Syria and Palestine.

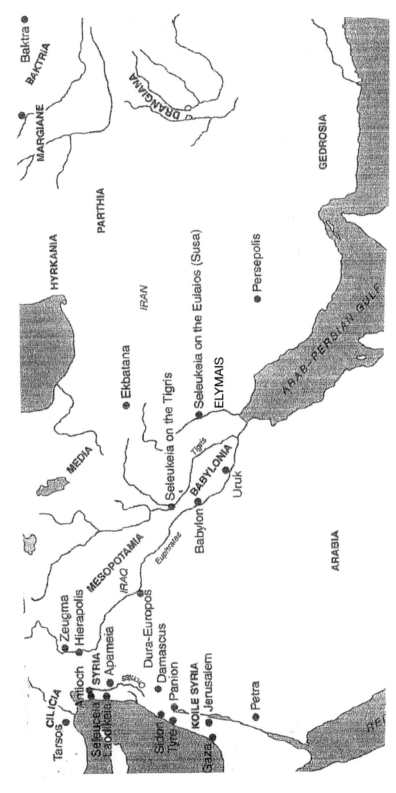

The Seleukid Regions.

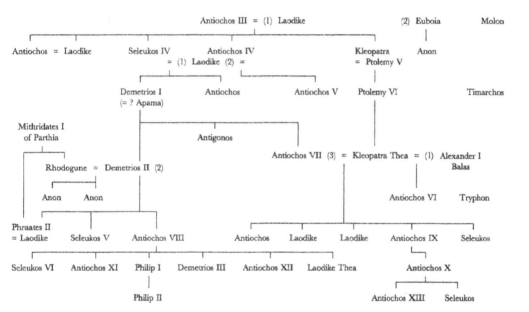

The Later Seleukid Dynasty.

Introduction

The Seleukid kingdom was a permanent and powerful fixture on the international landscape of the Hellenistic world for a century and a half before it suffered serious political damage. Even the removal of Asia Minor in 190 and Baktria in the 250s from its control had not caused much real reduction in its power, for Asia Minor had been held only temporarily and the Baktrian area was far distant from the centre of events and had always been semi-independent. But from 150 BC onwards, as can be seen retrospectively, the kingdom was clearly in decline, though it took another generation for this to become wholly clear to contemporaries.

This decline was an event which had been devoutly wished-for by the kingdom's numerous enemies, and it is not obvious which of the many enemies or other issues may be assigned to the primary cause. The kingdom was, of course, hardly unique in being surrounded by enemies, and it certainly took those enemies a long time to destroy it. So some responsibility may be claimed by those neighbours: the Ptolemaic kingdom in Egypt, with which the Seleukid kings fought a long series of wars for two centuries; the Parthian kingdom, which nibbled away at its territories in Iran and the east; the Roman Republic, which in fact only turned up at the last minute to snatch a choice morsel; even the Armenian kingdom in the north, and the Arabs in the desert – all of these had some part to play in bringing the kingdom to an end. But none of them can be said to have struck the fatal blow, unless it be Armenia and the Roman Republic, who successively seized its last territories, though only after it had been reduced to a minimal size.

A more convincing case for the kingdom's failure has been seen in its internal affairs, in particular in the civil wars which were generated by competition within the royal family, and in the rebellions and insurrections by communities aiming at some sort of independence from royal control. The problem with such explanations is that these disputes and these communities had existed from the beginning of the state, so an explanation has to be found to why these particular elements became toxic in the period after 150 BC.

Of course, no one would suppose that locating a single cause for the disappearance of a long-lived state could provide a satisfactory explanation for its demise. We are all accustomed to multiple causes of such disasters (and for many of the inhabitants of the kingdom its replacement by Roman and Parthian rule was a distinct change for the worse, certainly in the two or three generations after the conquests). It has been, however, normal to select a major cause, and so to relegate the rest to minor or contributory status. Rome has always been a favourite cause of the kingdom's destruction, and so have the civil wars. The Jews have been cast as villains or heroes, depending on one's point of view. What has not been done is to consider the matter whole, and from both the Seleukid point of view and that of its enemies.

The existing discussions of the reasons for the fall of the Seleukid kingdom are few, and, by now, old. The two main accounts of the history of the kingdom, by Bevan[1] and by Bouche-Leclercq[2] both date from before the Great War, and a good deal of work has been done on the kingdom since then – and even they scarcely provide an intelligible account of the end. Bevan, for instance, consigned the last two generations to a single chapter entitled 'The Last Convulsions', thereby simultaneously implying a terminal illness and avoiding a serious investigation. Since then the major work has been numismatic, by Bellinger in an obscure journal,[3] which has now been largely superseded by a comprehensive, if often indecisive, coin catalogue by Arthur Houghton and his team.[4] Yet this is hardly an adequate account of what must be seen as a major geopolitical development in world history, one which is comparable to the collapse of the Parthian power in the third century AD, and even of the fall of Rome in the fifth, or of the Arab conquests in the seventh century.

Other considerations of Seleukid history, a subject which has revived somewhat in recent years, have concentrated more on particular aspects of it, or on particular regions. So my own contribution has been on the cities of Syria, while three recent books have looked at 'Syrian identity', the governing elites of the kingdom, and 'space, territory and ideology'[5] or have dissected the kingdom, either as separate chapters, or as separate articles, without providing a full overall examination of its history.[6]

The several causes which have been suggested for its fall all have a degree of plausibility about them, though no single one can be assigned the dominant role. So the first thing to be done will be to consider the situation of the kingdom in the period preceding the beginning of the final Seleukid collapse, which I take to begin about 150 BC, and to have become irreversible from 129 BC. This period therefore (150–129) is the crucial one. Such a consideration may indicate just what influence each had in the generation or so preceding that collapse.

There is, however, even before detailing these elements, a preliminary comment to be made, to set the Seleukid kingdom's fall in to some sort of context. The extinction of states in the Hellenistic world was by no means an unusual phenomenon. In many cases it was due to annexation by the Roman Republic, so that Roman power gradually spread south and east at the expense of such well established states as Carthage, Syracuse, Macedon, the Attalid kingdom, Bithynia, and others. The Ptolemaic kingdom had also done its part in this, by annexing the Cyrenaican and Cypriot kingdoms. So these states were by no means as well established as their age might suggest. By contrast the Seleukid state was fissiparous, shedding sections which became new states rather than absorbing them, and even in victory it tended to impose supremacy, not direct annexation. This is one aspect which also needs to be considered. That is, the Seleukid kingdom was different.

Annexation is one method of removing states, but disruption from within was much less usual. Epeiros disintegrated in 231, when, by abolishing the monarchy, its constituent communities reverted to the separated political condition they had enjoyed before the monarchic unification. Macedon, by contrast, was deliberately broken up by the Roman Republic in 167, but reunited itself twenty years later when a plausible royal pretender popped up. The Romans gave in, removed the pretender, and then annexed the kingdom as a now reunited whole and made it a province. If one is keeping score, therefore, extinction by annexation is twice as likely as internal collapse.

The procedure here, therefore, will be to consider the apparent disruptive and inimical forces acting on the Seleukid kingdom in the first half of the second century BC (which is also the second half of the kingdom's existence), then to look at the kingdom's period of disruption in the third quarter of the second century, and finally to look at the kingdom's final half century or so, to see which of these forces, if any, still had influence. For one aspect which is generally ignored is the fact that even after the disasters of the period 150–129, the kingdom lasted for two more generations (129–75) as a local state, and that this was centred on North Syria, a wealthy land which later became one of the most important regions of the Roman Empire. It was rich and populous enough to have continued to exist as an independent state; why did it not?

Chapter 1

The Beginning of the End (187–170 BC)

T he kingdom which King Seleukos IV inherited on the death of his father in Iran in mid-187 was large, wealthy, and powerful. It was, however, faced with major problems. The death of Antiochos III cannot have been altogether a surprise, though no doubt it was unexpected, and after a long reign, a shock: he had been king for thirty-five years, longer than any other king of his dynasty; he was relatively old at fifty-six for his time, while he repeatedly exposed himself to danger in war. His death occurred in the process of attempting to seize a treasure from a temple in Elymais, an action to which the local people quite reasonably objected.

He died in the middle of an expedition into the eastern parts of his kingdom, where a delicate diplomatic arrangement he had made twenty years before had recently broken down. The kingdoms of the Parthians and the Baktrians had recently acquired new kings, and so they were no longer tied by diplomatic treaties to Antiochos. His purpose in marching to the east was, it may be conjectured, to restore the situation by making a new arrangement with the new kings. The treaties of peace which he wanted to renew with the new kings had lasted only until the death of one of the parties, and the deaths of Euthydemos I of Baktria about 200 BC, and of Arsakes II of the Parthians about 190 BC were the triggers for the new expedition.

The death of Antiochos himself had also ended the peace treaties with several western powers. The peace of Raphia with Ptolemaic Egypt, agreed in 195 and ratified by the marriage of Antiochos' daughter Kleopatra to Ptolemy V would probably hold, since Ptolemy was fully occupied in combatting a major rebellion within Egypt. (The marriage did not constitute a political alliance: no such arrangement in the Hellenistic international system maintained peace.) There was also a peace treaty with the Attalid kingdom in Asia Minor, which was now also ended, though King Eumenes II was, like Ptolemy, hardly going to use the freedom from the treaty to attack the Seleukid kingdom, since he was fully occupied in ensuring his control over the territories he had recently been awarded, at Antiochos' expense, within Asia Minor. His neighbours in Bithynia to his north and Kappadokia to the east were unhappy at Eumenes' sudden growth in power; Eumenes was in fact at war more or less continuously between 187 and 179.

But the main peace treaty which came to an end with Antiochos' death was that with the Roman Republic. This was a power which had, during Antiochos' lifetime, expanded from controlling peninsular Italy to holding all the western Mediterranean lands and dominating Greece and Macedonia. It had defeated in succession three rival great powers, Carthage, Macedon, and Antiochos III himself. By 187 the Romans were the superpower of the Mediterranean political system, more powerful than any single state within range, and probably more powerful than any combination of its rivals. The republic's failure to expand its direct control east of the Adriatic Sea was no doubt puzzling to contemporaries, but also relieving, and was probably due to the frontier problems in Spain and Italy. The military reach of the Roman army was in fact limited: the expedition against Antiochos had required some delicate diplomacy in Greece to allow its forces to move further east, which might not be possible again – and the Seleukid kingdom was now even more remote than before. These rivals were all able to relax their vigilance as a result of Roman forbearance, at least for the time being, but the spectre of Rome certainly hovered over all of them.

This was, from the new king's point of view, an encouraging vista, but the present inability of his neighbours to launch an attack on his kingdom would not necessarily last very long. Above all, once Ptolemy V put down the Egyptian rebellion he would be free to attempt to recover Palestine and Phoenicia – Koile Syria – from Seleukid control – and by 187 the rebellion was almost finished. Seleukos had to be vigilant.

Seleukos IV had been made joint king along with Antiochos III several years earlier (on the death of his elder brother), and was a well experienced commander and ruler.[1] However, as the preceding paragraphs will have suggested, he faced a difficult situation on his accession to sole rule. The complex web of peace agreements his father had constructed had fallen apart as soon as the news of his death spread. This had one advantage, in that the restrictive and expensive clauses of the Roman treaty – payment of 12,000 talents of silver over ten years, abandonment of a navy and of the war elephants – were no longer applicable and so not a drain on resources. On the other hand, suddenly every neighbour – Egypt, the Attalids, Rome, Parthia, Baktria – was at least potentially hostile.

The major change was in the west. It was quite possible that Rome would act to enforce the terms of the treaty with Antiochos III. The Senate had twice in the last half-century declared war on Carthage, or rejected a negotiated treaty, in order to obtain better terms, and demanding that Seleukos negotiate a new agreement would be much the same. As it turned out, on this occasion the Senate apparently did nothing. It is possible that Seleukos paid some of the instalments – Antiochos will have paid one or two by the time he died, plus the initial 2,500 talents indemnity in 189, but by the end of Seleukos' reign, by which time all should have been paid according to the treaty, he was well in arrears. (If Antiochos had paid two instalments, each would have been 1,200 talents; with the indemnity, Rome would already have received almost 5,000 talents – perhaps this was enough to be going on with.) One hold the Romans had on Seleukos was that his brother Antiochos was held in Rome as a guarantee of payment, though it is unlikely that this consideration weighed very heavily with Seleukos – and such a hostage was hardly useable in any real sense.

Elsewhere in the west the Egyptian rebellion was brought to an end in 186–185 with the defeat of the dissident pharaonic state in the south, and the capture of the pharaoh, and with the final suppression of the concurrent rebellion in the Delta, followed by a decree of amnesty.[2] But the rebellion had caused much damage to the country, and King Ptolemy V was a cautious man. He was urged by some of his courtiers to initiate a revenge Syrian war to recover the Palestinian and Phoenician lands lost to Antiochos in the last Syrian war, but he resisted such pressure. Nevertheless Seleukos was clearly under threat from both Rome and Egypt, neither of whom would bother to reassure him, and as a result he was unable to move far from Syria, which is where any attack would arrive.

The situation in the east was as unstable as in the west, but rather less directly threatening. The new King Demetrios I of Baktria had turned his attention to India, by which we may understand that land's north-western borderlands and the upper Indus Valley. A king called Sophagasenos had ruled in the Paropamisadai in Antiochos III's time and had been one of those with whom Antiochos had a treaty. It seems likely that either he was dead by the 190s or that Demetrios had used the freedom of manoeuvre which his father had lacked (because of the treaty) to seize Sophagasnos' kingdom. From there he was able to move into India.

This move into India meant that the aggressive Demetrios may have been seen as only a minor threat by Seleukos IV. We do not know what contacts there were between the two men, but it is possible that they came to some agreement, though even so Demetrios himself died in about 185. If they had made contact this would restrict the possible activities of the new Parthian king, Phriapatios, who succeeded his father at about the time of Demetrios' death. Parthia was boxed in on the west by the Seleukid kingdom and on the east by the Baktrians, and both of these were more powerful states than the one he ruled. Phriapatios remained quiet, so far as we can see, for his whole reign. On the other hand he did adopt the title of King, the first of his dynasty to do so, according to his coins.[3] This may have implied that he had achieved some notable military victory, for this was the usual necessary preliminary to such a claim, though who he fought is not known.

There was real trouble in Susiana, or perhaps in Elymais, which was where Antiochos had been killed. A fragmentary record dated to 183 notes that the Governor of Susa was involved in some way with enemies.[4] There is no more information in the note than this bare fact but it was surely part of the aftermath of Antiochos' attempted raid on the temple in Elymais. Trouble of some sort was very likely to reverberate locally for a long time, especially since the king had been defeated and killed. Local pride was considerably boosted by such a victory.

Internationally, therefore, Seleukos seemed to be trapped, but not under immediate threat. He was unable to move to the east, as his father had begun to do, because of the latent threat in the west, though it may well be that he made contact with the Baktrian king – though Demetrios' early death will have meant that any treaty made with him would have to be renegotiated with his successor. Demetrios' move against India had been relieving to the Seleukid king, even if it was unpleasant for the Indians. In the west Seleukos was faced with hostility from the Romans and Egypt which immobilized him. Only, as it turned out, in Asia Minor did he have some room for manoeuvre.

The threat to be apprehended was military, though it would probably be preceded by hostile diplomacy. The hostility of Ptolemy V could be taken as read, but a straight military contest with Egypt was unlikely to result in defeat – unless Egypt was assisted by another, and equally hostile, power. In this the continuing association of the Attalid kingdom with Rome was the main Seleukid problem, since simultaneous attacks from south and north would be militarily disastrous. The Seleukid military power was not great enough to withstand such an assault, when combined with the need to stand on guard in the east, and to garrison the many provinces. That is, the Seleukid kingdom was militarily overstretched (as it always had been). The solution was to remain quiet, provoking no one, or to be assertive and see off one enemy at a time. Seleukos chose the first option, having seen his aggressive father suffer ultimate defeat.

This does not mean, however, that Seleukos did nothing. It was incumbent on him from the moment he succeeded as sole king, to be active diplomatically wherever possible in order to secure his kingdom by deflecting any political enemies. As early as 187, and so in the second part of the year (for Antiochos

III died in June) he sent an embassy to meet the Achaian assembly with an offer of ten warships and a request for either an alliance or at least a statement of friendship. Polybios says it was to be 'a renewal of alliance', but there is no evidence of any earlier alliance so it was perhaps a renewal of the peace, for Antiochos and the Achaian League had been on opposing sides in Antiochos' war with Rome, and therefore they will have made peace at the time of Antiochos' treaty with Rome in 188.

The Achaians, wary of gifts from kings who were at enmity with Rome, accepted the renewal of the treaty, but refused the ships.[5] Seleukos may thus be said to have achieved a useful diplomatic success. Achaia was the most powerful single state in Greece, now that Aitolia had been crushed by Rome, and that Philip V of Macedon had been confined to his kingdom. On the other hand, Achaia's actual power was minimal; the treaty was thus of little use in the power game, though useful in the less helpful area of public opinion. It also lined both states up against Eumenes of Pergamon, who had made the offer of a gift of the island of Aegina, and had also been rejected.

Seleukos' envoys also visited Athens in 186, possibly the same men who had been to Achaia, possibly a separate embassy; but Athens was another useful place for influencing public opinion within Greece.[6] The two embassies add up to a careful, perhaps insidious, diplomatic assault on the solidarity of the Roman position in Greece; Seleukos could also point out that he was no longer bound by the limitations of his father's treaty with Rome.

A neglected aspect of this diplomatic campaign is the ten warships, and a consideration of what the offer meant will provide a way to discuss the actual enforcement, or otherwise, of the terms of the Treaty of Apamaea. In that treaty Antiochos III had been permitted to possess no more than ten triremes, and was to be prevented from sailing any of them west of Cape Sarpedon in Kilikia. It is evident that Antiochos had made no attempt to reduce his navy to the treaty level, and Seleukos quite openly offered some of the ships he had inherited to Achaia. He will scarcely have offered to give away his last ten ships, so it is all but certain that he had many more than that – and that they had been inherited from his father. That is, Antiochos III had made little or no effort to comply with the naval articles of the treaty, and it is therefore likely that other elements of the treaty had been similarly ignored – the prohibition on keeping war elephants, for example. Others of the provisions of the treaty were also never implemented – including the requirement to surrender five named individuals, at least two of whom were politically active in later years. It may also be pointed out that Rome made no attempt to oversee the implementation of the treaty. It is likely that the good sources of this period of Seleukos' rule – Livy and much of Polybios – would have included any references to any embassies sent to check in Syria on the numbers of warships and elephants there, but there is nothing. Either Rome did not care, or it was understood that when Antiochos III died the treaty lapsed.

Eumenes of Pergamon was involved in a succession of wars in Asia Minor from 186 onwards, first fighting off an attack by King Prusias of Bithynia, then against King Pharnakes of Pontos. Neither of these kings really measured up to the Attalid kingdom in terms of military power, and it is likely that they were at least encouraged and possibly directly helped by allies. Prusias was the brother-in-law of Philip V of Macedon, who was a long-time enemy of the Attalid kings; Pharnakes was Seleukos' uncle (the brother of his mother) and this may have contributed to Seleukos' near-intervention on the Pontic side in the war.

The war was fought between 183 and c.179, and until the end it was going Pharnakes' way. Eumenes three times asked for Roman help but only received ineffective visits by delegations of senators, all of which Pharnakes either ignored or rebuffed.[7] It was therefore only after Eumenes realized that he would have to fight his own battles that he organized an army and took the offensive, in the end successfully defeating Pharnakes, whose pretensions subsided as a result.[8] At some point in all this Seleukos gathered an army and marched it towards the Taurus passes, though he went no further than the approach march.

This episode is recorded only in undated items on Diodoros and Polybios.[9] One of these refers to an offer to Seleukos by Pharnakes of 500 talents. Diodoros claims that Seleukos called off the expedition because he recalled the terms of his father's Roman treaty. These have then been linked to suggest that Seleukos was bribed by Pharnakes to intervene, but then 'lost his nerve'. The problem here is that Seleukos is regarded with general contempt by modern historians, who believe that he should have been much more active. A Seleukid king who was not on some campaign is derided as 'lazy' or 'weak'.[10] Yet when he actually takes some action he is accused of 'losing his nerve'. It is better to investigate in more detail.

A less derogatory interpretation would accept that the 500 talents subsidy was intended to pay Seleukos' expenses; if he took the bait and intervened actively in the war it is likely that Pharnakes would have won; the Attalid forces were not likely to withstand Seleukos' army for long. But such an intervention by the Seleukid king would put Pharnakes under a serious obligation to his nephew, so he would not be likely to ask for such help until he was in a clear danger of defeat, and that was not until the last months of the war, either towards the end of 180 or early in 179.

It was in 179, in all probability, that Eumenes finally won his war, and imposed a peace treaty. The end was sudden, for Pharnakes had been fighting only weak opponents until then, and as soon as he was defeated his allies fell away. It is perhaps at this point that Seleukos' expedition was called off. This was not because of the terms of his father's treaty – which, apart from being inoperative after his death, did not say anything about military expeditions into Asia Minor – nor because he 'lost his nerve', but most likely because he found that Pharnakes, the man he was marching to help, had been so badly defeated that he had given up the struggle. It may be, in fact, that the difficulty of marching an army through the Taurus passes was one of the factors involved, for the passes were usually blocked by snow in the winter. (It may also be that the prospect of Seleukos intervening speeded up Eumenes' own campaign, where Roman talks had failed to.) The peace which ended the war was made some time fairly early in 179, so it was likely that Eumenes will have known of Seleukos' preparations and intentions, and so finally decided to fight in order to pre-empt a Seleukid march and intervention.

From 180 onwards major changes were under way in several of the states when ordered the Seleukid kingdom. In that year Ptolemy V was murdered in a court conspiracy by a group of courtiers. He had been pressed yet again to launch a Syrian war. He gave what was probably his usual non-committal answer, that he was thinking about the matter, but was then asked where he would find the resources for such a war; he pointed to the wealthy men at the court and described them as his moneybags.[11] The prospect of being taxed to pay for a new war was sufficient to frighten some of them into killing the king. He is said to have been poisoned, but that is a type of death which was all too easily confused with other and natural causes, so the accusation of murder must be held to be not proved.

The king's death nonetheless did delay any attempt at the recovery of Syria. At the same time, the murder of the king, supposing it is accurately reported, would suggest he was seriously considering the prospect of a new Syrian war. Ptolemy's widow, Kleopatra Syra (Seleukos' sister) became regent for her children; she was unlikely to attack Syria, not because of her relationship with Seleukos, but because a regency was always an unsteady political base for foreign action; she needed her full attention on matters in Egypt, and the (probable) murder of her husband only demonstrated that necessity.

The next year, 179, Philip V of Macedon died. His court had been upset recently by the execution of Demetrios, his son, but in the event, he was succeeded smoothly enough by another son, Perseus. Almost at once Seleukos' daughter Laodike was betrothed to the new king, an arrangement which was so rapidly concluded that it may well have been in train already before Philip died. As already noted, such dynastic marriages are no real indication of political alignments in the long run, but at the time they were agreed and carried out it may be assumed that the two kings were at least politically in agreement.

This connection was not in the least surprising. The two royal houses had frequently intermarried in the past and in the 180s and 170s they were both at enmity with Eumenes (and in a more muffled way, with Rome). In fact, Eumenes was surrounded by enemies – Bithynia, Pontos, Kappadokia, Seleukos, Rhodes, Achaia, Macedon. No wonder he appealed to Rome for help whenever he was threatened. The Romans provided no military help, but the constant despatch of senatorial delegations made it clear to all that Eumenes was their man. So the Seleukid-Antigonid alignment was less than an alliance, but more than a mere distant friendship. The marriage was celebrated by a naval procession, in which ships of Rhodes carried the bridal party from Syria to Macedon, with great publicity.[12] The ring around Eumenes was further strengthened when Perseus' sister was married to Prusias II, who had succeeded his father as king in Bithynia about 182.[13]

In none of this – Egypt's ambitions or Seleukos' diplomacy – was any heed being paid to Roman views. This is not to say that Rome was not interested in what was going on. Apart from the various embassies sent to Asia Minor in vain attempts to sort out the war there (but nonetheless showing Roman support for Eumenes), a major embassy led by T. Quinctius Flamininus went to the area in 183; he was probably accompanied by two other senators, though their names are not provided. He had been part of an embassy to Achaia a little earlier, accompanied by Q. Caecilius Metellus and Ap. Claudius Pulcher,[14] and it would be most economical to assume that it was these men who went on to see Prusias with him. They, or he, also went on to visit Seleukos, or so it is said.[15] There is, however, no indication of what he or they did on this embassy, which suggests that they did nothing worth noting (other than encouraging the suicide of Hannibal); indeed it is not even certain that Flamininus reached Seleukos.

The one item in which Rome and Seleukos were mutually involved during his reign was the exchange of Seleukos' brother Antiochos for his son Demetrios as 'hostage' at Rome. 'Hostage' is probably the wrong word, since there is no indication that any threat whatever was made against either while at Rome, or that their presence at Rome had any effect on Seleukos or his policies. Antiochos had been sent to the city in 189 as part of the guarantee for the peace settlement and had stayed on there, clearly from his later life and preferences, quite happily. Rome at some point demanded or requested that he be changed for Demetrios – or it may be that Seleukos decided to swap the two.[16] In theory Demetrios was the more valuable of the two as a hostage, since he was the son of the reigning king, but it seems that the original choice of Antiochos had been Rome's at a time when he was the heir presumptive after Seleukos, and before Antiochos III's death. In the event, the change proved to be immaterial, since events took a different course than expected.

It was, of course, possible for Seleukos to refuse the Roman demand, but there was no point in such an antagonistic gesture; also it would be useful for a future king to have experience of Rome and to make friendly contacts with important Romans. Seleukos had another son available to succeed him if Demetrios was detained or died. Seleukos did not know, of course, that he would be himself dead in a couple of years. It is worth emphasizing that neither Seleukos nor his successor seems to have been constrained in any way in their policies or actions by the absence of either hostage in Roman hands.

Demetrios' name has occasioned speculation that he was named to emphasize Seleukos' connection with Macedon, where, it is suggested, the name was known in the royal family, and so the transfer of the name was a diplomatic gesture.[17] The point about the Macedonian royal name is quite correct, but it is beyond belief that Seleukos was conducting a sort of megaphone diplomacy by naming his son in such a way. In fact, the names Antiochos and Seleukos were not the only ones in use in the Seleukid family; the eldest son of Seleukos II had been named Alexander, though he took the throne name Seleukos on his succession; a son of Antiochos III was named Mithradates for his Pontic grandfather; later Philip became a royal name in the family. The name Demetrios was also used in the Seleukid family, as the father of Stratonike, the wife of Seleukos I and Antiochos I, and as the husband of Stratonike the sister of Seleukos II. The choice of Demetrios as a royal name is not to be endowed with any diplomatic significance. It may have been intended that, like Alexander/Seleukos III, he would take up one of the traditional throne names when he succeeded.

The changes in the royal families of the western states further reduced the possibilities of a serious attack being made on the Seleukid state. Macedon was both friendly and distant; Rome was clearly not interested in events east of Pergamon; Egypt after 180 was in the hands of Queen Kleopatra as regent for her three infant children, and she was unlikely, after the apparent death of the king at the hands of those who did not wish to launch a new Syrian war, to initiate such a war. In the east, also, Demetrios I of Baktria was now dead, and it seems that one of his legacies was a divided monarchy; it seems that several kings now ruled simultaneously at this time and that Baktria was politically divided. In Parthia Phriapatios still ruled, perhaps until about 170, but as the third generation from the inception of the Arsakid dynasty in 247, he was probably now old; certainly he did not begin any hostilities that we know of.

In 176, however, Kleopatra Syra died. She left three children, two Ptolemies and a Kleopatra. The eldest boy had been technically king since his father died, but he was still too young to rule. The condition of the court meant that none of the more prominent members of the aristocracy was prepared to be regent in Kleopatra's place – or it may be that none of them would allow one of their fellows to rise so far. However it was, two obscure bureaucrats were put in place, Lenaios, a former slave from Syria, and Eulaios, a eunuch who had been Ptolemy VI's nurse. It was Eulaios who was the senior of the two; he even had coins minted in his name. The authority which these two wielded was clearly very limited, though they attempted to strengthen it by proclaiming Ptolemy VI a god and marrying him to his sister within a year. They also adopted the policy rejected by Kleopatra Syra of aiming to recover Syria.[18]

The occupation of king or king's heir had thus been revealed in the years after 180 as one which was particularly hazardous. Not that this would need to be emphasized to any Seleukid king. Of Seleukos IV's six predecessors on the throne, two had been murdered, one died in an accident while on campaign, and two had died in battle; one heir had been executed. In 222–221 the dynasty had been reduced to a single teenage male, who was faced by two energetic rebel usurpers. Only one Seleukid king had died a 'natural' death. Seleukos IV stood a good chance of dying violently, and in fact he was about to be enlisted among the murdered.

Seleukos had married his sister Laodike, the former wife of their elder brother Antiochos (the Young King), who had died in 193. Seleukos and Laodike had three children, possibly more, of whom Demetrios was the eldest son, and was hostage in Rome. There was another son, Antiochos, who was even younger than Demetrios, and, of course, their sister Laodike, whose marriage in 178 suggests that she was the eldest of the three. At court, Seleukos relied to a large degree on his chief minister Heliodoros of Antioch. He was one of the overbearing type of minister, like Hermeias, whom Antiochos III had finally got rid of only by murdering him. Heliodoros, contemplating a submissive queen and heirs to the throne who were children, decided not to wait for his own Hermeias-type fate, and murdered the king instead. According to the Babylonian chronicler, the murder took place late in 175.[19]

Heliodoros' action in killing the king is not explained in any source, except as a conspiracy; no doubt he would need accomplices, but why he should have acted is not known. It does seem that Heliodoros had been well rewarded by Seleukos, who had a statue to him put up at Delos – the honour was usually the other way about; a possible accomplice is Artemidoros, a royal Friend who put up another statue, also at Delos. Heliodoros had certainly been in his high position for several years, since he made a rich presentation to Apollo at Delos in 178.[20]

It is normally assumed that Heliodoros aimed at the throne for himself, but if so, he did not succeed, nor did he make any overt move to take it. It would not be unknown for this ambition to stir in a high Seleukid official – Hermeias may have felt it, his contemporary Molon certainly did, and Antiochos III's cousin Akhaios achieved it in Asia Minor. But Heliodoros either did not wish to go so far, or he intended to move slowly. His involvement in the king's death may not have been widely known at first, so it would be better for him to stay in the background, covered by Laodike as regent, for some time – in the end he did not get that time. Coin evidence implies that Laodike was made regent for her second son Antiochos, who was only four or five years old. A gold octodrachm from the Antioch mint shows them both, implying that she was protecting her son.[21] It may be assumed that Heliodoros therefore continued as the minister in charge of the government; he may have intended to eliminate queen and king later; we do not know.

There is an alternative explanation, however. The sources for the theory that Heliodoros was the murderer of the king are the usual later historians – Polybios, Diodoros, and Appian. The Babylonian chronicler does not assign a cause, which is said by the westerners to be poison. But poison was a cause of death easily confused with a natural cause: indigestion, a heart attack and so on, even malaria. If Heliodoros was innocent of this particular crime, then the stories of his being the murderer come from later official Seleukid sources – that is, from Seleukos' brother and successor Antiochos IV. He killed Heliodoros, and so he could control the information which was put out about the death. We know he was a ruthless man, as his later conduct shows. The more the situation is considered, the more likely it seems that Antiochos was the real villain, and it is quite possible that he was the origin of the story of the murder of his brother.

The royal succession in the Seleukid family had been, as noted above, by direct succession from father to eldest surviving son for a century when Seleukos IV died. It had thus hardened into a custom, but it was by no means set in stone. The actual process could take place in one of two ways, either of which would be expected to be followed. Antiochos III had made his eldest son Antiochos the Young King joint king when he went off to war in the east in 211; after the young king died, he made Seleukos joint king, once again before setting off to war in the east. Alternatively, a son could be nominated as the next king by the current one as he was dying. The first method was clearly preferable because it gave the heir time to become experienced at governing and commanding; the danger was that the heir would become impatient and aim to supplant his father by contriving his death.

The process clearly broke down when a king was unexpectedly murdered, or died suddenly. Seleukos IV had not nominated an heir, perhaps because one of his sons was held in Rome, and he would not wish to increase his hostage value. His sudden death prevented him from nominating a successor. In the event the succession of his second son Antiochos was the correct dynastic move, even if it was contrived by his (presumed) murderer, given that Demetrios was unavailable; proclaiming Antiochos as king pre-empted any Roman intrigue. On the other hand, there was no precedent in the Seleukid family for a regency for an infant king.

There can be no doubt, though, that the rightful successor of Seleukos IV was Demetrios, but he was in Rome, and so far as is known, there was no attempt by Laodike or himself to get him to Syria – certainly we may assume that Heliodoros would not want him back. But even if Demetrios did return, he would still need a regent, for he was only about ten or eleven years old. The obvious person to be regent, apart from the mother of the two boys, was their uncle, Antiochos, the third son of Antiochos III, whom Demetrios had replaced as hostage at Rome. It has been suggested that the child Antiochos was the elder son of Seleukos, because he had the dynastic name, but his portrait on the gold octodrachm indicted a younger child than the ten or so years known for Demetrios.[22] At the same time, the lack of fuss about the passing over of Demetrios – he did not do anything about gaining the throne until after his uncle Antiochos was dead – might also suggest that he was the younger; it also suggests that the process of succession in the family was understood to be internal to that family, and that no outsider had any voice in the matter.

Antiochos had been in Rome until he was exchanged for Demetrios, and by 175 he was living in Athens. He was clearly wealthy, and was awarded honorary Athenian citizenship.[23] He had probably been living in the city for some time, perhaps two or three years. Athens was a very useful place from which to keep in touch with events all around the Mediterranean, and in particular with Syria. There were numerous Phoenician merchants who had come to settle in Athens, or at the Athenian island of Delos.[24] And, of course, Seleukos had sent envoys to the city ten years before and he and Heliodoros had honoured each other at Delos. It was a city which had become friendlier towards the Seleukids since Antiochos III's adventure in Greece in 191, when its internal affairs were disturbed by his nearby presence, and it was a major diplomatic, cultural, and mercantile centre.

After Seleukos died Antiochos was the only adult male of the royal family left alive. If anyone was entitled to be regent he was. There had been no need for such an office in the dynasty's past so far, since all royal successions had gone to adults, but there were precedents in Macedon and Egypt. The Egyptian cases were not encouraging, for it had become the practice for non-royal regents (such as Sosibios and Agathokles in the 220s) to kill off all other members of the royal house on the accession of a minor, leaving the infant king as the only possible king and themselves as the guardians – access to the king, and control of access, being the crucial element. In Macedon, however, the usual procedure was for a regent to make himself king, but then to vacate the position to his ward when the latter was old enough. The most recent example was the childhood of Philip V between 229 and 221, when his cousin Antigonos Doson took the royal title and then conveniently died when Philip was seventeen. This procedure would suit Antiochos perfectly.

The problem was for him to get to Syria and survive. Heliodoros was surely alert to the possible arrival of either Demetrios or Antiochos and would have no compunction about killing them – if he was the late king's murderer, of course. If he went to Syria Antiochos needed protection for himself until he gained political control. He acquired support and protection from perhaps the least likely source, Eumenes of Pergamon. The deaths of two of Eumenes' enemies in the last four years, Philip V and Seleukos IV, had been helpful, but Eumenes was still surrounded by enemies, symbolized by the marriages between the Macedonian and Seleukid and Macedonian and Bithynian royal houses. He spotted an opportunity in the presence of Antiochos in Athens in 175, and invited him to Pergamon. There the two men, and Eumenes' brothers Attalos, Philetairos, and Athenaios, concocted a scheme to get Antiochos to Syria in safety and keep him alive for a time when he got there, by escorting him across Asia Minor under the guard of a detachment of Attalid troops. He was taken as far as the border – presumably one of the Taurus passes – and sent on his way into Syria with a bodyguard, money, a diadem, and the royal insignia.[25] Reasonably enough, the rest was up to him.

The dating of all this is provided by notes made by a Babylonian scribe who compiled a list of kings a generation later. He reported that Seleukos IV died on the tenth day of the sixth month in the year 137 of the Seleukid era, which translates to 3 September 175. By November Antiochos was in charge in Antioch (only dated by the Babylonian eighth month, 23 October to 20 November). In the interval he had crossed into Asia Minor from Athens, concocted the plot with the Attalids, marched to Syria, removed Heliodoros from power, and had him executed for the murder of Seleukos, and made himself co-king with his nephew. He also married Laodike, his brother's widow (and his own sister), and adopted her son as his own.

This information is acquired from a small notice in Appian, from a decree of Athens congratulating Eumenes on his help for Antiochos, described as a friend of Athens, and of whom there was already a statue in the city, and from the Babylonian scribe's notes. As such, some of the details seem to be wrong. The Babylonian, writing afterwards and when all this was well in the past, made a few mistakes regarding the relationships in the royal family, but it is reasonably clear what happened. He was hampered by the repetition of the name Antiochos for the new king, for his nephew/stepson, and for the son of the new marriage, but given the dating, the 'son' of Antiochos IV must be his stepson, since Antiochos and Laodike were not married until after the former's accession. None of the other sources were any closer in date to the events, except perhaps the Athenian decree, which does not go into any detail on events in Syria.

What had happened was a major *coup d'etat*, with large effects both internally within the Seleukid kingdom and internationally. Within the royal family this was the first regency in a century and a half; it was not the first joint-kingship in the dynasty by any means, but it was the first in which the subordinate king was not the son of the senior man. The marriage of Antiochos and Laodike was fruitful in that at least one child was born of it, a son called (almost inevitably) Antiochos; there were also perhaps other children, though we do not know how many or of what sex. By this time it may be that Laodike was almost past childbearing age. She had been married for the first time in about 195, probably at the age of fifteen or sixteen; by 175, she was in her late thirties; she had been seriously ill in 181, to the extent that a strong rumour that she had died had reached the compiler of the Babylonian *Astronomical Diaries*; three years later he reported that 'Seleukos, his wife and his sons' were presenting offerings at Babylon, so she had evidently recovered.[26]

In terms of internal politics the seizure of the throne by Antiochos IV probably seemed at first like the sort of regency which Antiogonos Doson had held for Philip V, but once Antiochos had a son of his own – presumably not before late 174 or 173 – his stepson's life and title were clearly in danger, and when his own son had survived long enough to be clear of childhood diseases, the stepson was killed, apparently by one of Antiochos' thugs, a man called Andronikos.[27]

Whether Antiochos IV appreciated it or not, this turned out to be a decisive breach with previous custom in the royal family. There had been killings and rebellions and murders in the past. The eldest son of Antiochos I was executed on his father's instructions, presumably for exhibiting a too-obvious ambition; the brother of Seleukos II made himself king in Asia Minor, thereby rebelling. But both of these crises had been overcome and the line of direct succession had been preserved from the death of Seleukos I to that of Antiochos III – in little under a century. Now that direct line had been usurped.

Two kings, Seleukos IV and his son Antiochos, had been murdered within three or four years; the direct heir to the throne was now Demetrios, but he had been ignored, and was in exile in Rome; Antiochos IV and his stepson were thus both usurpers. There were obviously good reasons for Antiochos IV's actions, but it is nevertheless a fact that once the custom of direct inheritance had been broken, it could be broken again, and it was to be broken repeatedly in the next century. And since the integrity of the royal family was the one element which held the kingdom together, the usurpation of Antiochos IV and his subsequent actions began the process of the disintegration of the kingdom.

Chapter 2

The Wars of Antiochos Epiphanes (170–164 BC)

In 170 Antiochos IV arranged the death of his stepson, murdered by Andronikos.[1] His own son by Laodike was now old enough to be reasonably likely to survive, so his stepson was now dispensable. His wife, if she still lived, was by this time at least 40-years-old. In fact, she is not referred to again, and may well have been dead. She is not, for example, mentioned in any of the notices in the *Astronomical Diaries*, though it has to be said that there are very few notices from Antiochos' reign which are relevant.

The unusual way Antiochos had seized power will have required him to take care in his internal policies to ensure that any opposition was blocked. The methods he used are not directly known, but will have involved the usual armoury of expedients of kings – bribery, promotion, execution, exile. The only source which gives any hint of his methods is the biblical book of Daniel, written by one who opposed him. In the guise of a prophecy, Antiochos is described as 'contemptible' and his methods as 'fraud' and 'stealth', and 'scattering wealth among his opponents', a series of accusations which are as vague as could be imagined, but which sound quite like the normal policy for Hellenistic – and any other – rulers, at least when the author's prejudices against Antiochos are taken into account.[2]

Whatever his precise measures, it is clear that Antiochos succeeded in establishing his rule firmly where it mattered; he governed, says one (late) source, with a firm hand, whatever that means.[3] One of the measures he will have taken fairly early in his reign was to move around the provincial governors, either to eliminate any opponents or to disrupt any possible conspiracies which were brewing; we know of only two of these moves: Timarchos of Miletos was made Governor of Media (and so quasi-viceroy of the 'Upper Satrapies', and his brother Herakleides was treasurer at Antioch.[4] However, it is not known when these men were appointed. They were in office at the end of his reign, which may mean that they had been relatively recently promoted; Herakleides at least seems to have been an official under Seleukos IV, though Timarchos is not known of earlier.

It was external affairs which preoccupied Antiochos most, as they did most Hellenistic kings. This meant his relations with the Attalid Eumenes and

Ptolemy of Egypt, as his closest neighbours, with Rome in the west, and with Parthia and Baktria in the distant east. We have no evidence of his contacts in the east, as it happens; this will in the first instance be the responsibility of the Governor of the Upper Satrapies – Timarchos, in other words, in this reign.

Antiochos' experience of living at Rome had perhaps given him an exaggerated respect for the Senate, but he was obviously aware that Rome's relations with his brother had been strained. A Roman delegation was sent to contact him, presumably in 174, soon after he became king, but its composition is unknown. The members reported back with details of the men in favour with the king, and presumably also with an assessment of the strength of his position.[5] They may also have suggested to him a way of achieving something Seleukos had not bothered to acquire, a renewal of the treaty of peace and alliance of 188.

In 173 Antiochos accordingly sent Apollonios, one of his courtiers, to Rome with some at least of the unpaid part of the indemnity which had been part of the Apamaean treaty agreement. Apollonios, who, like Herakleides and Timarchos, came from Miletos, had been a friend of Seleukos IV, and was Governor of Koile Syria and Phoenicia in 175–174 – that is, he governed the former Ptolemaic part of Syria during the time Antiochos was seizing power in Antioch; he was clearly one of those who joined him as soon as he arrived.[6] He and Herakleides, amongst others, will have been able to describe Seleukos' Roman policy, and to provide an account of the sums already paid, and of the outstanding balance.

Antiochos, no doubt prompted by the Roman delegation, and in consultation with his council, resolved to buy off Roman hostility. Apollonios took with him to Rome a large sum of money, said to be the unpaid part of the indemnity. He then asked that the defunct treaty of alliance, which had expired in 187 on the death of Antiochos III, be renewed – Livy makes it clear that it was the alliance and friendship which was being renewed, not the terms of the peace. As a sweetener a consignment of gold vases worth 500lb in weight was presented to the Senate. The Senate, perhaps with some relief at this gesture of friendship from Antiochos, accepted the gifts and agreed to renew the treaty of alliance. Apollonios was treated with consideration, assigned a house to live in, and given a large cash gift.

The renewal of the treaty meant little in reality, but it will have reassured both the Senate and Antiochos that neither was particularly hostile to the other. It will have been known in Rome that Antiochos had been helped to the kingship by Eumenes and his brothers, who were already Roman allies. With a crisis brewing in Greece and Macedon, where Antiochos' nephew-in-law Perseus was now seen by Rome as a major problem, the agreement with Antiochos meant that he was unlikely to involve himself in the crisis. One of the results was a much more aggressive Roman policy towards Perseus, and war within two years.

How much Antiochos paid the Romans is not known. Livy says it was the whole amount of the unpaid indemnity, but he gives no figures, where he has rejoiced in such sums in other places. Antiochos' father had paid no more than two instalments before he died (188 and 187), which left at least 9,000 talents unpaid. It is highly unlikely that Apollonios took so much with him – it is surely probable that such a sum arriving all at once at Rome would have provoked a record in at least one of the historians. The Seleukid state's disposable tax income was probably about 3,000 talents annually; Seleukos IV may have been parsimonious, not spending much on military campaigns, for example, but Antiochos is unlikely to have emptied his state coffers merely to please Rome. And only a couple of years later he was able to finance a major war.

The only possible clue as to the amount paid over comes from *II Maccabees*, which claims that 2,000 talents was owed to Rome by the king as late as 165, and was paid out of the proceeds of the sale of Jewish captives into slavery, so it was claimed.[7] But *Maccabees* is not a reliable source for Seleukid or Roman affairs, and the whole story looks like a concoction based on misunderstood items. The problem with *Maccabees'* story is not the sum of money mentioned, which is well within the likely range, but that other and more reliable sources say that Apollonios' embassy in 173 paid over the full outstanding sum – and so there was none still owing in 165. It would have been helpful if any other ancient source had bothered to quote actual figures, but it is quite possible that no one really knew, except perhaps the treasurers in Antioch and Rome, how much had been paid and how much had not been paid. Given the emerging Macedonian crisis the Senate and Antiochos had a joint interest in paying something and in accepting that the debt had been liquidated. We can probably disregard the Maccabean claim, since it is in a book full of distortions and inventions. Livy's source was clear that the Senate accepted in 173 that the money brought by Apollonios was enough to discharge the debt.[8] It is likely that Rome had never expected to be paid anything after Antiochos III's death. Rome's coffers were thus now conveniently filled just before the city set about attacking Macedon.

At the same time, the ability of the Seleukid kingdom to pay over such large sums shows that it was a rich state. The end of Antiochos III's war with Rome had involved the immediate payment of 2,500 talents to secure the armistice, and then a promise of 12,000 talents to be paid over ten years as the indemnity. The aim was evidently to drain Antiochos' immediate war chest – the 2,500 talents – which would prevent him from restarting the war, and then to maintain a drain on his treasury to render him weakened for the future. Apart from the fact that Antiochos' death after the delivery of the first two instalments soon stopped any further payments, these fines Rome imposed on her defeated enemies were inevitably much less than they could afford. Seleukos' reign had seen the full restoration of Seleukid finances, and would probably have done so even if the indemnity payments had continued. Antiochos' contribution to Rome's war chest in 173 must have amounted to some thousands of talents – the 2,000 talents of *II Maccabees* may well be near the mark, though as a source it is most unreliable. There is no sign that Antiochos' finances were strained afterwards.

Friendship with Eumenes of Pergamon carried with it automatically friendly contacts with the states to which Eumenes was also friendly. Antiochos sent gifts to a variety of Greek cities, including Ilion, Kyzikos, Delos, and his former home, Athens. One of his courtiers, Eudemos of Seleukeia-on-the-Kalykadnos, travelled about making contacts with a number of places – Byzantion, Rhodes, Kalchedon, the Boiotian League – and received honours from them in return. Like his brother, Antiochos maintained friendly relations with the Achaian League, and with individual cities of that league. Besides Delos, the other great Greek sanctuaries at Delphi and Olympia benefited from his generosity.[9] All this was perhaps less important diplomatically than it seems. It was by this time part of the necessary diplomacy of the Hellenistic world to be generous to Greek cities; it did not imply much in the way of power, since none of them, not even the Achaian League, was in itself powerful. It may be that much of these contacts was Antiochos craving recognition in Greek public opinion, but this had no real effect otherwise.

The participation of Eumenes in Antiochos' seizure of power was a major diplomatic shift. The two kings were now allied and linked by treaty, and this provided Antiochos with the renewal of another aspect of the policy of Antiochos III, giving the new king strong diplomatic cover on his westward flank, making it possible for him to indulge in actions elsewhere without fear of being attacked from Asia Minor. This had not been a condition available to Seleukos IV. In addition, just in case none of these new diplomatic arrangements lasted, the approaching Romano-Macedonian war would clearly preoccupy everyone around the Aegean, as well as Rome, for several years. Antiochos was free of the hostility and potential hostility by states to his west that had made Seleukos' policy in the region so difficult.

On the other hand, Antiochos' coup had stimulated a new hostility from Egypt. Antiochos' new position, and his guardianship of his stepson-nephew, may have raised fears in Egypt that he might try to attain the same position with regard to his other nephews and niece, Ptolemy VI, Kleopatra, and the younger Ptolemy. At some point between 174 and 172 Apollonios son of Menestheus, the Governor of Koile Syria and the man who went as ambassador to Rome in that same period, went to Alexandria to congratulate Ptolemy VI on some significant event – *II Maccabees* says it was his formal enthronement – and there he mingled with and talked with the Ptolemaic courtiers.[10]

The choice of Apollonios as envoy to congratulate the enthroned king sent a mixed message to the Alexandrian government. He was certainly high enough in Antiochos' counsels for his presence to be a high compliment to Ptolemy VI and his regents; he was also, or had been, governor of the territory which the king's regents were planning to recover, and whose loss, as he found in his conversations, was still resented. So Apollonios' embassy could be seen as a compliment, or as an insult, or as a warning, even as a threat; it was no doubt intended as all of these, and the regents could choose which of them to accept.

While in Alexandria, Apollonios heard enough to understand that it was the intention of the regents to make an attempt to recover Koile Syria in the near future. Yet this was not, and could not be, the fixed intention of the regency government in the sense of a plan awaiting implementation on a particular date. It was also obvious to Apollonios that Eulaios and Lenaios were widely disliked and despised among all sections of Alexandrian society – their servile origins would ensure this – and it was by no means obvious that they would be able to carry the government with them into a war. After all, the last time such a policy seemed to be likely, King Ptolemy V had been murdered. Eulaios and Lenaios were surely living in fear of the same treatment.

Antiochos at some point made a tour of the old Ptolemaic province, no doubt as a way of impressing his authority on the locals, and in particular on any who were minded to support the idea of a Ptolemaic restoration. He visited Joppa and Jerusalem, and no doubt other places, and his army was stationed for a time in Phoenicia.[11] The region in contention consisted of a coastal plain in which there was a string of Greek-type cities, including the capital of the area, Ptolemais-Ake. Inland were the Judaean Hills, a rural area centred on the temple-town of Jerusalem. This was a semi-autonomous area where the temple high priest exercised local jurisdiction. Beyond the Jordan River and the Great Rift Valley was a region of high plateaux with a line of small cities which had developed during the Ptolemaic rule. It would be surprising if there was no nostalgia for Ptolemaic rule in this whole territory. In fact one prominent man, Hyrkanos, who was of a family which had become rich as Ptolemaic tax-collectors, had built a palace and a rival temple to that in Jerusalem in the Transjordanian lands, at Iraq al-Amir.

Probably Antiochos was aware of tensions within the Jewish community in Judaea. The high priest, Onias III, the current representative of a line which stretched back to the sixth century, was 'a zealot for the laws', which was a way of saying he was a religious conservative, but he was also in conflict with a growing number of Jews who wished to adopt Greek ways and language. In 174 this group petitioned Antiochos, probably during his tour of Palestine, to be allowed to form themselves into a private organization called the 'Antiochenes in Jerusalem', which would live by Greek ways. Antiochos agreed, and they built themselves a gymnasium, the characteristic Greek educational institution; it was near the temple, and even some of the priests of the temple were members.[12]

Onias objected, and one of the measures Antiochos took to get the 'Antiochenes' established was to depose Onias and replace him with another high priest, Jesus, who preferred to be called Jason – a Greek name. Onias went into exile, curiously enough choosing to go to the sacred grove of Daphne near Antioch as his residence – a Greek sanctuary of Apollo. In Jerusalem Jason's policy was to attempt to hold a balance between the traditionalists and the hellenizers, but he was outflanked by a more fervent group of the latter. They went to Antiochos and persuaded him to replace Jason by one of their people, a man called Menelaos. Jason fled into exile, like Onias, but only to stay with Hyrkanos, across the Jordan at his palace-temple at Iraq el-Amir.[13]

The ease with which the extreme hellenizers had persuaded Antiochos to appoint Menelaos was a reflection of a standard and long-established Seleukid policy. From even before the acquisition of Syria the kings had encouraged the foundation of Greek-type cities, either as new foundations, or as made-over 'native' cities with Greek institutions of government. Their kingdom was littered with cities sporting royal names – Antioch, Apamaea, and so on – so when Antiochos was asked to encourage another hellenization project in Jerusalem he willingly complied, probably without too much investigation of the circumstances, and no doubt in the hope – or expectation – that this would solve any problems in Jerusalem and Judaea. The replacement of high priests was also standard practice in other places, and perhaps he considered it similar to the replacement of provincial governors. One of the royal prerogatives, inherited from the pre-Alexander past, was the appointment of high priests at Jerusalem.

For the Jews, however, there were now three high priests, and their loyalties had become uncertain and divided; further, the man with the least support, Menelaos, was the one of the three who was in office. His party organized the murder of Onias, but this merely alarmed Jason, who may have assumed that he was next.[14] However, instead of fleeing farther away – Daphne, a sacred area, had not been far enough for Onias – he returned to Jerusalem, and was welcomed into the town by his supporters; Menelaos, outnumbered, took refuge in the citadel.[15]

All this went on in isolation from the events in the wider kingdom, but it inevitably became involved in them, the king being the obvious link. Antiochos became involved in his Egyptian war, which we call the Sixth Syrian War, and Judaea lay on the flank of his main route connecting Egypt with the centre of his power in North Syria. He had made certain that he was fully informed about developments in the Alexandrian court. A Roman embassy toured the eastern states in 173/172 to make certain that none of the powers there would interfere in their Macedonian war; they noticed the war preparations in Alexandria and were content to understand that a war with Antiochos was intended – both states would thus be kept busy, and unable to interfere in Greece.[16] But when the Romano-Macedonian War actually began, it was realized in Alexandria that there was no hope of any Roman help in a Syrian war – it seems that the regents were not as alert to such developments as Antiochos. An embassy to Rome suggested an Egyptian mediation in the war in Greece, but this was never something Rome would accept.[17] It was clearly a device to encourage Roman interest in protecting Egypt, but Rome was quite unconcerned in doing so. And meanwhile, in Egypt, Antiochos' war began.

The Egyptian regents had successfully sidelined any opposition in the court by convening a mass meeting in Alexandria to promise that the war would result in a swift recovery of Koile Syria, and that this would cause the collapse of the Seleukid kingdom.[18] (In this, had Koile Syria been retaken, they might well have been correct.) And, just to ginger up their supporters, the three royal children were proclaimed joint kings and queen, and Ptolemy VI's *anakleteria* – his coming-of-age (he was about sixteen) – was celebrated. It was probably the news that Antiochos had caused the murder of his stepson – which took place in about 170 – which brought the regents to their decision for war, on the assumption that such a deed implied dissension within the Seleukid kingdom and the growth of opposition to Antiochos.

The Egyptian developments had to be in public, since the only way the regents could acquire some sort of validation for their war was to bypass the court's opposition. But it was all so publicly performed that Antiochos knew full well what was intended, and did not wait. He mustered his army in Palestine, and when it was clear that the Ptolemaic forces were about to move into Sinai in their preparations to invade Palestine, he marched to pre-empt them. At a point not far from Pelusion, the Ptolemaic starting point, he defeated the Ptolemaic army. A brief armistice followed, and then Antiochos seized Pelusion, by a ruse, though not until the armistice had expired; this is condemned by Polybios as unfair; but the historian was always rather pro-Ptolemaic, and had curiously naïve ideas about waging war. If he wished, Antiochos could now invade Egypt.[19]

The first result of the defeat was the overthrow of the Egyptian regency. It seems that Eulaios proposed to spirit Ptolemy VI off to Samothrace, but this probably never happened.[20] (It would have put him very close to the Roman war, and was presumably intended to put the king under some sort of distant Roman protection.) This would have left the regents in Egypt in control of Kleopatra and the younger Ptolemy, with the elder as a sort of hostage, and was probably a move intended to blunt opposition at home. It is quite likely that Ptolemy VI, who grew to be an intelligent and forceful man, was the one who prevented the move.

Eulaios and Lenaios now disappeared, probably killed, and were replaced by two soldiers, Komanos and Kineas. Antiochos moved into Egypt and occupied much of the Delta area, including Memphis, the old capital. A delegation of Greek envoys turned up at Antiochos' camp trying to mediate, but they were instead treated to a detailed and precise exposition of the Seleukid case for retaining Koile Syria. Then Antiochos moved forward to blockade Alexandria.[21] Ptolemy VI went to see him, alone, perhaps hoping to trade on their family relationship; they came to some agreement, but this was repudiated by the Alexandrians, who now proclaimed the younger brother, Ptolemy VIII, as their king. Antiochos laid siege to the city, apparently on behalf of Ptolemy VI.[22]

Antiochos had no wish to become involved in a lengthy siege of the city, still less to have his army storm into it. He withdrew from most of the country, leaving Ptolemy VI at Memphis and Ptolemy VIII and Kleopatra in Alexandria, though he kept control of Pelusion, the essential gateway into Egypt.[23] He presumably hoped that the three kings would continue to fight each other. In this he was mistaken, for they were quickly reconciled.[24] The Ptolemaic government in Alexandria had already appealed for help to Rome and to Achaia, without result; it clearly had no hope of resisting another Seleukid invasion, which the reunification of the royal family had made inevitable.

It was at this difficult time that Antiochos was informed of the changes which had taken place in Jerusalem, where the appointed high priest, Menelaos, had been overthrown by one who had been deposed. Jason had originally been given refuge by Hyrkanos, who was a known, or at least a suspected, Ptolemaic sympathizer, and when he returned to Jerusalem and reclaimed the high priesthood he quickly resumed control there. This, therefore, had the air of a rising in favour of the active Ptolemaic enemy, and was certainly a defiance of Antiochos' royal authority. In all this Antiochos and his advisers were probably wrong, though there is no proof either way, but to the king it looked very like a rebellion in a time of war. Antiochos decided he could not afford to ignore what had happened, and certainly his appointee as high priest had been overthrown by Jason, whom he had dismissed. He sent his army into the Judaean Hills, seized Jerusalem, looted the temple treasury, and defeated Menelaos' opponents.

The only sources for this are Jewish, and one of them dwells lovingly on the details of what was taken from the temple, while the other claims vaguely that many people were killed. It is characteristic of such sources to be more concerned at their material losses than the human casualties. One of the latter seems to have been Hyrkanos, for it is at this time that it is best to locate his suicide, which is explicitly linked to his opposition to Antiochos – and it may be that this constitutes some indication that there really was a Ptolemaic element in the troubles (which in the circumstances would hardly be surprising). From Antiochos' point of view this was a successful operation: he had suppressed an incipient rising, and acquired considerable wealth with which he could finance the continuing Egyptian war. Menelaos was reinstated, his authority more tarnished than ever.[25]

The news of the reconciliation of the Ptolemaic siblings brought a new Seleukid invasion of Egypt. Antiochos sent a force to capture Cyprus, where it defeated an Egyptian fleet and then conquered the island with no resistance, no doubt helped by the fact that that the Ptolemaic governor, Ptolemaios Makron, swiftly joined him.[26] The land army invaded Egypt again. Antiochos was met at the border by a Ptolemaic delegation hoping to negotiate a peace, but he demanded Cyprus and Pelusion and the land around it as his price. This would have kept open the invasion doorway into Egypt, and thereby reduce the kingdom to complete political dependence on the Seleukids. The terms were refused.[27]

Antiochos marched his army into Egypt again. There seems to have been little fighting, and the Ptolemaic government retreated once again into Alexandria. Antiochos reached Memphis, and received the submission of Upper Egypt, the area which had been in rebellion against Ptolemaic rule until the recent past. He had coins minted in his name; he issued at least one official Egyptian document in his own name; a governor was appointed for Memphis. How far this was an indication that Antiochos' policy was now to aim at the annexation of Egypt is not known; perhaps it was a type of psychological warfare, aiming to frighten the Ptolemaic rulers into fearing that they might well lose everything.

Alexandria was threatened again, and Antiochos camped at Eleusis, a little to the east of the city.[28]

Antiochos' intentions are in fact impenetrable at this distance. It is usually assumed that he did not really want to annex Egypt, though with his army in control of all of the country except Alexandria, he must have been tempted. A union of the two kingdoms would certainly hoist the Seleukid king into the first rank of powers; Egypt's financial resources would more than make up for the loss of Asia Minor.

There were, however, weighty objections to such a course. Joining Egypt to the Seleukid kingdom might well overbalance the joint kingdom. Almost inevitably Alexandria – supposing he could capture it – would become the seat of government of the joint state, and this would leave much of the eastern territories even more neglected than they already were. There may have been little serious resistance to his second conquest, but the prospect of permanent Seleukid rule would only stimulate it; Egypt would have to be occupied by the Seleukid army for at least a generation. Internationally it would skew Seleukid policy back towards the Mediterranean world when it had just been shifted much more decisively towards the east – and Antiochos was probably already considering an eastern expedition. And if the Seleukid kingdom once again became deeply involved in Mediterranean affairs, it would very quickly run up against Rome.

Rome, having defeated all its rivals in the past thirty years, and even then was in the process of finally destroying Macedon, would scarcely take kindly to the simultaneous appearance on its eastern horizon of a power equal in rank and vastly more wealthy than it was. Antiochos, of all the Seleukid kings, with his experience of life in Rome and his knowledge of the Roman politicians, was surely the one who would be most conscious of this. So also were the Ptolemaic officials and kings. Indeed it was to Rome that they had already appealed for help, more than once, though by doing so in the middle of one of Rome's more difficult wars they achieved only the appointment of an unknown minor envoy, T. Numisius, to investigate and possibly arbitrate, and he may not even have left Italy.[29] At the same time, Rome was awake to the problem.

As the Macedonian war was heading for an end, during 168, much higher ranking envoys had been appointed, but they were not going to involve themselves in Egyptian affairs until the war in Greece had been fully won. C. Popilius Laenas lingered in the Aegean for some time while M. Aemilius Paullus systematically destroyed the Macedonian army at Pydna. The decisive battle was fought in June 168, and this was the signal for Popilius to set off for

Alexandria. There, Antiochos was unable either to take the city or to persuade the Ptolemaic government to agree to any sort of terms short of his complete evacuation of Egypt – which he could not do until he was guaranteed peace – though it might have been better if he had simply declared victory and marched out. He had to consider his own position in his own kingdom, where no doubt there were still plenty of men who considered him a usurper and resented the murder of his stepson. He had also to remember that if he annoyed Rome enough his nephew Demetrios might well be sent to Syria, and his subsequent arrest when he arrived would certainly stir up just the sort of loyalists he must have feared.

The arrival of Popilius Laenas cut thorough the problem, rescued the Egyptians from Seleukid occupation (and looting), and rescued Antiochos from the dilemma he had ended up in. The scene is famous, as Popilius presented his apparently harsh terms to Antiochos, and then demanded an instant reply, drawing a circle around the king with his staff to enforce his demand and his time limit. Antiochos, of course, did not need such an insulting ultimatum to make his decision, and within a minute or so of his agreeing to the Roman terms, the two men were greeting each other as the old friends they were.[30] Indeed one might even suspect that the whole show may have been prearranged, since it resonated so well with Rome's view of itself as blunt and decisive, and with the general Seleukid resentment of Roman overbearing rudeness; Antiochos may well have received sympathy from his subjects at the necessities to which his position as a king had made him submit.

Popilius' terms were that Antiochos must evacuate all Ptolemaic territories, Egypt and Cyprus, though he was permitted – he could hardly be stopped – to carry off the booty he and his forces had gathered; no doubt even more looting accompanied the withdrawal. Much more valuable, however, was the fact of the treaty with the Ptolemies, so that he was protected once more on another border, as his father had been, from any attempt at recovery while both he and Ptolemy VI lived; it could be expected that the peace would therefore last for a good number of years. Rome, as mediator, might also be regarded as guarantor of the peace, should an attempt be made to circumvent it.

Antiochos had thus restored his ancestral kingdom to the position which Antiochos III had achieved in his last year, protected by treaty against any attack from Egypt or from Asia Minor. But this meant that Antiochos IV was also free to turn his attentions elsewhere, and for him that meant to the east. This was another of Antiochos III's legacies, for one of his greater achievements was to impose his domination over the eastern states, and he had been on his way to recover that position when he died. Antiochos IV could be claiming to revive his father's achievement.

The issue of Jerusalem had to be dealt with first, however. Jason had been driven out – he took refuge in Sparta – and Menelaos of the 'Antiochenes in Jerusalem' set about the next stage in the conversion of the place into a normal Hellenistic city. They must have had this aim in mind from the start, and the defeat of their Jewish opponents, symbolized by Onias and Jason, left the future in their hands. They now tackled the central element of the opposition, the temple. They applied to Antiochos to be allowed to convert the worship there from that of Yahweh to that of Zeus Olympios. Probably without giving the matter much thought Antiochos agreed – there is no sign of any of the events in Jerusalem at this time that any of the Greeks appreciated Jewish susceptibilities over the worship of their Yahweh (though in fact in the far distant past Yahweh and Zeus had been the same god, and 'Zeus Olympios' was a reasonably accurate translation of 'Yahweh' into Greek).[31]

The affairs of Judaea loom large in modern accounts of Seleukid history at this period, but that must not lead to the assumption that they did so at the time. For several years events there were of only minor importance in the kingdom as a whole, and even after Seleukid armies began to be involved in Judaea there is no sign that anyone higher in the government system than the Governor of Koile Syria became involved. Indeed, while the fighting went on in Judaea, Antiochos conducted large-scale expeditions elsewhere, leaving Judaea to the governor.

So, while in Judaea, an official called Apollonios set about establishing his authority in Jerusalem by building a castle, the Akra. Antiochos was planning a defiant celebration of his victories in Egypt, one to rival the Roman triumph which Aemilius Paullus had staged to celebrate his own victory over Macedon.[32] This took place at Daphne, outside Antioch, perhaps pointedly in a sacred place, rather than in the secular city. It was partly a sacred procession including an extravagant display of royal and private wealth, but mainly a boast of armed power, with at least 50,000 soldiers, foot and horse, chariots and elephants, in the march past. It is not known how it impressed the Romans, but Antiochos had imported delegations to the accompanying games from all over Greece, and Polybios was clearly impressed. He also finished his account with the waspish comment that it was all really paid for by the loot of Egypt.[33]

The account of the parade gives an idea of the composition of the Seleukid army, but to take it as a full description is to misunderstand what was being shown. Some of the units were in effect militias, only embodied when a great crisis arrived – Antiochos III had called these troops up perhaps two or three times in his thirty-five-year reign. So those on display were not fully representative of the normal Seleukid army, though they gave some idea of the potential of the kingdom. Equally important were those who were missing.

The frontiers needed to be guarded; the occupation of Judaea could not be relaxed; the forces in Media, and even those in Babylonia, could not be reduced for a mere parade, especially as their attendance at Antioch would involve an absence from their stations for several months. So what was on display was mainly the Seleukid army as available in Syria, Kilikia, and the nearby lands. This was substantial enough in all conscience – 50,000 troops would be the equivalent of eight Roman legions and more; there should have been at least that many soldiers in other parts of the empire, either permanently deployed as governors' guards and forces, or on the frontier stations, or available as militias.

It was in this period, after his Egyptian success, that the several stories of Antiochos' so-called erratic behaviour must have originated. The account of his participation in the Daphne games is clearly skewed to emphasize his odd behaviour – or behaviour which could be interpreted as odd. He dressed as a Roman at times, held elections in which he was a candidate (and won), conducted legal hearings in public, and armed and drilled a unit of his forces in the Roman fashion; he took the epithet, *epiphanes*, implying near-divinity. None of this is really any more than an exuberant king's indulgence, a celebration of his success, and can hardly be held against him. Exaggeration in the sources is to be expected because the two main sources for these stories are Polybios, whose Ptolemaic and Roman sympathies are both evident, and the *Commentaries* of Ptolemy VI, as quoted much later.[34]

There is no mention of Antiochos' wife in any of the celebrations, though this is not necessarily evidence that she was no longer alive. Yet one might have expected her to be noted at the Daphne parade. If alive she had surely been angered by the murder of her son, and could well have cut off relations with him. He consoled himself with a woman called Antiochis, said to have been a concubine, and suspected by at least one scholar, from her name, of being a member of the royal family. Antiochis' description as a concubine does not preclude the possibility that she was really Antiochos' wife – either in succession to Laodike or bigamously. The latter condition was hardly a crime, nor very unusual, among Hellenistic royalty.

It is certain that Antiochos had two children by Antiochis, called Alexander and Laodike – royal names again, though not exclusively so – and he allocated the revenues of two cities in Kilikia, Tarsos and Mallos, for the upkeep of his paramour and her household, at which the cities objected violently enough for them to be said to have been in rebellion. It is typical of the sources for Antiochos' reign that this comes from an unreliable source, and that we do not know the full story or what resulted from the cities' resentment. But the children existed.[35]

Some of Antiochos' internal policies were rather more traditional in intent and scope. It has to be said that we lack any evidence for his direct involvement in these policies, but since they began under his kingship it seems safe to credit him with them, either by initiating or by accepting them. The old Seleukid policy of founding new cities had largely fallen into disuse in the previous reigns: neither Antiochos III nor his two predecessors can be seen to have made any moves in this direction, Seleukos II and Seleukos III because they were involved in a long civil war, and Antiochos III probably because he did not have the necessary manpower resources for any such projects. But Antiochos IV and his brother tried a different approach.

The purpose of the new cities founded by his predecessors had been largely defensive, to encourage the immigration of men and their families from Greece who would populate the cities, and so would be available as soldiers. The policy had come to a halt partly because of the civil wars and invasions of the 240s and after, but also because there was no longer a surplus of population in Greece to draw on, especially after the damage caused there by the Roman wars and those of Philip V.

But the initiative of the 'Antiochenes in Jerusalem' came from a group of men who were Jews in origin but Hellenes in culture. This was a new version of the older urbanizing policy which had converted likely local settlements into Greek cities partly by imposing a Greek ruling class on them. Many of the cities of the eastern provinces had begun as such local cities, with immensely long histories – several of the cities of Media were in this classification, including Ekbatana. There were some in Syria, such as Damascus and Hierapolis and the Phoenician cities. In the old Ptolemaic province of Koile Syria this was in fact the origin of most of the urban places, for the Ptolemies had not been enthusiastic about cities with any sort of autonomy.

Antiochos adopted two other policies for encouraging city life and growth. He awarded royal names to several towns which had developed in the previous century or so without the benefit of a formal foundation by one of the kings. But if a city was awarded a royal name it will have also had a formal Greek constitution imposed on it, with the usual magistrates and local government, whose members would speak Greek. It is likely that Seleukos IV had begun this process in Koile Syria – which, after all, had only become formally Seleukid at the peace treaty of 195. Antiochos III had evidently had no time or perhaps no inclination for such work, but Seleukos clearly had both, and Koile Syria was a prime candidate for native settlements to be converted, since such a move would help cement the loyalty of the places to the Seleukid dynasty, or at least their control by the dynasty.

Seleukos awarded his own name to four places, all in Koile Syria. Three of them were in a small region east of the Sea of Galilee: Abila, Gadara, and Seleukeia-in-the-Gaulan. The first two were long-established towns whose promotion was evidently intended to create a better fortified and larger group of settlements loyal to the Seleukid dynasty in a strategic area. They were in a region which had a number of small cities already; their presence would help to reinforce Seleukid authority in the area. The third town was a little to the north. The Gaulan (the modern Golan) was a region of rich grassland where nomads long gathered and held an annual fair. To be sure, the evidence for this is considerably later, but a rich grass resource would always attract nomads, and it may be that the city was intended to be a centre for their meetings, and perhaps a place where taxes on their transactions could be collected. The city, however, did not prosper, and a century later it was referred to as a village, thus implying that no formal civic organization then existed.[36]

The fourth place converted to a Seleukid city was Gaza. This development is not in the least surprising. The intention was obviously to strengthen the defences of Palestine against the possibility – or rather, the probability – of a Ptolemaic attempt to recover the lost region. By making it a specifically Seleukid city the place would be presumed to be loyal, though it was undoubtedly also occupied by a substantial garrison; but an autonomous local government could help to reduce the burden of a garrison on the general population, and would provide a mechanism for resolving disputes, should any arise.[37]

All of these were foundations which were pre-existing urban places, perhaps in some cases actually aspiring to city-status even before Seleukid attention was drawn to them, such as Gaza and Abila.

But the predominant element in them all is their strategic usefulness. Gaza's position is obvious, a vital strategic place, astride the main route between Egypt and Palestine, the essential door which, in the hands of the ruler of Palestine, kept the route shut, and, in the hands of Egyptian rulers, opened the way for an invasion whenever they felt like it. The three new cities east of the upper valley of the Jordan were again close to the ancient route called the King's Highway, which ran south from Damascus to Amman and on to Arabia; they were also close to a branch of that road which turned west to cross the Jordan south of the

Sea of Galilee at the Jisr Bint Yakub (the Bridge of the Daughters of Jacob), and led into the Vale of Esdraelon and central Palestine and on to the coast.

Antiochos IV's work in founding cities was similar, though not quite so obviously strategic in intent, perhaps because the main work had been done by his brother. Two places in central Syria which already existed, but which were promoted to city status by him might be considered strategic. On the Phoenician coast Berytos was promoted by either Seleukos or Antiochos and received the name Laodikeia, perhaps named for their wife. Inland, in the Orontes Valley the old site of Hamath was refounded as a city by Antiochos, and called Epiphaneia after his chosen nickname. These were both important sites, Berytos as a port and as the seaward end of the best route over the mountains into the Bekaa Valley, and so on to Damascus; Epiphaneia-Hamath was a centre for that part of the Orontes Valley north of the Bekaa which had been a frontier area between the two Hellenistic kingdoms before 200 BC, and which could now be redeveloped. It was also a very high mound, a great tell, which was a ready-made citadel.[38]

Antiochos added three new cities, or rather promoted them by awarding them his name. The administrative capital at Ptolemais-Ake became an Antioch, though it is unlikely this had much effect on a city already necessarily well governed in the Greek style, and the new name did not last. Two others of these cities were in the region where his brother had been active. Gerasa, which was a Greek city which claimed to have been founded by Perdikkas, presumably in 323–321, was made into an Antioch, distinguished from the rest as 'by-the-Chrysorrhoas'; to the north, in the same area as the three foundations of Seleukos, 'Antioch-by-Hippos' sounds like a new foundation, but one which was close to an older settlement. The control of the great route was thus being reinforced.[39]

Antiochos planted at least one and perhaps two new cities on the Euphrates. Epiphaneia-on-the-Euphrates is fairly clearly his work from the name; there was also an Antioch-on-the-Euphrates, which may well be close to it, perhaps on the opposite side of the river. These were both close to Seleukeia-Zeugma, the most important city on the river, and so they probably acted as forward defences for the main city. If it is the case that the Seleukids had lost control of Kommagene to the north as Strabo claimed, this should be another necessarily strategic foundation; it may also be related to the independence of Armenia, which had been resumed since 187.[40]

In Syria there was just one more place which can be attributed to Antiochos, Antioch-in-Pieria. It is mentioned only once, in a very late source; if it existed it will have been somewhere in the neighbourhood of Seleukeia-in-Pieria, Pieria being a name adapted to Syria from the Macedonian original. It was probably the name given to the hills sloping down to the sea at the southern end of the Amanus Mountains or the northern end of the Bargylos, or both, and including the estuary of the Orontes. Antioch should be somewhere in this area, possibly at Rhosos, at the southern end of the Bay of Iskenderun.[41]

One of Antiochos' measures which stimulated the development of cities was to permit the establishment of local mints. These mints produced mainly copper or bronze coinage of low denominations, without any control over size or design, though they were stamped with a letter indicating the denomination – a single, a half, or a quarter of an obol. The mints, and therefore the cities, could make a profit on the issuing of these coins, which is one of the reasons they proliferated when Antiochos permitted them to be founded. He, of course, charged for the privilege. Many of the cities of Syria became mint-cities, noticeably the Phoenicians, the four great cities of the north, and several of those in Kilikia. This is perhaps an indication of the economic activity of the region; it is noticeable that none in Babylonia or Iran took up the offer, if indeed it was extended to them. This is less an indication of a lower level of economic activity, at least in Babylonia, than an indication of an exchange system which did not need small change in metal units, and was in many ways independent of coined money.

Investigations into the scale of minting activity, above all at the busiest mint, Antioch, have shown a close correlation between the production of coins and the wars Antiochos waged; an increase in minting, particularly of silver tetradrachms, preceded and accompanied his military campaigns. The transfer of a substantial quantity of silver to Rome in 173 does not seem to have had any effect, and the mint's production increased soon after, suggesting that the Seleukid government had plenty of precious metal in reserve (and that the sum handed over was much less than the total supposedly 'owed'). The highest level of activity came in the last years of Antiochos' reign, from 169 onwards, when he had fought in Egypt and in Judaea – though this was probably not a very costly matter – displayed his army in the great parade at Daphne and set off on his campaign in the east.[42] The loot of Egypt and the confiscated temple treasury of Jerusalem will have helped his finances, of course.

The great eastern expedition is an enterprise which is but poorly known. All we have are a few disconnected anecdotes and facts, onto which have been added some inferences, convincing or not, and some elaborate theories which can be ignored. A reasonable stab can be made at the sequence of Antiochos' actions, so far as they are known, in a geographical sense, and we have an approximate date for the end. But we do not know his purpose, or what sort of a force he took with him. This last is a crucial omission, since if we knew how large an army he had under his command in the east we could estimate his intentions. One of the anecdotes, when he was faced down by a gathering of hillmen, may indicate that he took only a small force with him; it is quite certain from later events that a large proportion of the main Seleukid army remained in Syria.

He took what now were almost traditional precautionary measures to ensure stability in the west while he was away. His son Antiochos was made joint-king, under a regent, Lysias, who had command of a part of the army.[43] The expedition began with an invasion of Armenia, which was in a position to cause trouble while the main Seleukid forces were preoccupied. Artaxias, the man who had been set in power as governor by Antiochos III, had made himself an independent king after Antiochos' death; now he was coerced into submission, and agreed to pay tribute once more; he may even have been captured by Antiochos' forces, but if so he was reinstated.[44] This was the standard technique of establishing domination, of course, since such a man would be bound by the treaty he had made while both of the principals lived.

It is a reasonable assumption that Antiochos' next move was into Babylonia, marching his army south along the Tigris, and calling at both Seleukeia-on-the-Tigris and Babylon. We have no evidence of this, since the obvious source, the *Astronomical Diaries,* do not survive for the relevant period, but he is recorded at the very southern end of Babylonia, at the city of Alexandria. Three separate notices in the *Natural History* of Pliny the Elder seem to mark his presence. One claims he explored the Arabian shore of the Gulf, and another says that a man called Noumenios commanded the king's fleet in the Gulf.[45] At this point, of course, we can begin to suspect that either the notices are confusing Antiochos IV with his father, who did exactly that in the Gulf (and in Armenia), or that Antiochos IV was deliberately copying his father's itinerary, but in reverse.

The third explanation, and one which makes sense, is that Antiochos IV was reinforcing or recovering the positions his father had attained by compelling the renewed submission of Armenia and of the Persian Gulf regions. Both of these had been forced into a condition of submission, and were freed by Antiochos III's death; it would always need a royal visit to renew that submission. If this is so we therefore have a glimmer of a clue as to what Antiochos' purpose was in this eastern expedition: to recover the authority his father had exercised. His presence in the east would also be a useful stimulus to loyalty to other regions, and was something his brother had not been in a position to do. His achievement in securing diplomatic protection in the west had thus been the reason he was able to march east. The celebration at Daphne had been not merely a gesture of one-upmanship to outshine Paullus' triumph in Rome, or a statement of victory over Ptolemaic Egypt; it had been the start of a new eastern expedition.

The third item of work Antiochos did in southern Babylonia was to refound the city at the mouth of the Shatt el-Arab, where the joint waters of the Tigris and Euphrates reach the Gulf. The place was originally one of Alexander's cities; Antiochos refounded it, probably with some effort, and renamed it Antioch. It had a mint, which started producing coins at this time. It was in a difficult situation geographically, liable to be flooded when the rivers rose, but the new founding was successful, though it changed its name again later.[46]

The great city of Iran, Ekbatana, was also renamed, as Epiphaneia, which suggests that this may well have been another stop on Antiochos' campaign. It was the major city of Iran, the ancient Median capital, and it was an obvious destination for any royal visitor to Iran. In that case, we may assume that Antiochos took his army into Iran by way of the Bisitun Pass, marching up from Seleukeia-on-the-Tigris. This was the place the Babylonians called 'the royal city' and a visit by the king to Babylonia necessarily demanded a call there, and one to Babylon, where religious ceremonies would be conducted, just as Ekbatana was the Iranian 'royal city'. Renaming it Epiphaneia was perhaps more a compliment to himself than to the city; just as with Ptolemais-Ake the name did not last.[47]

Either after visiting Ekbatana or directly from southern Babylonia, Antiochos entered Elymais, where he attempted to raid a local temple for its treasure. Again, there is a curious echo of his father's attempt on a temple in the same region, though it was not apparently the same temple, the earlier one being of Bel, and this of Nanaia. In this case the king did not get anywhere near his victim, for the local people were clearly warned and gathered defensively. Antiochos pulled back, which tends to suggest he did not have the full Seleukid army with him – or that he did not trust his own military skills.[48] But if he had only a detachment with him, one would have expected him to have returned later in full force.

When all these events took place is not known, but the time frame is between 166 and 164. There is no reason to believe that he delayed for very long in setting out after the celebration at Daphne in the summer of 166, and we know he was in central Iran by late 164. Within that period of over two years he could have performed these tasks in any order, though it is more likely that the Armenian expedition came first, then Babylonia, the Gulf and Arabia, then Iran. The gradual move east and the final venture into central Iran, however, does imply that he was intent on a further expedition into Parthia and Baktria. On the other hand, he was at Tabai in south central Iran in November 164, and he could well have intended to move south into Karmania and then round into Arachosia, which would be more or less the reverse course of his father on his return in 207–206. This route would bring him into conflict with one or more of the Baktrian rulers. The only thing we may conclude is that he had not finished his expedition and that the eastern kingdoms were the obvious targets for another move eastwards. It is surely all but certain that the king was also thinking of India.

Speculation is all we have left, for in November 164, at Tabai, he died. Various diseases have been suggested, without any proof for any of them. Several sources decided that he died because of his religious policy, such as it was. The Maccabees went into imaginative detail, gloating most unpleasantly on his supposed suffering, with no evidence at all, and ignoring the fact that his policy towards Judaea was motivated by politics and not religion; elsewhere his raid on the Elymaian temple is said to have brought down the wrath of the goddess whose temple it was – ignoring the fact that he did not actually carry out a raid there. Once again we have to admit ignorance of everything except the basic fact of his death.[49]

Antiochos' reign was in the short-term a success. He had conducted a successful war against Ptolemaic Egypt, in the process reducing that kingdom to international impotence; he maintained good diplomatic relations with the powers of the west, the Attalids and Rome; he cultivated his good reputation in Greece; he had brought some marginal areas into his kingdom once more, though the smouldering guerrilla war in Judaea was still not finished. But in a longer view the methods he had used to obtain power proved to be a political cancer, as did his killing of the rightful king, his stepson Antiochos. He also left two dire legacies to cause future trouble: as he was dying in Iran he gave his royal insignia and his ring to a commander called Philip, who then claimed to have been made regent, despite the existence of Lysias in the west, so setting up the kingdom for a new civil war. And there were his children by Antiochis the 'concubine', whose exclusion from the royal inheritance eventually caused another civil war.

Chapter 3

The Advent of Demetrios I (164–159 BC)

In the western parts of the Seleukid kingdom, that is, in Syria, Koile Syria, Mesopotamia, and Kilikia, Lysias had been governing since the departure of Antiochos IV to the east in late 166 or perhaps early 165. Lysias had with him the joint-king Antiochos V, who became the sole king in 164. He was about 10-years-old when his father died so Lysias continued to govern, but now in the new king's name, as his regent.

While Antiochos was campaigning in the east, Lysias had been attending to the problem of Judaea. (This was obviously not his only problem of government, but it is virtually the only matter of which we have any information.) Before Antiochos left, little had happened in Judaea to disturb the Seleukid central government, but matters developed into a crisis as Antiochos was preparing for his expedition. With the conversion of the Jerusalem temple to the worship of Zeus Olympios a set of royal officials fanned out over the Judaean countryside to enforce the worship of the new god – and even perhaps to show how it was to be done. They required the prominent men in each settlement to sacrifice on a Greek-type altar, since they would be the men who would become the local priests of the cult. The man who ordered this is said in the first instance to be Apollonios, who was made administrator by Antiochos in 167, but he derived his local authority in such matters as the worship from the high priest Menelaos.[1]

This change was not universally popular, though it seems that large numbers of Jews co-operated without difficulty.[2] Some refused, either by absenting themselves from the sacrifices or by other means. For those who were particularly obdurate, withdrawal into the desert was a popular move. In one case which is recorded in some detail, Mattathias, a prominent man of the village of Modiin in the north-western area of Judaea, not only refused to sacrifice, but drew a weapon and killed both the man about to make the sacrifice and the official in charge.[3] Afterwards he received no support from his fellow villagers, apart from his six sons, and they all soon took refuge in the nearby Gophna Hills, the local equivalent of withdrawing into the desert.[4]

Mattathias' stroke had been against a man operating as an agent of the high priest Menelaos. He was quite likely a fellow Jew, and the conflict of which this was an incident was essentially one between Jews. The sons of Mattathias – the old man died not long after the murders – were joined by some others in their hills and they then set about persuading the rural population to accept their views. Menelaos' men retaliated, and violence was used by both sides. The most effective were the Maccabee brothers (the sons of Mattathias) and their associates, who roamed the countryside, overthrowing altars, terrorizing their opponents, and intimidating neutrals.[5]

Menelaos appealed for help to Apollonios, who collected an army from Samaria, a Macedonian colony city. The force he had was essentially the local militia, so the fight which developed was between a group of Jews who had experience only in terrorizing civilians and farmers, and a civic militia with little more military experience than their opponents. The battle was brief and ended when Apollonios was killed, targeted right at the start by Judah Maccabee. This was a technique Judah, the eldest of the brothers, who had emerged as the leader of the insurgents, was to use repeatedly. With their commander dead, the Samarian army fled.[6]

The death of Apollonios brought the whole matter to the attention of the Governor of Koile Syria, who was based at Ptolemais-Ake. He appointed a professional soldier, Seron, to mount a new attack. With a rather larger and perhaps a better army, though he was in fact outnumbered in the fighting, Seron marched up into the Judaean hills by the route through the two Beth Horon villages. This was a long, narrow, and difficult route, and Judah succeeded in ambushing and destroying the attacking force. Seron died in the fight, probably deliberately targeted in the same way as Apollonios; many of his men were killed, probably mainly in the subsequent pursuit.[7] The Maccabean forces assiduously collected the weapons their enemies dropped in their flight; Judah had seized Apollonios' sword, and used it throughout. Nothing emphasizes the amateurism of Judah's army more than this need to arm the soldiers from the enemy's weaponry.

Judah was now able to attract even more volunteers. He held an assembly at Mizpah, almost in sight of Jerusalem, where he organized his force into divisions and regiments, appointing commanders of thousands, hundreds, fifties, and tens, and indoctrinated the soldiers, especially the recent volunteers, with a loyalty to the old version of Judaism which he imagined had operated before the recent changes.[8] He was given time for all this because this was the time when Antiochos held his great parade at Daphne, which must have gathered up a lot of the local troops, and then was organizing his eastern expedition. When he left he allocated a substantial part of his army to Lysias – *I Maccabees* says it was 'half' the army – and gave him general instructions to deal with the Judaean rebellion.

A new governor of Koile Syria was appointed, and also a new commander of the expeditionary force for Judaea, respectively Ptolemaios, son of Dorymenes and Nikanor, son of Patroklos. Nikanor collected his army from the available forces in southern Syria, and from the civil militias of the various cities, and set up an armed camp at Ammaus in the plain below the Judaean hills. From there he had the choice of two separate routes towards Jerusalem. Like Judah, he spent some time training his forces, many of whom had probably hardly ever held a weapon. At Mizpah Judah purged his army of those with families and of the evident neutrals.[9] He wanted only fanatics in the coming fight.

Nikanor may have had the choice of two routes into the hills, but Judah had a better viewpoint in the hills from which to spy out what he actually did. A large detachment, under Gorgias, was sent up by the valley of the Wadi Ali. This was reported to Judah who brought his own forces over the hills – avoiding the valleys – and attacked the camp at Ammaus by surprise. Gorgias' forces reached Mizpah to find the campsite empty, and when they returned to Ammaus they found that it had been destroyed.[10]

Negotiations followed; a long-drawn-out process because any agreement had to be referred to the king in the east, and because several parties – Lysias, Menelaos, Judah, the Governor of Koile Syria, at least – were involved. Menelaos made concessions, Lysias made concessions which the king refused to agree to; a tentative agreement with Menelaos was repudiated by Judah and the army. The Maccabees and their forces insisted on nothing less than their full demands, and since they had been victorious so far, they had no reason to compromise. By the time this had all become clear, and that it was impossible to reach an agreement, a full year had passed since the fight at Ammaus.[11]

In the summer of 164 Lysias himself came south with the main army. He chose to avoid the difficult approaches made by the earlier invaders, and marched his forces to the southern end of the Judaean hills, to approach by an easier route past the small fort of Beth Zur. The approach was methodical and therefore slow. It had taken most of the autumn to reach the point of attack, but while the attack on Beth Zur was being prepared, the Seleukid army suddenly retired.[12]

Since the Maccabees had raided the Seleukid army a short time before, they chose to claim that this raid had frightened the bigger force away, and exaggerated the number of casualties they claimed to have inflicted. In fact, the retirement took place because Lysias had just received news that Antiochos IV had died in Iran, and that Philip and the other part of the Seleukid army was marching west; some of them had already reached Antioch when Lysias returned to the city; the intentions of Philip were not clear, but no doubt Lysias got some idea from the men he had found in Antioch.

The chronology of all this is unclear, but it seems unlikely that Lysias would have set off on an expedition into Judaea had he known that Philip was on his way west. His ward, Antiochos V, was now sole king; Lysias faced being trapped between two rebellions, though they were still well apart and hardly likely to co-operate, so the obvious thing to do was to eliminate one of them quickly. Keeping control of the Seleukid government was clearly Lysias' priority, and therefore confronting Philip and his army came first; hence his retirement from the Judaean war.

Judah Maccabee had therefore gained a respite, and he used it to attack and capture Jerusalem, where the temple was 'cleansed' of the 'pollution' of the worship of Zeus, and Menelaos was besieged in the Akra.[13] This was not a difficult operation, since the city had been left unfortified by Apollonios when he built the Akra. Without any siege equipment or machinery all Judah and his men could do against Menelaos was to build a wall to surround the fort to prevent sorties of the garrison and to attempt to induce a famine.

Judah sent raiding expeditions out in all directions, across the Jordan, into Galilee, and into the lowlands, no doubt mainly to gather loot and weapons and food, but also in some cases to collect Jews who felt that they were under threat – because of Judah's violence. Much of the detail of this in the books of Maccebees is invented or exaggerated or both, but the war had certainly now spread from the Judaean hills into the surrounding countries.[14]

The threat from Philip pinned Lysias down in north Syria for some time, perhaps for much of the winter of 164–163, but eventually Menelaos and some of his fellow besieged left the Akra – the siege was clearly no more than a loose blockade, despite the wall – and went to Antioch, where he convinced Lysias that it was now urgent that the siege be relieved, and the insurgents be defeated. He marched south, bringing the new king with him, and approached once again by way of Beth Zur. The fort there was quickly taken and the Maccabean army, which had massed a little to the north at Beth Zakaria, was defeated with little difficulty. (The Maccabees made a great point of the exploit of the youngest of the brothers, Eleazar, who attacked an elephant, dying in the process, but this only disguised the comprehensive defeat of the army.) Judah and his soldiers scattered. Lysias captured Jerusalem, and relieved the siege of the Akra. A diehard group put up a forlorn defence of the temple, without success. Then Lysias had to return north, taking the high priest Menelaos with him. Philip approached.[15]

Philip managed to reach and occupy Antioch while Lysias was away in the south, but Antioch was only one city, albeit an important one; it was the person of the king which was crucial to the result, and he was in Lysias' hands. The story as retailed in Josephos' version is that Antiochos had not only given Philip the royal insignia but had charged him with the guardianship of his son, and with his education. But this is clearly Philip's version, as is the story that he was given the royal insignia – retailed by Josephos because Lysias was the Jews' enemy – and we do not need to accept it whole. He certainly carried the royal insignia, but then he was in command of the army which he was returning to Syria. The rest may be disregarded. It is hardly likely that Antiochos set up a civil war between the two men to initiate his son's reign – that was all Philip's doing.

Philip's precise purpose is never stated, other than to take up the guardianship of the boy king Antiochos V. But one must recall that Antiochos IV had begun that way (as had Heliodoros before him), and within a few years he had dispensed with his charge and made himself sole king. It seems quite likely that Philip had the same scenario in mind. He failed. Lysias' army retook Antioch and inflicted a defeat on Philip's forces. We do not know the details, other than the recapture of the city, but it seems safe to assume that Philip died, either in or after the fight.[16]

In Judaea a new high priest was appointed. Menelaos was sent into exile at Beroia in northern Syria (and not much later was killed).[17] The new man was Alkimos, and he found that Judah's old terrorist tactics had been revived. However, Alkimos' own arrival helped rally the Jewish opponents of the Maccabees, and he also attracted some others who had broken with them. This time Lysias did not come to the rescue: he was otherwise engaged in defending his position.

Lysias was probably a scion of a family which had been established in Asia Minor back in the time of Seleukos I. They were responsible for the foundation of two cities, Lysias and Philomelion (named for the alternating names of the male heads of the family). The family had probably lost its position in Asia Minor when the Attalids took control. They were thus notably Seleukid-loyalist, and Lysias the regent certainly fulfilled the trust placed in him by Antiochos IV.[18] Lysias seems to have founded another city somewhere in Judaea during his time as regent; it was probably essentially a fort, perhaps named informally by the soldiers – but it was another Lysias. As regent he clearly had difficulty in holding on to his authority. This was not a position which had any tradition in the Seleukid family history (unlike in the Ptolemaic and Antigonid families). Philip clearly had felt entitled to make a grab for it; there may have been others.

So far as can be seen Lysias did not change the personnel of the government, except in one case, where the Governor of Koile Syria, Ptolemaios Makron, was dismissed after the rejection of the peace terms by the Maccabees. He was vulnerable anyway, since he had betrayed his Ptolemaic employers when Antiochos IV invaded Cyprus. He was clearly dismissed as the man who had advocated compromise with the rebels, and when that policy failed, thanks to Maccabean obduracy, he had to go.[19] Otherwise it seems that the officials appointed by Antiochos IV generally stayed in post. But they had owed those posts to the dead king, and may well have felt a certain independence from Lysias.

Lysias' lack of authority was presumably somewhat reversed by the defeat of Philip and the reconquest of Judaea, but his power was still fragile. This was demonstrated by a visit by a Roman delegation in 163. Roman senatorial travellers regularly turned up in Syria when a new king took office, no doubt in part as a courtesy to congratulate the new king, but also, and mainly, to investigate his policies and intentions. As the period since the victories at Magnesia and then at Pydna lengthened, these delegations became more arrogant. They were generally most concerned to see if the Seleukid government had any intention of adventuring westwards. In 166–165, perhaps in the aftermath of the great parade at Daphne, whose concentration of forces must have seemed threatening, Ti. Sempronius Gracchus arrived; when he returned to Rome he reported that Antiochos was not a threat after all, since he was intent on going to the east.[20]

A new delegation therefore arrived in 163 to check on the policies of the regency. It consisted of three senators, of which the most forceful was Cn. Octavius. He was clearly a coming man in Rome, having commanded the Roman fleet as praetor in the Macedonian war with some success, and was consul in 165. Whether or not he had instructions to this effect is not known – though Polybios claims he had – but he started issuing orders that the terms of the Treaty of Apamaea should be enforced. This is most likely to have been his own idea; it may be that he had been told to assert Roman power, but he cannot have been told to enforce the provisions of a treaty which had been defunct for over twenty years.

Nevertheless Lysias felt constrained to obey, or at least to make gestures in that direction, such was the erosion of his authority. Naval vessels were burned and war elephants were killed. The only way the beasts could be killed was apparently by hamstringing them and then letting them die, presumably of starvation and thirst, and in agony. The most efficient method is to drive an iron spike into their brains, and it is highly unlikely that the mahouts did not know this, so perhaps Lysias contrived this even less pleasant method because of its results. The maimed animals complained loud and long, to the distress of everyone within earshot.

Public opinion in Syria swung violently against Octavius, and probably against Lysias as well. One man, Leptines, assassinated Octavius in the gymnasium at Laodikeia-ad-Mare. Leptines claimed divine inspiration, no doubt as a way of escaping punishment; a Greek rhetorician, Isokrates, began raising a mob to finish the job by murdering the other Roman envoys, but they got away – and Lysias would scarcely permit more murders. Public adulation of the murderer prevented him from being arrested, and Lysias had to report the murder to Rome. The Senate actually did nothing, perhaps embarrassed by Octavius' earlier behaviour, which was clearly even more overbearing than was usual with Roman envoys.[21]

These Roman envoys had been prejudiced against Lysias even before they had reached Syria. They had passed through Kappadokia, where the new king, Ariarathes V, who had succeeded his aged father in 163, had a complaint about Lysias. He claimed that his mother, Antiochis, and his sister, had been killed in Antioch, and that Lysias was responsible. Antiochis was a daughter of Antiochos III and was an assertive woman, as one would expect with a Seleukid princess. She had apparently moved to Antioch when her son became king in Kappadokia, taking her daughter with her. While there she, or her daughter, had evidently fallen foul of the regency government, and had died, or been murdered. Ariarathes later described this as an 'abominable crime'.[22]

What the women had done to deserve such a fate – if they really were murdered – is not known, but if it was the doing of Lysias it was presumably something political. There are two obvious possibilities: Antiochis was now Antiochos V's nearest female relative, and she might have made a bid to become the king's official guardian; or she was somehow involved in the adventure of Philip aiming to do this. (Her daughter, if young enough, could well have been a prime candidate for the wife of the young king.) Ariarathes clearly held Lysias responsible in some way for their deaths, either directly or indirectly, or in failing to ensure their safety. He had sent envoys to Antioch before meeting the Romans to recover their bodies for burial in the cenotaph of the kings of Kappadokia, but he was careful to avoid accusing Lysias until after this mission was successful.

So, apart from Philip, it seems likely that Lysias had also faced a threat to his position from Antiochis, Kappadokian queen and Seleukid princess, and that he had dealt with it in the usual way of threatened politicians – he could well have learned what to do from Antiochos IV. The next threat, however, was one he could not defeat so easily.

Demetrios, son of Seleukos IV, had been in Italy since the early 170s, before his father died. During the reign of his uncle he had not apparently made any attempt to return to Syria or to claim the throne which he, as he made clear later, felt should be his. It would have been suicidal to arrive in Syria to make the claim while Antiochos IV was in control. Until 170 Demetrios also had the fate of his brother to consider, and when the young Antiochos was killed when he was actually joint king, it was even more likely that Demetrios, almost adult by then, and virtually unknown in Syria, would be despatched as quickly should he attempt to claim the kingship.

With Antiochos IV's death, however, the position changed. Now Demetrios was the senior adult male in the Seleukid family, just as Antiochos had been in 175; and he was still the rightful king if primogeniture was the accepted mode of succession. But, unlike Antiochos, who was free to decide his own actions in 175, Demetrios was constrained by his detention in Italy. When he heard of Antiochos' death he went to the Senate to ask for release from his hostage status, but was refused. Polybios explains that the senators felt that a weak and unstable government in the Seleukid kingdom was in their better interests, an interesting comment on both Roman fears and latent Seleukid strength when ruled by a vigorous king.[23]

Demetrios cast around for advice, receiving contradictory suggestions. When news came that Octavius had been murdered he tried again with the Senate, but was again refused. This time he understood the finality of the refusal, and so set about plotting to escape. He was introduced to an envoy of Ptolemy VI, Menyllos, who agreed to set things up by hiring a Carthaginian ship which lay at Ostia, supposedly to take him home to Egypt. Demetrios' foster father, a man called Diodoros, had arrived in Italy, and reported on the condition of affairs in Syria, suggesting that Demetrios had only to land to be accepted. A trio of brothers, sons of Apollonios, a man who had served Seleukos IV but who had refused to serve Antiochos IV, were enlisted as helpers. A plot was organized which allowed Demetrios to apparently disappear from Rome on a hunting expedition for several days, something he was in the habit of doing.

He went on board the ship at dawn and sailed at once. It was four days before his absence was discovered, and a meeting of the Senate decided that they could do nothing about it; they sent off another delegation of senators, headed once again by Ti. Sempronius Gracchus, to wait in Asia Minor to see how Demetrios' venture turned out. It is clear that the Senate did not really care one way or another, what happened, though some pleasure was probably felt at the likelihood of further disruption of the Seleukid kingdom. There was a general dislike of the method Demetrios had used to escape – the sort of complaint made by men who were unable to do anything definite – not that he had been given any choice.[24]

As Diodoros had predicted, the arrival of Demetrios immediately punctured the remaining prestige of the regency government. On landing at Tripolis, Demetrios at once put on a diadem, so proclaiming himself king. In Antioch the troops, under whose command we do not know, arrested Lysias, King Antiochos, and his even younger brother (this last is unknown otherwise) and set out to bring them to Demetrios. He sent a message that he did not want to meet them, and the troops obediently killed all three. This looks bad, but it is unlikely that anyone expected him to do anything else. At least there were now no family competitors left, or so he must have thought.[25]

Demetrios was faced with much the same sort of problems as had confronted Lysias: the rebellion in Judaea, a military rebellion in the east, and the interference of Rome. But in addition, because of the way he had become king his diplomatic relationships in the region were now different. We do not know much about Lysias' diplomatic situation, except that he was at enmity in the end with Ariarathes of Kappadokia. He was appointed regent by Antiochos IV, so in theory he should have been able to count on Eumenes of Pergamon as a friend, though we do not know if he did. The treaty with Ptolemy VI ended with Antiochos' death, but Egypt was in the midst of a political crisis in 163, and was not in any condition to mount a new attack to recover Syria. Demetrios had also been given help by Menyllos, which may indicate Ptolemaic support for his coup, but either way he did not have to worry about his southern front.

Demetrios, on the other hand, had brought with him some diplomatic baggage of his own. His mode of leaving Italy had prejudiced the Senate against him, though it seems that Ti. Sempronius Gracchus' senatorial delegation, which waited in Asia Minor to see what happened, suggested that this was a suspension of Roman hostility; if he secured rapid control of the kingdom and looked to becoming seriously powerful, no doubt Roman attitudes would change. But the friendship with Eumenes of Pergamon, which had sustained Antiochos IV, was undoubtedly finished. In Egypt, Demetrios had made friends with Ptolemy VI on one of the latter's visits to Italy, and it might be assumed that for a time at least, that personal relationship would continue – but neither king would allow that to stand in the way of action should his kingdom require it.[26]

The internal situation in the kingdom is symbolized by the changeover of officials. The three sons of Apollonios, who had assisted him in Italy – one of them described as his foster brother – had been exiled because their father would not work under Antiochos IV; now these men would work for Demetrios, and given the circumstances he was very likely to favour them at the expense of any of Antiochos' men who continued in government under him. At the same time we know of some officials who had worked with Antiochos but who now refused to work with Demetrios. It is evident that the split which had occurred in the royal family had spread down the social ladder to the official aristocracy.

Demetrios identified the Judaean problem as either the most urgent, or perhaps it was the issue he felt he could deal with first and easiest. Demetrios, of course, would find it necessary to impose himself at once, assert his power and so convince everyone that he was in control. He presumably knew of the presence in Asia Minor of the senatorial delegation, and would wish also to impress them, if only so that they would go away. And the Judaean rebellion was tailor-made for an early success: a minor affray, a virtually unarmed enemy which had been defeated already, a long-standing dispute, and a solution which was obvious, and had been tried already only not to the full extent necessary for a clear victory. All it needed was a clear plan and the resolution to win.

Demetrios was appealed to by the high priest Alkimos, who was the most likely victim of the revived rebellion. A substantial army commanded by a competent general, Bakchides, was sent to Judaea. At first Bakchides attempted to negotiate, and met a group of moderates so-called, referred to as Hasidim, though he evidently was unable to distinguish their attitudes from those of the Maccabees. They did say that they did not accept the authority of Alkimos as high priest. Since Alkimos was installed by royal decree, this made them rebels, so they were executed.[27]

After this any planned negotiations with the Maccabees were never even started, so Bakchides campaigned against them, driving their forces into their traditional refuge in the Gophna hills. He managed to kill considerable numbers of fighters, but none of the Maccabee leaders was caught. It may be that Bakchides found no one left to fight, and assumed that the rebellion was suppressed, or perhaps he was recalled by Demetrios to face the new threat of Timarchos from the east, but he did withdraw, taking his army with him. The rebellion once again revived. Another appeal for help went to the king from Alkimos. Another army under another general, Nikanor, arrived.[28]

The Maccabean forces had been defeated, and then once more negotiations were attempted. An elaborate and unbelievable story, involving Judah being enlisted as a friend of the king (*philos*), marrying and settling down, is spun by the Maccabees books, designed to cast the blame for the breakdown of the talks on everyone but the Maccabees. But any agreement which the Maccabees would accept was never going to be acceptable to Alkimos and his party, and when this became clear Demetrios refused to ratify the tentative agreement Nikanor and Judah had reached.[29]

Fighting restarted. Nikanor received reinforcements from the surrounding lands, but probably none from the main army in North Syria. It is a measure of the increased military confidence of the Maccabees that Judah was now willing to risk another pitched battle; perhaps Nikanor's force was also perceived to be less powerful than Bakchides'. Once again, Nikanor as commander was the first target in the battle; he was killed early on, and his army then disintegrated and fled. The anniversary of the battle has been celebrated by the Jews ever since, as 'Nikanor's Day' – March 161 – though the sequel was a disaster for them.[30]

The main reason for the Jews' victory was less the competence or otherwise of Demetrios' commanders than the small size of their armies. It seems clear that Bakchides had been in command of a larger force than Nikanor, whose reinforcements were probably militiamen from the lowland cities rather than the professionals whom Bakchides probably commanded – the same make-up as the defeated armies of Apollonios and Seron. And the reason for the shortage of forces is that the Judaean war was by far the less important conflict facing Demetrios. He also, like Lysias in 164 and 163, was faced by a much more dangerous enemy, the Governor of Media, in this case, Timarchos.

It is not clear when Timarchos was appointed Governor of Media, but he was first made Governor of Babylonia. His brother, Herakleides, had been Antiochos IV's treasurer, and it may be that Timarchos was made governor early in Antiochos' reign, in which case he cannot have supported Philip in his campaign against Lysias.[31] It is thus perhaps more likely that he was given the post in Media by Lysias in succession to whoever held the governorship at the end of Antiochos' reign, for this man must have either supported Philip or been removed by him.

Herakleides seems to have been one of those officials who refused to serve Demetrios. As a result he had to go into exile, but his brother had substantial armed forces under his control. Timarchos advanced with some care and deliberation. He can be traced first as Governor of Media (and therefore as viceroy of the eastern provinces), then in Babylonia, where he minted coins in his own name, and thereby claimed the royal title. At some point he contacted Rome, possibly through Gracchus and his delegation in Asia Minor. He is supposed to have bribed the senators wholesale – which seems unlikely – but he did receive an ambiguous decree of recognition in return. The story in Diodoros implies, however, that he did this before raising an army in Media, and this cannot be accepted as it stands. One can well believe, however, that Rome interfered. Alternatively his brother Herakleides went to Rome on his behalf and secured the decree. Given the likely attitude of senatorial annoyance with Demetrios, bribery was hardly necessary.

Timarchos may have also minted coins at Nisibis in Mesopotamia, and may have contacted Artaxias of Armenia, though presumably only to neutralize a threat to his flank rather than to make an active alliance. Eventually he faced Demetrios' army and was defeated. He is said by Diodoros to have marched as far west as the Euphrates crossing at Seleukeia-Zeugma, which was perhaps where the battle took place.[32]

The timing of all this is as unclear as the events themselves, but it seems that it was not until 160, perhaps early in that year, that Timarchos was finally defeated. By then Judah Maccabee had been in control of all Judaea apart from the Akra in Jerusalem, for a year after his defeat of Nikanor. Demetrios, victorious in the north, turned at once to dealing with this other rebellion. This time, now that the government was not distracted, a clear plan was made to ensure that the rebellion was first defeated, and then was unable to revive. Judah, who must have known that whoever won the war in the north a new attack would eventually come, had contacted Rome, but received neither encouragement nor help.

Rome was unusually prominent in the minds of all those involved in the extended Seleukid crisis which followed the death of Antiochos IV. Yet all the appeals produced no reaction worth mentioning, and certainly nothing effective. Timarchos was 'recognized' as king, but received no help, which is what he needed. Roman encouragement was perhaps enough to keep him going, but not enough to give him victory. In Rome this might well have seemed enough – the kingdom would continue to be disrupted. In the same way, Judah Maccabee cannot have expected anything concrete to come from his appeal; the only assistance which would be of use to him was a Roman military expedition, and this was never going to be mounted. Lysias had clearly been intimidated by Octavius, and had hastened to apologize when the Roman was killed. Roman reaction to all this was negligent or non-existent. The only man involved who showed indifference to Rome was Demetrios, and he was the one man who knew Rome and the senators at first hand. (The same indifference may be said to have been shown by Antiochos IV, whose presentation of money to the city had an element of contempt in it.) The more familiar with Rome a politician was, the less it was feared; only those far off thought it was worth appealing to.

Demetrios reappointed Bakchides to the task in Judaea, and gave him a substantial army. He climbed up to the plateau by an unexpected route on the

Jordan side, and his army took up a position on the plateau top before Judah knew he had arrived. In order to bring the Maccabean army to a fight Bakchides sent out raiding parties to ravage the countryside. Judah, who by this time had been the effective ruler of Judaea for a year, had no choice but to co-operate with the invaders by gathering his own army and marshalling it into a regular formation for battle. The two armies faced each other for a few days, then Bakchides shifted his army forwards until they were so close together that, even if he wanted, Judah could not get away; at the first sign of retreat, or retirement, Bakchides would attack. For the first time Judah and his army were facing a competent general and a competent professional army.

The two armies were arrayed in the standard Hellenistic pattern, infantry in phalanx formation in the centre, cavalry on the wings. Bakchides initiated the fight by advancing his infantry, spears levelled. Judah led his left wing cavalry in a charge against the Seleukid cavalry opposite them, in which Bakchides was. This was again Judah's normal tactic of aiming to kill the enemy commander at the start. But he had done this too often: Bakchides carefully retreated before the attack, drawing the Maccabean force along, and then brought the whole of his cavalry from both wings to deal with the Jewish cavalry separately from the infantry. Judah was killed, and probably almost all of his cavalrymen as well. The infantry battle was a slower defeat for the Maccabean army, and when the news of Judah's death reached the foot soldiers, the survivors broke and fled. The victorious cavalry were available to harry the rout.[33]

Bakchides then implemented a new plan of occupation of Judaea, which had probably been arranged with Demetrios before the expedition set out. It had not been possible to do this earlier because of the various threats to Lysias and to Demetrios from other enemies, but now, with no distractions, and with manpower available at last, Bakchides set about establishing a firm grip on Judaea.

The Maccabean supporters were chased down, though probably most of them simply faded back into the general population. The defeat was serious enough to ensure that no immediate renewal of the insurgency was likely, especially now that Judah was dead. The Seleukid forces established a series of forts and fortified towns, controlling the roads and approaches. The Maccabean leadership devolved onto another brother, Jonathan, who failed to hold a position in Judaea and soon removed himself to beyond the Jordan. Later he became established, apparently quietly, at Michmash in the north of Judaea, where he remained for several years. He had attempted a new rising by seizing a place called Bathbasi, but Bakchides blockaded his forces into surrender.[34]

In 159, therefore, when Alkimos died, Judaea was reduced to the peace of a military occupation by enemy forces. Alkimos was not replaced. The hereditary succession the Oniad dynasty of high priests had been broken fifteen years earlier, and neither of the two last incumbents, Menelaos and Alkimos, had been of that family. Demetrios had evidently decided that the post should be left unfilled, presumably because to appoint anyone would only rouse opposition from somewhere.

Demetrios had therefore survived the dangerous first years of his reign, defeating Timarchos' rebellion, and successfully bringing an end to the rebellion in Judaea. But he was still faced, like his father, with hostility from Asia Minor. In Egypt, Ptolemy VI was regaining control of his kingdom and had given refuge to the surviving Oniad, Onias IV, who developed a rival Jewish temple.[35] The civil wars of the Seleukid kingdom had attracted the greedy attention of his neighbours, while the killing of Timarchos, whether by execution or in battle, had roused in Herakleides his brother an anger which could only be appeased by Demetrios' destruction. The poisonous legacy of Antiochos IV continued.

Chapter 4

The Problems of Demetrios I (160–150 BC)

Demetrios I had begun his rule with some successes. He had survived a rebellion from the east, and he had put down the Jewish insurgency in Judaea. The reactions of his neighbours, who had no doubt contemplated his defeat and death with equanimity, if not anticipated pleasure, is not known directly, which means they did nothing. The report by Gracchus and his fellow senators to the Senate when they returned to Rome could only be that Demetrios was firmly seated in power and the kingdom was at peace.

However, with his accession the Seleukid dynasty was reduced once more to a single adult unmarried male. It was therefore necessary that the new king should marry as quickly as possible, and produce a male heir, but the choice of possible wives was very limited. None of the foreign dynasties who might be regarded as of a suitable rank had daughters available. The only Ptolemaic female was Kleopatra II, but she was one of the trio of monarchs, and was already married to her brother; the Antigonid line had been extinguished; the Attalids were now diplomatically hostile, probably had no women available, and were anyway not in the habit of sending daughters to be queens elsewhere; Ariarathes of Kappadokia was probably hostile as well after his dispute with Lysias. There was only one woman who was both available and of the properly distinguished birth, Demetrios' own sister, Laodike.[1]

This was a delicate diplomatic matter, however. Laodike was the widow of King Perseus of Macedon. She had survived the Macedonian debacle of 167, though both her husband and her children had died or were imprisoned in Italy after the Roman conquest. Laodike had probably been sent back to Syria by the conquerors, in or about 167. She is said to have been offered in marriage to Ariarathes of Kappadokia, which may have been a gesture by Lysias aimed at repairing relations after the breach with Kappadokia after the deaths of Antiochis and her daughter.[2] It has to be said that this identification is not secure. Demetrios' wife was certainly called Laodike, and it has not been possible to find another woman of the right name, age and birth other than Demetrios' sister. (This argument is not by any means watertight, of course, but it is a useful and in many ways persuasive hypothesis.) It would thus seem that brother and sister were married, probably as soon as Demetrios had made himself king.

The practice of sibling marriage was, of course, well established in the Ptolemaic dynasty, and had become a Seleukid practice with the marriage of Demetrios' mother Laodike, to her full brother Antiochos the Young King in about 195; Laodike was then subsequently married to her two other brothers. So Demetrios' marriage to his sister was within the practices of the dynasty, quite apart from the lack of suitable women elsewhere. Their eldest son, Demetrios (II), was a young teenager in 148 when he began to campaign to unseat the usurper Alexander Balas, and was thus born before 160. Once he was born, of course, the dynasty was on its way to safety. Two other sons were born of the marriage, Antigonos and Antiochos.

Demetrios' reign may therefore be said to have begun with several successes, but he faced some formidable problems from then on. Internally the east was disturbed. Twice in five years a general from Iran had brought an army west as far as North Syria only to be defeated. The result in the east must have been a severe depletion of the Seleukid military power, and thus of imperial security there. It neither case does it seem that a royal expedition was sent to the east to settle affairs there. Neither Lysias nor Demetrios could afford to leave Syria. Externally Demetrios, unlike Antiochos IV and Lysias, faced the hostility of his western neighbours, which was why he was unable to attend to the east. It would be best to look at the eastern territories first, then the problems of the west.

The eastern territories began with Babylonia, the valley of the Tigris and Euphrates rivers, a region with a strong traditional loyalty to the Seleukid house, whose kings had planted several Greek-type cities there including one of the great cities of the Greek world, at Seleukeia-on-the-Tigris, but at the same time they had carefully cultivated an image as Babylonian kings, attending regularly to the ceremonial required by a royal presence at the greater temples, and they had been rewarded by a steadfast Babylonian loyalty. Even during Timarchos' time of success a cuneiform tablet from Babylon had used the name of Demetrios in the dating formula, yet Timarchos had minted coins at the city in his name as king.[3] This was a wealthy region, one of the main financial resources of the monarchy, but it was, as several military campaigns showed, virtually undefendable, being easily invaded from both east and north (and, soon, from the desert as well). Timarchos had overrun it with ease, coming through the mountains from Iran, and it fell back into Demetrios' control just as quickly when Timarchos was beaten and killed.

Beyond Babylonia, Iran was only partly under Seleukid control. In the north-west was the kingdom of Media Atropatene, ruled by a dynasty descended from a Persian nobleman of Alexander's time; in the north-east was the Parthian kingdom, an amalgam of nomads from the north and locals long domiciled there, and including at least two Greek cities originally founded by Alexander or an earlier Seleukid king. It is this kingdom against which Antiochos IV was campaigning when he died in 164. In the south, the region of Persis, around the former Persian imperial centre of (ruined) Persepolis, was semi-independent under a local dynasty. Susa and the region of Susiana/Elymais had also seen trouble at the time of Timarchos' rebellion. The city had a prolific mint, but Timarchos produced no coins there, even though both Antiochos IV and Demetrios I did. Instead, an otherwise unknown man, Hyknapses, an Iranian name, is recorded on some bronze coins from the city. He was presumably a local lord who seized the moment of confusion caused by Timarchos to set himself up in the city as ruler, in emulation of Persis. He did not last long, and was removed when Demetrios' power returned.[4]

The main strength of the Seleukids in Iran lay in the centre, along the great ancient road which led from the Bisitun Pass which led up through the Zagros Mountains from Babylonia, towards Baktria, beyond Parthia. There was a cluster of Greek cities just east of the pass, and several others along the road, including the main political centre of Seleukid Iran, at Ekbatana, renamed by Antiochos IV as Epiphaneia. But Seleukid authority only reached to some way east of Rhagai (near modern Teheran). The next city along the road, Hekatompylos, was one of the Parthian capitals. Power radiated, in other words, from the cities, and it was control of them which was essential. But Seleukid control of Iran had thinned out in the last generation thanks above all to the western adventures of Philip and Timarchos. Attention by the central government was required, though Demetrios was unable to provide it.

Still further to the east, beyond the Parthian kingdom, was the kingdom of Baktria, ruled by one or more Macedonian or Greek dynasties. It was a turbulent land, which had to withstand nomad attacks from the north, occasionally fight the Parthians on the west, and yet had sent armies to invade India to the east. The internal history of the kingdom is not really very clear, but by the 160s there were at least two antagonistic dynasties fighting each other, and the Parthians had taken advantage of this to seize parts of the kingdom, along their mutual border.[5] This took place at the expense of King Eukratides I, who ruled in the 160s and perhaps until about 155. The event is important for the Seleukid kingdom since the growth in power and territory of the Parthian state and the breakdown of the Baktrian kingdom gave Parthia a larger population base and less to worry about to its east. With the Baktrian kings preoccupied with each other and with India, Parthia might be able to turn to the west. It was no doubt this which had persuaded Antiochos IV to undertake an eastern expedition. For the time being the Baktrian turbulence had to be watched in case it spilled over into a Parthian war, and the memory of Antiochos' invasion from the west, which had reached into Parthian territory, was still fresh. But the nomad threat to Baktria from the north was growing, with the movement westwards of the Yueh-chih nomad state, and if the Seleukid power weakened further, the Parthians were clearly available to take advantage of it as they had of Eukratides' Baktrian preoccupations. Antiochos' expedition had obviously bolstered the Seleukid position for a time but Timarchos' adventure following on the withdrawal of Antiochos' army by Philip, had given some idea of the basic Seleukid weakness, and can only have made it worse.

Demetrios kept the administration of the kingdom as it had been under his predecessors, and this included keeping many of the provincial governors in their offices. These were important, well-connected men, and most were happy to continue in their posts. It was fortunate that no other governors rebelled with Timarchos. The Babylonian governor had fled to Seleukeia during the troubles, and this presumably meant he was loyal to Demetrios. Further south, in the sub-province at the head of the Persian Gulf, the governor was Hyspaosines, whose origin may have been in Baktria. He had been appointed by Antiochos IV when the king campaigned in the area, and he used the new city of Antioch-on-the-Erythraian-Sea, the former Alexandria which had been refounded by Antiochos, as his governing centre. Hyspaosines remained in office throughout both Timarchos' campaign and Demetrios' reign, clearly as a loyalist.[6]

The governor of the sub-province of Kommagene, Ptolemaios, also remained in that office for thirty years after his appointment in 163, through the disturbances of every reign, and a series of civil wars. Kommagene was essentially the valley of the Euphrates River where it came through the Taurus Mountains, and was therefore a frontier over against the kingdoms of Asia Minor, Kappadokia and Armenia, and beyond them the Attalids of Pergamon. Ptolemaios was appointed by Lysias on behalf of Antiochos V, but he must have shown a rapid loyalty to Demetrios, since the decisive battle against Timarchos in 160 took place very close to his province; had he been disloyal he could have been easily removed. No doubt this guaranteed his position for the rest of Demetrios' reign. He was sufficiently independent to conduct a campaign over the border into Melitene at one point, without drawing any complaint from

Demetrios – but then Demetrios himself had troubles in the area, and it might be that Ptolemaios was actually operating on behalf of the king. Either way the episode implies a certain independence in the governor. And if he ran a tight ship in his frontier land, he could be more useful there than if he was moved on or retired, and every king seems to have appreciated his quality – or it may be that he had implanted himself so firmly in the province that it would be dangerous to remove him.[7] After 152 no king was interested in disturbing matters any more than absolutely necessary.

The sources for identifying governors, their territories, and their careers, are almost non-existent, so it is not possible to discover anything resembling a career path for them, nor is it possible to follow individual men from post to post, except in cases such as Ptolemaios of Kommagene, or in occasional throwaway comments by the historians. Some men will have been replaced as the casualties of Timarchos' rebellion (or his collaborators, if there were any) were identified; some, like Ptolemaios, will have been left in post. By the late 150s it would have been reasonable for Demetrios to assume that he had the loyalty of all the governors, most of whom by then were probably his appointees. But they were all necessarily mature men who had started their careers perhaps twenty years earlier, as subjects of Antiochos IV, so their loyalty may well have been partial and provisional. One at least proved to be actively disloyal.

The defeat and death of Timarchos had been a legitimate defence of his kingship by King Demetrios, and could be expected to have settled the matter; earlier revolts – by Molon or by Akhaios – had ended in the same way, with no repercussions. But Timarchos' revolt had an afterlife, and produced a problem which grew so that it eventually overwhelmed Demetrios.

Timarchos came originally from Miletos in Asia Minor,[8] and his brother Herakleides, who had been a high official of Antiochos IV and Lysias, had been dismissed by Demetrios on Timarchos' rebellion.[9] Not surprisingly, he became Demetrios' active enemy after his brother's death. It is probable that Herakleides was the fount of the conspiracy which began to form soon after Timarchos' death in 160, for he seems to have been the one who sought out the children of Antiochos IV and his 'concubine' Antiochis. They were living at Ephesos and he persuaded the elder, Alexander, to make his claim for the Seleukid kingship.[10] It is, however, not only in memory of Timarchos that Herakleides organized the plot. It is likely – though it is not possible to prove this – that Herakleides was also acting in memory of Antiochos IV and of Antiochos V, the child who had been killed at Demetrios' orders in 162 – and perhaps also in memory of Lysias.

Herakleides was especially dangerous because he had full knowledge of the people in Demetrios' court and administration, and of the government system. He was therefore working with full knowledge of his enemy. Demetrios had disturbed the governing system as little as possible, of course, and it is likely that he had not removed many of the officials and commanders who had been in position when he took over. Continuity was in his interest. Timarchos, for instance, had been put in post as governor of the east by Antiochos IV or Lysias, and had at first been left in post by Demetrios. Some others no doubt went, such as Herakleides, but there was only a limited pool of administrators and it was in the king's interest to keep as many of them in position as he could. But Herakleides knew these men, and could appeal to them in some ways. The ground was well prepared for his plot.

Having contacted Alexander, and presumably persuaded him to make his claim, Herakleides brought the two children to the Pergamene court. The new king there, Attalos II, had succeeded his father in that year, 159. These kings had no doubt been annoyed by the loss of their ally Lysias, and before that of Antiochos IV, but the success of Demetrios I was a serious blow, and threatened to cause trouble in Asia Minor – as it did. Attalos proved to be fully willing to become a part of Herakleides' plot. He dressed Alexander in royal robes, saluted him as king,[11] and set him up with a mountain chieftain called Zenodotos on the Attalid-Seleukid border in the Taurus Mountains of Kilikia.[12] Both of these actions were virtual declarations of war by Attalos on Demetrios. Zenodotos actively campaigned, with little effect, for his guest, but his methods were those of a raider from the hills into the valleys, and this was not a very effective way of persuading the people of the lowland, Zenodotos' victims, to accept a new king.

Just to the north of this affair was the kingdom of Kappadokia, already annoyed with the Seleukid kingdom over the deaths of the Queen Mother Antiochis and her daughter. The change of ruler from Lysias to Demetrios does not appear to have calmed the relationship. A series of incidents over the 150s kept the antagonism going. Ariarathes V was deposed by his brother Orophernes in a plot in which Demetrios took part, and his return to his throne in 154 was just as disturbing.[13] Ptolemaios of Kommagene invaded Kappadokia at some point in Demetrios' reign, attacking the town of Melitene.[14] The result is not known, but no Kappadokian riposte happened.

There were thus two conflicts going on in the same region, and it is only reasonable to connect them. Since Ariarathes of Kappadokia was antagonistic to Demetrios he will have been supportive of the plot to replace him with Alexander, and will no doubt have also supported Zenodotos and his raiding activities. Since Zenodotos was a proxy for Attalos and Ariarathes, Ptolemaios was presumably also a proxy for Demetrios. And Ptolemaios' raid was much more damaging than those of Zenodotos.

In other words, for most of the period from 159–154 (when Ariarathes regained his kingship) Demetrios was successful in fending off Alexander's pretensions, at the cost of an occasionally active guerrilla war in the mountains. This may well be the reason Herakleides turned to Rome for help. He took Alexander and his sister to Rome in 154, and presented them to the Senate, where they made a good impression, though the Senate was only marginally interested, and provided no material support for their pretensions – just as it had with Timarchos, or later with Judaea.[15] This lack of interest, however, was both a lack of support for Demetrios and a clear sign that Rome would not interfere in the plotters' activities. It was, in a way, a green light to proceed.

It was at this point that Demetrios made a grievous mistake. Until 154 he had been successful in foiling the plotters, though their activities did mean that he was pinned down in Syria, so that the wider problems of the empire could not be dealt with except at long range. Demetrios allowed himself to become involved in another plot, this time to seize control of Cyprus, part of the Ptolemaic kingdom of his friend Ptolemy VI. One reason may have been the result of the visit of Alexander and Laodike to Rome, whose result was an obvious Roman lack of interest in affairs in the Eastern Mediterranean; it was a green light for others besides Herakleides.

Demetrios' aim was to suborn the Ptolemaic Governor of Cyprus, who would hand the island over to Demetrios' control, just as Ptolemaios Makron had done for Antiochos IV in the Syrian War in 168. This was done, of course, clandestinely, but it failed, and Demetrios' involvement became known. As a result he did not gain Cyprus, but he did gain Ptolemy VI's enmity. Ptolemy was now necessarily at least suspicious of anything Demetrios did, if not immediately hostile to him.[16]

This was Herakleides' opportunity. He could now count on the enmity towards Demetrios of three kings. Of these Attalos was publicly committed to Alexander's cause, but Ariarathes, only just restored to his throne, was probably less so, though he would no doubt be happy to see the end of Demetrios, or at least his defeat. But it was Ptolemy who was the key. Of the three he was the only king with a credible military power, and perhaps even more important, naval power, for it was this which had been lacking so far in the plot. The details of the discussions between the conspirators are not known, but during 153 Ptolemy was persuaded to join them.

There was another dimension. It was necessary to ensure a quick and fairly extensive foothold within the Seleukid kingdom both as a means by which Ptolemaic forces could gain access and as a sign that there was support in the kingdom for Alexander. This meant Palestine, since Ptolemy's forces would need to march in from Egypt, and he would not want his advance to be held up at Gaza.

Indeed, it may be that Ptolemy did not wish to intervene himself in the coming conflict. It would suit him, as it would suit the kings in Asia Minor, and the Romans, if the Seleukid kingdom simply collapsed into civil war, the more prolonged the better. Ptolemy had spent much of the past decade and a half recovering control over Egypt, from rebels and from his obstreperous brother; he knew, far more than most contemporaries, the vagaries of military conflicts. He was persuaded to involve himself in the plot only to a degree. It had to be shown that the plotters were able to accomplish at least something themselves. They had not, of course, done very much so far, other than plot.

This meant that the plotters had to gather an army and had to gain access to the kingdom by suborning a governor or a garrison somewhere. Then they had to get their army to the kingdom, land it, and perhaps defeat Demetrios' army. And this meant also that Alexander had to take part as commander of the expeditionary force. Only by doing so, and winning, could his claim to the kingship be taken seriously. All this necessary preparation explains why it took two years from the accession of Ptolemy to the plot until the landing. In the end it seems that Ptolemy had also to make a decisive contribution.

This theorizing rests on the events of 152. The recruited force of Alexander landed at Ptolemaios-Ake.[17] This means that the plot had recruited a substantial mercenary army, and that it had gathered a sufficient force of warships to transport them. These last could only have come from Ptolemy, who was the only power in the region with sufficient ships – an early danger will have been that the Seleukid fleet might intervene, and it had to be deterred, at least. Second the landing took place at the strongest place in Palestine, the government centre at Ptolemais-Ake, and the city and the citadel immediately surrendered. This in turn implies that the governor and the garrison and its commander had been successfully suborned before the landing. All this will have required a good deal of money. Neither Herakleides nor Alexander can possibly have had enough personal wealth to hire an army and bribe a Seleukid governor and a city garrison. They had presumably been subsidized from the wealth of Egypt and Asia Minor.

Alexander the pretender's parentage is less certain than I have assumed earlier. In this we are enmeshed in rival accusations and assertions. Alexander himself asserted that he and his sister Laodike were children of Antiochos IV; his opponents, led by King Demetrios, accused him of lying, and asserted that he was actually nothing more than a man who looked rather like Antiochos, and that he had been put up to make the claim for the kingship by his unscrupulous backers. So far, so familiar in dynastic politics. But Attalos II knew Antiochos IV, and he accepted that Alexander was his son; Ptolemy VI knew Antiochos and married his eldest daughter to Alexander; when he had actually become king, Alexander's sister, Laodike was married to the king of Pontos, Mithradates V.[18] None of these rulers would be likely to make these contracts if Alexander was a mere lookalike. He must therefore have had other qualities which convinced them. They might have promoted him as king to spite Demetrios – which it certainly did, and which happened again later with another pretender – but Ptolemaic daughters were too valuable dynastically to be given out to mere lookalike pretenders. We may accept that Attalos and Ptolemy – and Mithradates of Pontos – were convinced of Alexander's, and therefore of Laodike's, genuineness.

At the same time, it is obvious, if only from the timing of events, that the installation of Alexander as king in Antioch was not the first priority of any of those involved except Herakleides and Alexander himself. Attalos may have helped to place Alexander with Zenodotos in the Kilikian borderlands in 159, but it was not until another seven years had passed that Ptolemy took a hand openly. When active measures were finally taken it was only because the conditions were right for the backers, and that Demetrios' situation was seen to be weakened by his foreign policy failures, and by his internal unpopularity. And it turned out that he was unable to respond when attacked.

It was the participation of Ptolemy VI which was crucial to the enterprise. Rome may have indicated that it would not oppose Alexander's adventure, but the Senate was clearly not interested in doing anything concrete to further it. It was clearly immaterial to Rome who ruled the Seleukid kingdom, but the Senate was certainly interested in making trouble for it. Attalos II had had to submit to Roman supervision on several occasions in the past, and in all cases it was designed to prevent him from becoming more powerful or gaining territory, or crushing a local enemy, so Rome would certainly look askance at his direct involvement in a war of conquest in Syria, if it could give him greater power.[19] It is not even likely that he was militarily capable of undertaking an expedition that far, and there is little doubt that the Seleukid army would make short work of the Attalid forces. Ptolemy, on the other hand, was a free agent, who had defied or ignored Rome in the past when it suited him.[20] He could certainly launch a war in Syria, either by himself or by proxy, without Rome being able to do anything about it.

So, once Ptolemy's financial and military resources were involved, the plot had enough support to be launched. In 152 Alexander seized control of Ptolemais-Ake, the government centre of Palestine.[21] In order to do this he must have had a force of soldiers, a squadron (at least) of ships – for he arrived by sea – and the assurance that he would not be opposed in the city. The garrison of the city had been subverted by the plotters. Josephos claims that the garrison was disenchanted with Demetrios because of his 'arrogance and unapproachableness', which is scarcely convincing, but then Josephos was hardly interested in the reasons, being mainly concerned to write Jewish history. The importance of the soldiers' treason was, of course, that they provided Alexander with a powerful well-fortified base fairly remote from Demetrios' centre of power, which was North Syria. They also supplemented the mercenary force he had with him, recruited by Herakleides.

The mercenaries hired for Alexander's immediate support could have been recruited in Greece and Asia Minor, but the finance for their initial wages must have been provided by Attalos or Ptolemy, or both. Alexander must have commanded an army of several thousands of men, for he had to have overwhelming military strength at Ptolemais, in order to deter the immediate counter-attack which he would expect Demetrios to launch. Since Demetrios did not do this, even though he had some thousands of troops available in the Palestinian area, Alexander's forces were clearly the stronger. The ships which brought him and his army to Ptolemais were presumably supplied from the Ptolemaic navy. It would be a nice ironic gesture if the expedition had been launched from Ptolemaic Cyprus. Other men could have reached Cyprus through Attalos' new port-city of Attaleia in Pamphylia, which had been founded during the 150s.

Josephos, quoting a Greek source, probably Nicolaos of Damascus, ascribes Alexander's initial success to the treason of the garrison of Ptolemais-Ake, which in turn is taken to be a result of the king's unpopularity. This reason for the treason is only supposition, and is not sufficient. It is notable that the Governor of Koile Syria is not mentioned either by name or by office. This presumes he was loyal to Demetrios; he must have been either driven out or otherwise eliminated. The date of Alexander's landing was in the 160th Seleukid year, which equates to the twelve months from spring 153 to spring 152 BC; the landing is generally assumed to have taken place in the spring of 152.[22]

Josephos then claims that Demetrios replied by gathering an army and that he then 'lead it against him', a sentiment repeated in *I Maccabees*.[23] But this was clearly not the case. Demetrios did not appear with an army in Palestine. There was no battle, and none is recorded for the next two years. Instead the two sources concentrate on the diplomatic contest between the rivals for the support of Jonathan Maccabee and the Judaeans. Jonathan was contacted first by Demetrios, who released the hostages being held for Jewish good behaviour, and allowed Jonathan to return to Jerusalem, where he began to refortify the city. The garrisons which had been holding the various fortified posts around Judaea were then withdrawn. (Josephos says they 'fled'.) Only the garrisons of the fortress in Jerusalem and at Beth Zur in the south were retained.[24]

Disregarding Josephos' pro-Jewish interpretation, what we have here is a partial view of Demetrios gathering his forces. Jonathan, who had been living quietly in the countryside for the past seven years, was now clearly seen by Demetrios as a safe pair of hands, and when the garrisons were withdrawn, Jonathan was installed as a quasi-governor of Judaea. Demetrios thereby gained the use of some thousands of soldiers (he withdrew eight garrisons, each presumably several hundred strong), and hopefully established a strategic threat to Alexander's position, once the Jews were re-armed. On the other hand, Demetrios did not wholly abandon his control of Jerusalem, for the main garrisons, in the Akra of Jerusalem and at Beth Zur, were kept in place.[25] Beth Zur had been the point-of-entry to Judaea for more than one Seleukid army in the recent past; Demetrios, once he had finished with Alexander, clearly intended to return his garrisons to Judaea.

In reply, Alexander now contacted Jonathan himself, offering to make him high priest of the Jews, an office which had been vacant for several years, and whose appointment was within the king's gift. By accepting, Jonathan therefore aligned himself with Alexander's cause.[26] He also made it clear that his loyalty was for sale. Accordingly Demetrios is said to have offered extensive tax cancellations and concessions and an increase in territory, but these were rejected by 'Jonathan and the people', supposedly because it had been due to Demetrios that they had been conquered eight years before.[27] It is, however, likely that this offer was wholly imaginary, and that it was never in fact made. The concessions as stated were very generous, and it seems unlikely that they would be rejected merely because Demetrios had been doing his job as king years before. At the same time, no doubt the proximity of Alexander's forces and the absence of those of Demetrios would have had as much to do with their decision as any memory of bad treatment.

The only date included in all this is that of Jonathan's assumption of the office of high priest, October 152.[28] Demetrios' second offer, if it was actually made, came after that, perhaps a month or more later. But we cannot believe that these events in Judaea were the only things that occupied the two kings for two whole years or even for the six months or so between Alexander's arrival and the making of the deal with Jonathan. Both men were presumably gathering support elsewhere. Alexander, once he had successfully neutralized Jonathan and the Jews, would need to ensure his control of other cities in the region, notably those along the coast between Ptolemais and Gaza, each of which could supply a force of soldiers, garrison or militia. None of these cities could be allowed to stay with Demetrios if Alexander was to be able to move north.

These events are recorded in detail only by Jewish sources, which naturally concentrated on the revival of Jewish fortunes. We have two later sources, both of Roman imperial date, and both very brief and summary, Appian and Justin-Trogus; neither makes any mention of these events in Palestine. But then neither do they suggest any reason for the long delay in the actual fighting. It is, however, not difficult to guess the reason.

The Palestinian details, believable or not, are useful in providing a view of events in one small part of the Seleukid kingdom, and they can be taken as an indication of the sort of tensions set up in the kingdom as a whole by Alexander's intrusion. The jockeying for positions and the search for support by both men must be the main explanation for the two-year gap between Alexander's landing at Ptolemais in early 152 and the campaign which brought on the fighting and which ended in the summer of 150. Within Palestine the Jews under their new leader Jonathan were attached to Alexander, but having been largely disarmed, were of no military use for some time – apart from having Demetrios' garrisons in Jerusalem and Beth Zur, which, notably, Alexander did not tackle. Either they were too strong for him, or he left them to Jonathan – more likely he was happy to have them checkmate Jonathan, and reckoned that, if he won, they would become his own men and garrisons. That is, by failing to tackle these places Alexander was serving notice that he did not trust Jonathan. Meanwhile Alexander's efforts to secure his rear by taking control of the Palestinian coastal cities will have taken some time. The dates noted by *I Maccabees* indicate that this all took several months.

In the rest of the kingdom we have no direct information on reactions. Inference must be our guide. In Kilikia, for example, the two cities who had objected to paying their taxes to Antiochos IV's concubine Antiochis twenty years before – Antiochis was Alexander's mother – were no doubt supporters of Demetrios, whereas in the mountains Zenodotos had long been Alexander's champion. Again, this might indicate a paralysis in which each contender blocked his rival, but it surely required a considerable force of Demetrios' troops to both defend the kingdom and keep order.

In Syria the unpopularity of the king in Antioch must have made him clamp a strong garrison on the city. (He faced the annoyance of having the pretender to the Macedonian throne, Andriskos, appealing to him for support, and when he did not get it, stimulating a riot in the city; Andriskos was swiftly deported.[29]) The fact that he did not move south into Palestine with the army he is said to have gathered is perhaps an indication that his control over Syria was uncertain, and that much of his military strength was locked up in maintaining that control.

It could also be that it took some time for Demetrios to collect his forces. The main Seleukid military base was at Apamaea in Syria, but at a time of peace, the army was presumably spread towards the frontiers – the garrisons in Judaea are perhaps an example – and in the main cities such as Ptolemais. The strained relations with Ptolemy and Attalos would suggest that more troops than usual were on the Egyptian and Kilikian borders – and the former might have joined Alexander. Susiana had recently shown a disposition towards secession and the Parthians were stronger than before, so extra troops were no doubt deployed to the east. It will have taken some time to collect all the forces he needed, though two years seems to be rather much. Maybe there were expressions of support for Alexander in other areas which compelled Demetrios to leave strong forces in other garrisons, just as he did at Jerusalem and Beth Zur. There could be a hint of this in the words of Josephos, who says that Alexander gathered 'soldiers from Syria', as well as hiring mercenaries.[30] 'Syria' might mean Palestine, of course, which was part of Koele Syria and so the term could have referred to the city along the coast, and those inland across the Jordan. It might, however, also mean that men came to join him from the great cities in North Syria.

It may be that there is a clue to one reaction in some coins produced in Kommagene. These coins were minted in imitation of those of Demetrios produced in Antioch. They bear the date 160 and the legend 'King Demetrios Soter', and they are of a weight compatible with the official Seleukid coinage. In other words, they have all the appearance of official coins, and could be accepted as such. On the other hand, they are not official, but copies, as is shown by the mint mark the bear, which is a copy of the one used at the Antioch mint. Their origin is almost certainly Kommagene, since they are found almost only in that area, and, given the date, they were therefore produced by the longstanding governor, Ptolemaios. The date of their production – 60 SE (= 153/152 BC) – is obviously significant, considering the uprising led by Alexander at the time. They were produced, it may be said, partly as a means of payment for local forces (for Ptolemaios raided over the Taurus at some time which is not discoverable) but the date and the king's name makes it clear that the coins were issued as a gesture of loyalty towards Demetrios.[31] This was not an action taken by any other governor, it seems, but then Ptolemaios was not a normal governor. His ten-year tenure, so far, must have included other gestures of support for Demetrios, with the aim of conciliating the king and continuing his own local rule.[32]

This interpretation may also point to one of the elements which must have existed in this crisis, but which is largely hidden: the decisive influence of a fairly small group of men, courtiers, governors, city councillors, army commanders, in the support for one or other of the two contenders. It seems that Ptolemaios was clear in the support he provided to Demetrios (though he survived as governor through Alexander's reign), whereas the governor in Palestine was caught between the two.

Elsewhere, in Babylonia and Iran, we have no indications of support for either man. For what it is worth, Demetrios' name was still being used in dating formulae in Babylon in May and October 151.[33] It is another possible indication of sentiment that after Alexander succeeded in taking over the kingship there was no movement of support for Demetrios' children or in revenge for him, as there had been on behalf of Antiochos IV and V. It looks as though most people throughout the kingdom did not much care who was king, or perhaps could not do anything about it. Those who could affect the situation perhaps saw no reason to bother, the choice being less than enticing. What they required was competence, and it looks very much as though Demetrios had forfeited the confidence of many of those who counted. And then, of course, victory brought its own reward: when Alexander overthrew Demetrios, he thereby demonstrated the greater competence, and so he was acceptable to the opinion-makers – until he was perceived as having demonstrated his own incapacity.

Whatever the reasons for the delay in launching his attack, in 150 Alexander finally did so, marching his forces north into North Syria. This would argue that he felt he had a strong enough army by this time to tackle Demetrios' forces. Two battles resulted. There are brief accounts in Josephos and *I Maccabees*,[34] and mentions in Appian and Justin-Trogus,[35] but the most useful account is a fragmentary account by the Astronomical Diarist in Babylon.[36] In addition the pattern of coin minting seems to provide a helpful indication of Alexander's progress.[37]

(It is worth noting some characteristics of the Diarist's work. His object was to record various astronomical phenomena, which are useful for our dating purposes, but he also included information about prices of goods and he mentions such matters as famines and floods and plagues. He records political and military events in and around Babylon, and, using the formula 'I heard', reports matters gathered from elsewhere. The successive compilers were thus careful historians, scrupulous about their sources. The information is often unique, as well as being more accurate and detailed than most – above all the Diarist was contemporary with the events, which is not the case with any other source.)

The Babylon Diarist provides the date for the fighting. He recorded that the fighting took place in the third month of 162, which was June 150 BC. From a phrase which he used, it seems that Alexander moved part at least of his forces by sea and landed at Seleukeia-in-Pieria. This was a powerful well-fortified city, so it may be that Alexander had suborned the garrison or the city council beforehand. It was one of the cities also in which Alexander minted coins in his own name during the Seleukid year 162 – spring 151 to spring 150 – and therefore within three months of his arrival in the north. The other mints he used in this year were all in Phoenicia – Ptolemais-Ake, Sidon, Tyre, Berytos, and Byblos – which may mean that his voyage to Seleukeia had included calls at all these cities to establish his authority. But he did not, so far as can be seen, mint coins at Ptolemais-Ake before the year 162. Perhaps he did not need to, having been financed by Ptolemy and Attalos sufficiently well to avoid that task.

Demetrios, however, won the first of the battles which followed. Again the Babylon Diarist gives rather more detail than anyone else. He reports that Demetrios came out of Antioch – the only Syrian city in which he minted coins during 162 – with his troops, and with twenty-five elephants. (These had supposedly been killed at Octavius' order in 163 BC, but either the killing had not been completed, or Demetrios had acquired more.) The battle was a disaster for Alexander, but he and his army largely survived. Perhaps he was able to take refuge in Seleukia or another city, and he was certainly able to return to the attack within a few days – the Diarist gives the date as the 21st day of the third month. This time Alexander also had elephants with him, as did Demetrios. Where Alexander's beasts came from is not known, but it is evident that some manoeuvres and intrigues had taken place. The Seleukid war elephants were quartered at Apameia; perhaps Alexander used the time between the battles to seize that city. If he had ascribed the first defeat to Demetrios' elephants – and the Diarist's mention of them seems to imply their importance – then a swift raid might net those not used by Demetrios. In the new battle the two elephant forces 'defeated each other', as the Diarist neatly puts it. This was followed, or was accompanied by, a more conventional infantry fight. At the end of this Demetrios had become separated from his own forces, and he was surrounded by the enemy and killed, still fighting.

Chapter 5

The Destruction of Alexander Balas (150–145 BC)

Alexander capitalized at once on his success in defeating Demetrios, requesting a marriage alliance with Ptolemy VI.[1] This was a radical change in Seleukid marriage policy. The only comparable previous marriage between the two royal houses was that of Ptolemy II's daughter Berenike with Antiochos II and had ended in her murder, a Seleukid civil war, and a Ptolemaic invasion. (A Seleukid daughter, Kleopatra Syra, married Ptolemy V – and so was Ptolemy VI's mother – but this turned out well, and anyway scarcely affected the Seleukid situation.) This new marriage took place at Ptolemais-Ake, between Alexander and Ptolemy VI's daughter Kleopatra Thea; she was, if Alexander was Antiochos IV's son, his cousin. The instant request by Alexander and the instant response by Ptolemy suggest strongly that this was the fulfilment of an earlier agreement. That the ceremony took place at Ptolemais was a sign that Ptolemy's influence over the new king was likely to be strong, and indeed Alexander tended to live as much at Ptolemais as at Antioch, and there were at least two high officials in Alexander's organization who were seconded from the Ptolemaic system; these men, Ammonios and Hierax, were surely even more Ptolemy's men than they were Alexander's.

The triumph of victory and marriage was, however, not complete. Demetrios I was dead, and Alexander had captured and killed his wife Laodike and their eldest son Antigonos.[2] The deed is attributed to Ammonios. The killing of Laodike was presumably due to the fact that her status as the daughter of Seleukos IV and widow of Demetrios I (and of Perseus) made her a possible centre of legitimacy in competition with Alexander. Also, Alexander's marriage with the eldest daughter of the reigning Ptolemy imparted some much needed charisma to the former pretender, self-confessedly a bastard. In Seleukid terms Laodike's aura would have eclipsed that of Kleopatra.

Demetrios, perhaps with memories of his own adolescence in exile, perhaps anticipating defeat, had sent his two younger children, Demetrios and Antiochos, out of the kingdom for safety. They were sent, well supplied with gold, to Knidos in Karia, where a friend of their father's agreed to shelter them.[3] The choice of refuge was not an accident. Almost at once, the elder boy, Demetrios, began the process of recruiting a mercenary army with which to recover his rightful throne – as he would have put it. The younger boy, Antiochos, aged about 10 or less, was sent at some point to live at Side in Pamphylia, probably to ensure that assassins did not get them both at once, but also to have him close by if the elder boy succumbed.[4]

Knidos looks out at the southern Aegean towards Crete, one of the main sources of mercenary soldiers. The process of recruitment would seem to have been to find a commander first, in this case a Cretan called Lasthenes, who would then recruit and organise an army, something the boy Demetrios could hardly do.[5] No doubt this was expensive, hence the gold Demetrios I had provided. No doubt also the recruits were promised more pay when they were successful, and a share of any loot. The prospect of the riches of the cities of Syria was no doubt enticing; nevertheless it took two years and more before all was organized. The possibilities of spying, subversion, and other nasty tricks are evident, but this was also what Alexander had been doing between 154 and 152.

Alexander meanwhile had failed to live up to his promise. He had at first revived memories of the time of Antiochos IV, his father. His monetary policy was more generous than that of Demetrios, though that was more to publicize his success than for economic reasons, but he also needed to pay off his own mercenaries, and had a continuing need for a standing army. He gained a reputation for laziness and frivolity, just as Demetrios had acquired one for laziness and drunkenness.[6] It may have been an accurate representation, or it may have been mere rumour – or disinformation by his enemies – but in neither case does such a reputation necessarily preclude attention to matters of state. This had been Antiochos IV's reputation also; maybe it was hereditary, or maybe it was an attempt to demonstrate heredity where it did not exist; Alexander was under the constant necessity to insist on his claimed parentage. In Demetrios' case the claimed laziness did not lead to a neglect of his tasks; in Alexander's case, however, it may well have done. Yet when put to the task Alexander showed himself a capable man; he had after all been successful in stealing a kingdom, even if he had help.

Like Demetrios, but for different reasons, Alexander was pinned down in Syria and the west, and was compelled to neglect events in the east. Internationally, the circumstances of his victory had brought the kingdom back to the diplomatic condition of Antiochos IV's reign, with friendly powers in Asia Minor – the Attalids, possibly Kappadokia, and the marriage of his sister Laodike to Mithradates of Pontos – and Egypt. In theory this should have allowed him to give the attention to the eastern provinces which Demetrios had failed to do, but for two main reasons he did not do so. (His apparent laziness may have been publicized as part of this difficulty.)

One reason may have been the need to maintain contact with Ptolemy VI, and he seems to have spent much of his time in Ptolemais-Ake. Ptolemy would not want his protégé to escape his tutelage and/or control, and in all likelihood Alexander did not get much of a chance to demonstrate his abilities, supervised as he was by Ptolemy and perhaps blocked by Ammonios and the Ptolemaic officials. He had shown that he could win battles and could recover from a defeat. It may well be that had he had a direct opportunity he would have shown considerable abilities. But the most important reason for his continual presence in the west was the actions of the younger Demetrios, which constituted a clear threat to Alexander from 149 onwards, though it was not until 147 that he had enough of a force to attempt an invasion. So, despite the diplomatic resemblance of the time of Antiochos, in fact Alexander was in much the same position as Demetrios I had been.

The main result of Alexander's immobilization in Syria and Palestine was that the Parthians were able to make inroads into the kingdom from the east. It would seem that Alexander was able to gain acceptance in the rest of the empire quickly enough, and coins in his name were minted at such distant cities as Ekbatana in Iran, Antioch-by-the Erythraean-Sea, Susa, and Babylon, without any noticeable break from the reign of Demetrios.[7] Of course, everyone was half-prepared for a change because of the two-year stand-off between 152 and 150, although it seems unlikely that the mint masters would have prepared a portrait of Alexander for the new coinage before the news of his victory arrived – some seem to have used a portrait of Antiochos IV instead. A document from Babylonia of October 150 is dated by Alexander's name, so the news spread, as is only to be expected, fast enough.[8]

The governors of the provinces may or may not have been replaced by the new regime. Ptolemaios in Kommagene carried on, and the hyparch of the region around Antioch-by-the-Erythraean-Sea, Hyspaosines, who had been in office since the reign of Antiochos IV, also continued.[9] A new governor for Koile Syria was clearly needed, and a man called Apollonios Taos was appointed to the office by Demetrios II in 147, which probably means that there was no man in the office under Alexander.[10] If he lived much of the time in Ptolemais, it may be that a local governor for Palestine was not needed. Otherwise we know of no new appointments, though there were presumably some. The garrisons which had been removed by Demetrios were no doubt scheduled for replacement, though the posts in Judaea evacuated by Demetrios were not reoccupied, and the continuing crisis of the regime probably prevented any serious reinforcement of the depleted garrisons in the eastern provinces.

It took a year or more before anyone outside the kingdom made any attempt to exploit the change of king, but during 148–147 the Parthian King Mithradates I invaded the Seleukid territories in Iran. In 148 there was a viceroy of the east in office, Kleomenes, for his name was inscribed on the dedication of a sculpture of Herakles above the road through the Zagros at Bisitun.[11] The sculpture – Herakles is fat, soft, and self-satisfied, with a large cup of wine in his hand – is dated to Panemos 164 (SE), which is June 148, and will have taken some time to produce, though it could be that the governor merely added his name to one already made. Even so, it is clear that in mid-148 there was a governor in office for the eastern provinces, and since the dedication was to 'Herakles the Victorious', it may be assumed that Kleomenes had won a victory over an enemy, who was presumably the king of the Parthians.

During 147, however, King Alexander's men lost control of all Iran. The Parthians had already expanded their kingdom at the expense of King Eukratides of Baktria by the annexation of two provinces, and had pushed their power into Hyrkania, the agriculturally rich and well-watered land between the Elburz Mountains and the Caspian Sea. Now, despite his (presumed) defeat sometime earlier by Kleomenes, Mithradates conquered Media, the land south of the Elburz and north of the central Iranian desert. This was in fact only a relatively small part of Iran, for Media Atropatene to the north was already ruled by its own king and to the south, other events were taking place.

So the campaign of conquest by Mithradates involved moving westwards along the great Royal Road in the north-centre of the land, starting no doubt at Hekatompylos, already under Parthian control. He will have captured the Caspian Gates, a narrow pass supposedly guarded at each end, and then he will have captured Rhagai, and from there on the road was more or less clear as far as the group of major hellenized cities in front of the Zagros Pass at Bisitun, apart from the usual minor garrisons, which were clearly too small to withstand the full Parthian army. The great prize here was the city of Ekbatana, one of the four cities, the old imperial capital of the kings of the Medes and of the Great Kings of the Akhaimenids. With Ekbatana taken, no doubt the other nearby cities – Laodikeia (Nihavand), Kangavar, and Demavar, would also fall, but more important, possession of Ekbatana conferred a type of legitimacy from the point of view of the Medes, who still comprised the majority of the local population.

Mithradates was now faced with the pass itself, an area well organized militarily, and this was much easier to defend than the open Median plane.

No doubt the Seleukid forces now concentrated there, men were retiring from Iran before the Parthian attack and others were coming up from Babylonia. It is likely that there were some groups already in garrison at the pass as well. Mithradates stopped on the Median side of the pass.

Events in the south involved a repetition of those at the start of Demetrios I's reign, in that a local lord emerged and seized control of the city of Susa. The man this time was called Kamniskires, and he may or may not have been related to the earlier intruder Hyknapses. Judging by the city's coinage, he seized control during 147, the very year Seleukid authority in Media to the north collapsed.[12] Whether this was a joint move by Kamniskires in alliance with Mithradates, or one taking advantage of the other's victory, or even Kamniskires acting in the interests of the Seleukids, is not known, though the second of these theories is perhaps the most likely. Perhaps Mithradates' invasion (or the crisis in the west) had led to the removal or reduction of the Seleukid garrison in Susa (and from any posts they occupied in the surrounding countryside), at which point Kamniskires found he was strong enough to capture the city, perhaps even welcomed into it by at least part of the population. The general overriding reason for the successes of both Mithradates and Kamniskires was that the Seleukid military strength under Alexander in the east was reduced to cope with the simultaneous threat he faced in the west. Possibly the victory of Kleomenes had led to over-confidence and another reduction in manpower.

The secret of the Seleukid Empire was thus revealed, possibly inadvertently – that it was too big to defend itself against simultaneous attacks from east and west. It had in the past survived invasions from the west, and had succeeded in reducing the latent threat in the east, but in 147 it was attacked from three directions at once, from the west by Demetrios II, from the east by Mithradates and from the south-east by the uprising at Susa. Possibly Kleomenes' victory had been the last successful defence of the Median province, and had allowed Alexander to withdraw forces from Iran to face Demetrios. This is the sort of gamble which when successful earns a general great plaudits for skill, judgment and daring; when it fails, he is condemned for gambling foolishly. In the event Alexander almost succeeded, but his failure proved disastrous to himself and his kingdom.

These events may have begun in 148, or even 150, but they culminated in the loss of Seleukid eastern territories during 147, which was the very year Demetrios II landed in Syria to reclaim the kingship for himself and his family. Alexander was thus trapped. The fighting in 152–150 will have cost casualties among the Seleukid forces – the two battles we know of were anything but bloodless – and they certainly involved the movement and removal of troops and the evacuation of military garrisons. Some of those, as in Judaea, had not been replaced, which may be the result of political arrangements, but it may also be a result of a shortage of soldiers. It is surely this latter reason which led to the swift collapse of the Seleukid position in Iran, which had not been in danger for the previous century and more – it had even survived earlier reductions in military strength, when governors rebelled and marched their armies west to try to seize the throne, as with Timarchos. The reason the old posts and garrisons were not reoccupied, or that they continued in a weakened state, was presumably Alexander's need to keep his forces concentrated along the Syrian coast because of the threat of Demetrios II, which had been growing as he recruited his forces during 150–148. After all, this was exactly how Alexander himself had gained his throne, by bringing a mercenary army to a landing on the Syrian coast in a surprise attack, so he will have been especially sensitized to such a possibility.

That coastline is long, dotted with numerous cities and towns and other places where a landing at a defended place was possible. Only by garrisoning each city strongly could a proper defensive be mounted; a mobile reserve would also be needed. This would require a large number of soldiers, hence, no doubt, the weakness in the east. But it was simply not possible to be on full guard everywhere – and, as the garrison of Ptolemais-Ake had already shown, none of these garrisons could be fully relied on; so Alexander was probably haunted by his own subversive methods being turned on him. Demetrios, with his Cretan mercenary force under Lasthenes, landed in Kilikia, and did so while Alexander was at Ptolemais-Ake.[13]

The choice of Kilikia is interesting – quite apart from its distance from Alexander's command post. Two of its cities had resisted Antiochos IV's transfer of tax revenues to his mistress, and may well have been therefore hostile to Alexander, whose activities in the mountains before 152 also cannot have been welcome. It was also a region on the very border of the kingdom. Demetrios had therefore positioned himself in a place likely already unhappy with the new king, and from which he could retreat fairly easily. (Or, more likely, it was Lasthenes and Demetrios' other advisors who chose the landing place – Demetrios was still only 14 or so.)

Alexander raced north to confront this threat, going directly to Antioch where a sentiment in favour of Demetrios had developed. The city had been administered by two of Alexander's officials, Hierax and Diodotos, while Alexander stayed at Ptolemais, and this apparently annoyed the Antiochenes, who no doubt felt they were being somehow demoted from their earlier high status in the kingdom: they were normally governed directly by the king, and their city council; no governor of the Seleukis, the area of North Syria, is known of. In addition, Ammonios had become far too prominent in the general imperial administration for many tastes.[14] No doubt all the various threats had compelled a more than usually rigorous collection of taxes. At the same time, the absence of the court from Antioch will have annoyed the local chief men, and reduced the opportunities for profiteering by the merchants and shopkeepers. This could all be enough to make the return of Demetrios' family attractive to the citizens.

The city is said to have joined Demetrios' cause, and later to have risen to drive out Ammonios. These are clearly two different events with different purposes, and need to be located at different times. Alexander is explicitly said to have gone from Ptolemais to Antioch when he heard the news of Demetrios' landing in Kilikia.[15] Two reasons can be suggested, to gather his forces, and to quiet the city. These are not mutually exclusive, of course, but he did not need to go there for his forces, many of which will have been in other places. Accordingly his visit was most likely designed to regain control of the city, which Justin says had risen for Demetrios.[16]

Behind him, as he went north, Alexander's governor in Koile Syria, Apollonios Taos, defected to Demetrios and persuaded all or a large part of the local Seleukid forces to join him. He at once fell into a dispute with Jonathan Maccabee in Judaea, who remained loyal to Alexander. At first Apollonios had hoped to persuade the high priest to join him, or at least to remain neutral. Jonathan refused, and the two fought a campaign which ended with Apollonios' defeat in battle.[17]

As usual the most vociferous sources, Josephos and *I Maccabees*, concentrate on this sideshow, and this time we do not have the Astronomical Diarist in Babylon to help, for his diary for this period does not survive. Nevertheless the coincidence of a hostile landing by Demetrios' forces in Kilikia, the defection of Apollonios Taos in Palestine, and the revolt of Antioch against Alexander in North Syria suggests that there had been a successful conspiracy on behalf of Demetrios. Presumably the organizer was Lasthenes – according to Polybios, Cretans had the reputation for such plots.[18]

All these events were not sufficient to give Demetrios an early victory. Alexander recovered control of Antioch, and Apollonios was defeated by Jonathan and the new Judaean army. It seems that Demetrios was not strong enough to challenge Alexander directly, though Justin comments that parts of the Seleukid army, which had, after all, fought for Demetrios' father, also defected.[19] Once again, as in 152–150, there was a stalemate for more than a year, during which intrigues took place which we can only imagine. It was in this period that the immobility of the two sides in Syria permitted Mithradates and Kamniskires to conduct their successful campaigns. The stalemate was broken by Ptolemy VI, who moved into Palestine in support of his son-in-law Alexander.

Ptolemy, of course, had his own aims in this development. He moved along the Palestinian coast, taking over the cities one after another, and garrisoning them with his own troops. Jonathan's forces had sacked Ashdod after the victory over Apollonios Taos, and Ptolemy listened to the survivors' complaints, but did nothing for them – he and Jonathan were both allies of Alexander. The Ptolemaic garrisons left in the cities could be explained as a protective 'security' measure, but they were a clear sign of Ptolemy's basic purpose: he was aiming to recover the old Ptolemaic province of Koile Syria-and-Phoenicia. The clearest sign of this, apart from the garrisons he left in the cities, came when he reached the Eleutheros River, in the north of Phoenicia. This marked the old Ptolemaic-Seleukid boundary, which had separated the kingdoms until Antiochos III's conquest of Koile Syria in the Fifth Syrian War fifty years earlier. Jonathan had accompanied Ptolemy on his march north, but he was left behind at the Eleutheros, a clear indication both that Ptolemy regarded the border as still – or again – operative, and that Jonathan was now a subject of the Ptolemaic kingdom.[20]

Once he reached Antioch, Ptolemy accused Alexander of plotting his assassination. He claimed to have survived an attack at Ptolemais-Ake, which he said had been organized by Ammonios on Alexander's behalf.[21] Whether the plot actually existed is not known – we have only Ptolemy's word for it, and he apparently said nothing about it when he was at Ptolemais – but Alexander understood well enough that the accusation was a deliberate move against him, a means to sever the alliance between them. Ptolemy's basic purpose, it must be repeated, was to gain control of Koile Syria, which he had already done physically and militarily by his garrisons. He now needed to secure a treaty by which the territories were legally transferred to him. If he continued to support Alexander, he would never be able to take the province, since his public purpose was to restore Alexander's authority of his whole kingdom in the face of Demetrios' attack. So Ptolemy had to break with Alexander, and this was the purpose of the accusation. The next step would be to conclude a treaty with whoever emerged as the Seleukid king from the civil war – it might be Alexander or Demetrios, but Ptolemy was now in the position of kingmaker and could state his own terms. That is, like Mithradates and Kamniskires, Ptolemy was aiming to secure his own set of spoils from what he clearly thought was a failing state. Alexander, surely understanding all this, refused to surrender Ammonios, as Ptolemy had demanded, and this was the point of breakage.[22] However, the Antiochenes took the opportunity to rise once more, this time against Ammonios rather than Alexander, hunted him down, and killed him as he tried to escape.[23] (Ptolemy might have been the instigator of the riot, but merely by indicating his break with Alexander, he had made Ammonios a target.) Diodoros says that Hierax and Diodotos 'roused the Antiochenes', and Hierax at least was Ptolemy's man; Diodotos as a Syrian was more Alexander's.[24]

Ptolemy now followed this by ordering the divorce of Alexander and Kleopatra Thea, and then offered her, and his support, to Demetrios. Demetrios, who had so far failed to make much impression on Alexander's position as king, accepted at once.[25]

Alexander fled the city, took refuge in Kilikia, and there collected up his forces – those of his soldiers who were loyal, reinforced by local recruits.[26] He clearly aimed to return, which would betoken some serious unpleasantness for Antioch if he succeeded. Demetrios may or may not have been accepted as king, but he was clearly a good deal less capable than Alexander, and in the meantime both were threats. The answer, according to Hierax and Diodotos, was to make Ptolemy 'king of Syria'.

Hierax was an Egyptian, a Ptolemaic appointee in the Seleukid administration (like Ammonios); Diodotos was from Kasiana near the great military city of Apamaea, appointed and perhaps recruited by Alexander. They had been, until this point, committed to Alexander's cause, but once he left Antioch they switched to Ptolemy as being the man most likely to be able to enforce peace. Their plan put Ptolemy in a dilemma. They also had strong influence among the Antiochenes, those who counted politically at any rate, so that when they publicly offered the kingship of the Seleukid kingdom to Ptolemy, they appeared to have popular support – though this support presumably consisted of the city councillors, the wealthy, the courtiers, and so on, those in other words with a lot to lose in the event of a sack. The only means of expression among the population at large was to riot.

Ptolemy seems to have dithered, quite probably taken by surprise by the offer. His policy since the defeat of Alexander had been to support Demetrios – hence the marriage – though he had evidently not ensured that Hierax and Diodotos understood this. In the end he urged the claim of Demetrios, so rejecting the proposal. It is also likely that the Antiochenes fairly quickly cooled to the idea, and when, at another public meeting, Ptolemy promised to be a good counsellor to Demetrios, he was able to persuade the audience to accept his new son-in-law as their king. His price, of course, as it had been all along, was Koile Syria, which he had already garrisoned. It appears that Ptolemy took some time to consider the proposal, which means he was initially attracted to it, but it was an unknown quantity, while he held Koile Syria firmly. With this bird in hand, he rejected the one in the bush. Demetrios was also trapped: he either agreed to surrender Koile Syria or Ptolemy took the whole kingship, at least so he must have thought. He had no choice but to accept the lesser prize.[27]

Alexander had meanwhile recovered, recruited a new army, and begun a campaign against the territory of Antioch, ravaging the land, and in effect demanding that his opponents come out to fight. They did so, and the three kings met in battle by the Oenoparos River, north-east of the city. Alexander was defeated. During the fighting Ptolemy fell off his elephant, and was attacked by his enemies. He was rescued, badly injured, by his bodyguard. While the surgeons were trying to save him, Alexander took refuge with an Arab chieftain who then betrayed and killed him. Alexander's head, minus the rest of him, was the last thing Ptolemy saw as he died. Demetrios in this unexpected way was now king of his father's kingdom.[28]

Alexander's reputation, as relayed in the rather straight-laced historians' accounts, was poor. He was accused of laziness, and of dissipation, but the evidence is little more than rumour, and could well have been Demetrian propaganda. 'Lolling about among his concubines' is one accusation, but this is no more than one of the standard accusations made by ancient historians who have no evidence, and who suppose that this is what kings did. Instead it is best to consider the evidence of his actions as king.

In his campaign for the kingship he was guided by Herakleides, but he clearly made a satisfactory impression on Attalos, on many of the Roman Senate, and on Ptolemy, none of whom were gullible. In his campaign against Demetrios I in 152–150 he was patient and careful. His first battle was a defeat, but he recovered, reorganized, and won the second battle. As king, he no doubt enjoyed the perquisites of his position, but the threat from Demetrios II immobilized him and prevented him from attending to other crises, such as those in the east. When Demetrios and Lasthenes did attack, Alexander was quick to respond, securing control of Antioch, leaving Jonathan to deal with Apollonios Taos, and confining Demetrios to a small part of the kingdom. When Ptolemy broke with him he stood by Ammonios (who had probably originally been Ptolemy's man), escaped from the city, and then returned to the fight. Had he not been killed by the Arab chieftain he trusted, it seems very likely that he would have been able to recover his throne from the teenaged Demetrios, who owed his victory to Ptolemy's army – which soon disappeared.

It cannot seriously be claimed that Alexander had a real opportunity to show his larger abilities as king. In his reign a large part of the kingdom had been lost, his administration had become unpopular, and, of course, he could claim to have been under constant attack, and in the end to have been betrayed not merely by his Arab chieftain but by Ptolemy, whose part in the whole affair was devious in the extreme. Given the difficulties he faced, therefore, it seems unlikely that Alexander could ever have succeeded – though whether he should have made the attack on Demetrios I in the first place is another matter. But he deserved to be given credit for playing his hand as well as he could, and to have been estimated in his own terms and not in those of his enemies' propaganda and the words of later censorious historians.

Chapter 6

The Travails of Demetrios II (145–138 BC)

emetrios II, king at the age of perhaps 16, and given the epithet '*nikator*' – 'the victor' – which he may have taken seriously but which others no doubt used in an ironic sense, and married with a new wife, scarcely had the chance to prove himself before being overwhelmed by new troubles. He was beholden to his Cretan mercenary commander, Lasthenes, who seems to have adopted the official position of foster father – and on at least one occasion was addressed by Demetrios as 'father'. But Lasthenes had prior responsibilities towards the men he had recruited for the war, and he had to pay them from the revenues of Syria; other than that his interest in governing Demetrios' kingdom was minimal.

If the first reaction to the death of Alexander Balas was to confirm Demetrios as king, the first reaction to the death of Ptolemy VI was to appreciate that the agreement to deliver Koile Syria to Ptolemaic control was now void. Demetrios' forces advanced steadily south through the disputed territory, meeting no resistance from the Ptolemaic garrisons, either because they were overwhelmed, or they were without orders, or, more likely, because they had instructions from the new king, Ptolemy VIII, the dead king's brother, to evacuate the region.[1] (Ptolemy VIII was never interested in the empire, and evacuated the last Ptolemaic naval bases in the Aegean in the same year.) Within a short time, less than a month probably, the whole coast as far as Gaza was back in Demetrios' kingdom.

Demetrios II had won a surprising success, but much of his achievement had not been his own. The fighting had been done mainly by the mercenaries commanded by Lasthenes, though it is probable that a number of Syrian soldiers had been recruited during the campaign. The deaths of his two enemies, Ptolemy VI and Alexander I, had again not been his work, but were the results of battle and treachery.

The withdrawal of the Ptolemaic forces solved one problem, but there were plenty of others to bother him. The Parthians had overrun Media, pushing along the main Royal Road westwards, capturing the cities.[2] Their King Mithradates was evidently fairly careful in this campaign, but since it took two years to make this conquest it seems evident that he also encountered a good deal of resistance. At the same time, in the south of Iran the Elamite chieftain, Kabneskir (Kamniskires to the Greeks), had seized control of Susa (in 147) and took control of the Susian/Elymais region. He took the epithet *nikephoros* ('victorious') which also implies some fighting.[3]

The great prize in the eastern fighting, however, was wealthy Babylonia, which was held by Seleukid forces. These had no doubt obeyed Alexander Balas while he lived, but it was possible for Demetrios II to issue a proclamation in Babylonia in September 145, and a month later the Seleukid Governor of Babylon, a man called Ardaya by the Babylonian Diarist (probably originally Ardaios in Greek) was sent to campaign against Kabneskir, who had invaded Babylonia; it seems clear that Mithradates' progress had stopped in Media.[4] He is in fact known to have returned to the east during 145, leaving his brother Bagasis as his viceroy in Media.[5] His concern was no doubt to watch over events beyond his eastern border, where the last strong Baktrian king, Eukratides, died during 145, and Baktria had been invaded by nomad groups; this invasion might, and later did, spill over into Parthian territory.

So during 145 Demetrios recovered Koile Syria, and launched a campaign to recover Elymais from Kabneskir. Coins in Demetrios' name were minted in Susa late in 145, so it seems that Ardaya had conducted a successful campaign, but fighting was still going on near Susa a year later, so the victory was always partial.[6] And this, as it turned out, must be the verdict on the rest of Demetrios' work in that year. The reconquest of the Koile Syria region did not deal with the revived problem of Judaea, where Jonathan Maccabee had been raised up by his alliance with Alexander. And the death of Alexander had not solved the dynastic problem, since he had left a baby son, Antiochos, who was hidden with an Arab sheikh in the desert.

The victory at the Oenoparos River had killed two kings and made another, but elements of the regime of Alexander Balas had survived. Two of these men were officials of Alexander, Hierax and Diodotos. They were the two men who had engineered the offer of the Seleukid kingship to Ptolemy, a factor which may have marked them from the start as enemies of Demetrios to be sought out and if possible eliminated. Hierax was from Egypt and seems to have returned there; his loyalty to Ptolemy VI made him an enemy of Ptolemy VIII, who eventually had him killed. Diodotos, on the other hand, was Syrian, from Kasiana in the land of Apamaea. He also went home, remaining there quietly for some time without being disturbed, which suggests he had some helpful local support. He evidently knew where Alexander's son Antiochos had been parked.

Demetrios II was not liked by large sections of the population. Partly this was due to his being the son of his unpopular father, partly it was an inheritance from the regime of Alexander, but this became worse when he gave authority to Lasthenes and his mercenaries to collect taxes. This was presumably a way of ensuring that they were paid, and so a quick way to get rid of them, but, needless to say, the soldiers were not good at the task – or rather perhaps too good. They worked with enthusiasm, targeting first the former supporters of Alexander and operating mainly in Antioch. The Antiochenes responded in part by threatening to attack the palace. Jonathan Maccabee sent a Judaean force which joined the mercenaries in defence of the palace, and both were free with their weapons. Fires broke out, and the citizens were defeated. The soldiers wrecked the city; refugees spread throughout Syria.[7]

The king's defenders, Jewish and mercenary forces alike, took their loot and left, as, no doubt, did Lasthenes. The danger to Demetrios and his regime, physically and politically, was real. Whatever credit Demetrios had gained by his victory was clearly dissipated. Diodotos, probably in Kasiana, or maybe Apamaea, watched all this and decided he could use the confusion and the drastic reduction in Demetrios' armed forces to revive the cause of Alexander I in the person of his son. It may be that he collected his forces first before raising the child as a figurehead, but whatever the sequence of events he proclaimed a rebellion active in 144, after the various foreign forces had left.

He recruited a cavalry unit from Larissa, and was allied with the Arab sheikh who had guarded the child Antiochos. He established his first base at Chalkis, east of Antioch, where he could interrupt communications between Antioch and the east, and from where he could conduct raids in several directions. Demetrios played down the threat, and ordered his soldiers to arrest Diodotos, which they predictably failed to do. It was probably at that point – having defeated Demetrios' first counter-attack – that the child Antiochos was proclaimed king as Antiochos V, and coins were minted which showed that Diodotos had control of Apamaea as well as Chalkis. (It appears that the mint staff at Antioch had fled to Apamaea, for it is their monograms which appear on the Apamaean coins.) Diodotos went on to gain control of Antioch itself during 143.[8]

Demetrios retained control of Seleukeia-in-Pieria, probably Laodikeia, and most of the Phoenician cities. But at Laodikeia we have a source which claims that he instituted a reign of erratic terror. This evidently comes from a source hostile to Demetrios, but what it implies is not so much the individual caprice of the king in picking off enemies in the city at random, but the difficulty of maintaining control in the city at a time of civil war.[9] It would be reasonable to expect the same general conditions of internal disturbance to apply in other cities, both those controlled by Demetrios and those by Diodotos.

The conflict spread to Kilikia, where the mints at Tarsos and Mallos coined for Antiochos, and to Palestine, where Ptolemais-Ake's mint also coined for him.[10] In the east Kabneskir in Elymais recovered control of Susa from an army of 'Antiochos son of Alexander', which suggests that the Seleukid Babylonian forces had either joined Antiochos, or, perhaps more likely, had become divided in their allegiance.[11]

This was a condition which enemies would be expected to exploit. Jonathan Maccabee was one such, though he was not very good at it. He had already used some of his forces to operate in Antioch for Demetrios, relying on a vague promise of future benefits which never materialized. Now he took the side of Antiochos VI, and gained another meaningless concession, this time from Diodotos: the appointment of his brother Simon as governor of the land 'from the ladder of Tyre to the border of Egypt'.[12] This could theoretically imply Jewish control of all the Palestinian lowlands, but it never came to pass. There is no sign ever that Simon operated in that capacity – and it may be an invention of the author of *I Maccabees*. Jonathan moved his forces into the southern part of the Palestinian coastland, accepted the submission of Ashkelon – this was a city which submitted at once to whoever was locally powerful – and menaced Gaza. But Gaza, which had originally supported Demetrios, now seems to have aimed at independence, or at least it had no wish to be under Judaean control, and resisted. In the end the city also submitted and gave hostages.[13] Jonathan then had laid siege to Beth Zur, the southern gateway into Judaea, and Demetrios, clearly concerned at these Jewish advances, sent an army south.

Jonathan left Simon to engage the garrison at Beth Zur, and took his main army north to confront Demetrios' forces (not actually under Demetrios' command) near Tell Hazor. He was hoodwinked in the subsequent conflict by the old trick of the sudden appearance of a hidden part of the enemy army, which sent the Judaean forces fleeing. They rallied at a narrow part of the road along the west of the Sea of Galilee at Hamath Tiberias. Jonathan meanwhile made a dash for Jerusalem, no doubt to ensure that no coup was attempted after his defeat.

The Demetrian army did not pursue, but withdrew in the night, leaving their watchfires burning. The Jews claimed victory, but all that was signified was the ease with which the Judaean army had been defeated, and that Demetrios had a better use for his army elsewhere. Simon, however, did succeed in forcing the surrender of Beth Zur, and then marched his army into the coastland to seize

Joppa, probably in the name of Antiochos VI, but actually using Maccabean forces – and Joppa was an old target of the Maccabees.[14] This was a perfect example of a minor player using the civil war to advance his own agenda; but it also demonstrated the unimportance of the southern region to both sides.

The child-king Antiochos VI died in mid-142, under the surgeon's knife according to one version, murdered by Diodotos according to another.[15] The former is more likely, because Diodotos had nothing to gain from the king's death other than blame and unpopularity, and a political crisis. He responded by proclaiming himself king under the throne name Tryphon, and laid out a political programme of enhanced Macedonian-ness, emphasized by starting a new dating era – 143–142 became his 'Year I'; he put a picture of a Macedonian shield on his coins.[16] This had only moderate appeal, largely because Demetrios' control was clamped tightly on the rest of the land, with four of his generals operating in his territory: Dionysios the Mede in Mesopotamia, Sarpedon and Palamedes in Palestine, and Aischrion in Seleukeia-in Pieria.[17]

Tryphon's new programme was, however, a necessity now that Antiochos VI was dead; Tryphon personally had no claim to the kingship, so he needed a distinctive political programme to convince others to support him. The choice of emphasizing the Macedonian inheritance of the monarchy is interesting, since it implies a controversy at the time over such matters as the assimilation of Macedonians into the Syrian population and the hellenization of the Syrians. It was a version of the dispute which had been taking place in the Jewish community a generation earlier, and which had been theoretically resolved by the Maccabean victory – though as will be seen later, this controversy continued, even in Judaea. It seems clear that the issue was a constant area of discussion throughout the later Seleukid period, and, as the Jewish wars against Rome show, afterwards.

The death of the child-king and the new policy which resulted may, in fact, have raised doubts about Jonathan's allegiance – he had no stake in a policy which emphasized the Macedonian elements in the Seleukid government. Tryphon invited him to a meeting at Ptolemais-Ake. Jonathan agreed to enter the city with a guard of 1,000 men, but these were overwhelmed by the citizens, and Jonathan was captured. (This appears to have been a spontaneous action by the crowd, for the people of the city had no reason to like either Jonathan or the Judaean army – but they did hand over their main prisoner to Tryphon, which suggests collusion.) Tryphon travelled towards Judaea, parading Jonathan about and demanding acquiescence and support. Simon, who had swiftly established his own control of Judaea when Jonathan was taken, ignored him, and Tryphon eventually had Jonathan killed.[18] For the Jews this was paradoxically helpful, since Simon was much the more capable of the two brothers, while a dead Jonathan was a useful martyr. When Tryphon left, Simon took Demetrios' side – altogether the episode had been a disaster for Tryphon but because of the unimportance of the south it did not damage him too much.[19]

Demetrios' position was thus altered only marginally by the changes among his opponents. The situation in Syria remained a stalemate with each side unable seriously to dent the other's support. (Simon's change of side had little effect, even in the south.) Tryphon appears to have contacted pirates in Rough Kilikia, who will possibly have shared the profits of their activities in exchange for his sponsorship, but this was hardly going to increase his support in Syria.[20] For Demetrios the solution had to lie elsewhere, and the only region in which he had serious armed support – the only sort of support which counted – was Babylonia, and there his forces were fighting their own battle, so it was not possible to withdraw any force for use elsewhere. Then in 141 things changed in the east.

The army which Ardaya had used against Elymais in 144 had evidently been defeated in the end; Ardaya is not heard of again, and it seems likely that his forces had been seriously reduced in numbers. All this, and the continuing stalemate in Syria, attracted Mithradates, who had been in Hyrkania (we may assume) since 145, supervising the situation with Baktria and the nomads beyond his eastern borders. He now came west in early 141. For the first time, he brought his army through the Zagros Mountains, at the Bisitun Pass, and quickly captured Seleukeia-on-the–Tigris and Babylon. By June of that year this operation had been successfully accomplished.[21]

There was, so far as we can see, no resistance, and indeed Mithradates carefully sent messages ahead of his march, which were read out in the Babylonian cities, so that the population knew he was on his way. It was also clear that there was no army available to oppose the Parthian advance. Having achieved a peaceful conquest, Mithradates then set about consolidating his position by appointing new governors: the viceroy (the 'general who is above the four generals') was Antiochos son of King Ar'abuzana. Where Ar'abuzana ruled is not known, but he appears to have had an Iranian name, and the obvious possibilities are Atropatene and Adiabene; just as important is the fact that his son, who actually became the viceroy, had a Macedonian name. One of his subordinates – one of the 'four generals' – was Nikanor, appointed a few days after him.[22] It made sense, of course, to appoint Greco-Macedonians to a Greco-Macedonian area, and may have undercut any support Tryphon had in the area for his policy of emphasizing Macedonian-ness. (After all, the army in Babylonia had at one point supported Antiochos VI, and Tryphon presumably had some support there still.) But the appointment of locals as governors was also a practice inherited from the Seleukids – as in Armenia, and Judea – and is a clear indication of the basic Seleukid inheritance of the Parthians.

It was not the ideological Macedonian Tryphon who responded to this new crisis, but Demetrios. He took the decision to take a Syrian army east to recover Babylonia. To do this he obviously risked his position in Syria, but in the event little changed, and withdrawing his toxic presence may have helped to bring some stability to Syria. No doubt he consulted with those holding the cities still under his control, and this would include his wife, Kleopatra Thea, who held Seleukeia-in-Pieria in association with the general, Aischrion. She also lived there with their three children, who were clearly dynastically precious. Once the decision was made to move to the east, a period of preparation, of gathering troops and stores, and at the same time an active pursuit of diplomacy and intrigue in the east, followed. Demetrios will have heard of Mithradates' conquest of Babylon no earlier than July 141, and it was not until the beginning of the next year that he reached the border of Babylonia. It is clear from what then happened that he had made considerable and careful preparations for this new campaign.

The traces of the diplomacy and/or the intrigues conducted in advance by Demetrios are occasional and fragmentary, but in their total they are comprehensive. He had plenty of possibilities to work with. Mithradates' acquisition of Babylonia had lifted Parthia into a higher level of power, an empire stretching from the Euphrates to Central Asia, and therefore its neighbours were at the least apprehensive, and in some cases most likely fearful, of future attacks – the new empire was surrounded by enemies, just as the Seleukid had been. Baktria was reviving slightly under King Heliokles, the son of Eukratides I; Kabneskir in Elymais who had hoped to conquer in Babylonia, had been pre-empted there by Mithradates; Hyspaosines of Charakene was a Seleukid loyalist: all of these were obviously potential allies in a coalition directed at Mithradates. In Babylonia the Parthian occupation, no matter how soft and peacefully it had been begun, was no doubt increasingly resented as it continued, particularly by the ruling city oligarchies whose power was significantly reduced. The several Parthian vassal states might well fear the greater Parthian presence; and these might include, besides Charakene and Elymais, Atropatene, Adiabene, Persis, and perhaps others.

It was Demetrios' diplomatic task to bring these several actual and potential Parthian enemies into a coalition, and Justin lists the participants as: Demetrios, the Elymaeans (i.e. Kabneskir), the 'Persians' (that is, Persis), and the Baktrians.[23] The Persian ruler's name is unknown to us, but the Baktrian involved was probably Heliokles I, who by 140 was the ruler of one of the main surviving Baktrian states. In addition Demetrios could probably count on the residual loyalty of the Greco-Macedonian rulers of the Babylonian (and even the Median) cities. But the distances involved made communications between the partners very difficult and the co-ordination of their actions impossible; not only that but there were plenty of mutual suspicions between the allies which might open the way for Mithradates to split the coalition; each hoped for independence, and at least had ambitions to control Babylonia. To gather these four into a coalition was a major diplomatic achievement. It would be interesting to know just what promises Demetrios had had to make.

Mithradates remained in Babylonia throughout the second half of 141, and took his army back to Media in December 141 or January 140.[24] At that time Demetrios was probably at Nisibis in Mesopotamia, where he minted a large number of coins, and where he probably had had his winter camp.[25] The coins were no doubt minted so as to pay his army, and any other troops who came to join him. Nisibis (Antioch–in–Mygdonia) was just halfway from Zeugma to the Tigris, a good place for observation and for reconnaissance of the way ahead, and to investigate conditions in Babylonia. It seems likely enough that Demetrios was waiting for Mithradates to move east once more to deal with his continuing imperial problems, before he invaded Babylonia. (It may also be that Mithradates was waiting in Babylonia to see what Demetrios would do, and that he moved in order to bring the approaching crisis to a head.) But one of the problems with a far-flung coalition of jealous members is that each is in it for himself, and they are all competing with each other.

Even as Mithradates withdrew through the passes into Media, Kabneskir launched an attack into Babylonia, capturing and sacking the city of Apamaea-on-the–Silhu-River (near to modern Kut el-Amarna), clearly aiming not only to dislodge Parthian power, but to pre-empt his allies in seizing control of Babylonia. Nobody else was ready to join in the attack on the Parthian position as early as that, or was perhaps close enough to do so, or maybe was willing to tackle the Parthians. We do not know what part the Baktrians played in the crisis, but it seems likely that they stayed out of it; or they may have been successfully opposed by forces commanded by Bagasis who was the Parthian governor in Media; their inclusion in the alliance in Justin's list does imply that they took part in some way in the fighting. Kabneskir's attack, however, was not just on the Parthian position in Babylonia; it was also regarded as an attack on the Babylonians themselves. The Elymaians and the Babylonians were ancient enemies, and the Babylonians had no doubt that the Elymaeans were still their enemy. The viceroy Antiochos, no doubt buoyed up by local support, marched at once to defend his lands against the Elymaean attack.[26] At the very first move, the fissures within the coalition were gaping wide.

It is difficult to sort out what then happened, though the fighting seems to have come as far north as Babylon itself. Fighting of various sorts lasted throughout January and involved much of Babylonia. The advantage of operating from a central position was seized by Mithradates: while his viceroy Antiochos fought the Elymaean army in Babylonia, he himself took the army he had removed from Babylonia and invaded Elymais from the north, out of Media. It seems likely that this pushed the Persians, by far the weakest of the allies, into peace at the same time. At Susa the coinage of Kabneskir ceased during 140, implying that he had ceased to rule, and probably he was killed. His successor Kabneskir III, probably his son, was installed by Mithradates as his satrap of Elymais, either as the price for peace, or as a quisling.[27] Mithradates was quite consistent in the appointment of such governors: a local man of stature was always his first choice – Antiochos, Nikanor, Kabneskir III, the son of his recent enemy – and he was not apparently decoyed from this policy by rebellions and invasions.

Mithradates' move first into Media and then into Elymais had opened the way for Demetrios to move into Babylonia. How much the two kings knew of each other's marches or intentions is unknown, but the coalition orchestrated by Demetrios had obviously been aimed in part at distracting Mithradates from Babylonia, and while the latter was operating in Elymais, Demetrios marched into Babylonia from the north.

It is possible that a stage on his route is marked by the city of Demetrias, which was somewhere near Arbela in Adiabene, probably on the Lower Zab River, which flows from the Zagros to the Tigris. From this position he could survey the condition to Babylonia, receive reports, and plan his next moves. The founder of Demetrias is not known, but the name indicates that it was either Demetrios II or his father; the former's systematic campaign seems to make him the more likely author.[28]

The details of the campaign which followed are unknown, as usual, but the mint at Seleukeia-on-the-Tigris produced Demetrios' coins in 140–139, but then later in 139 it reverted to producing coins for Mithradates.[29] The fighting lasted a full year and more, from early 140 to mid-138, and must have initially involved the forces of Demetrios against those of Antiochos the viceroy. The latter is not heard of again, so presumably he was either killed or comprehensively defeated; this was probably one of the two battles Demetrios is said to have won, and it may well be the point at which Demetrios took Seleukeia-on-the-Tigris.[30] In the end Demetrios was defeated and captured, either by treachery during a peace conference, or by surprise attack; the latter explanation seems preferable, though it is uncomfortably reminiscent of the capture of his brother a decade later – and both explanations may be inventions. Mithradates paraded him in chains through the cities of his former kingdom, demonstrating to Demetrios' former subjects that their king was a lost cause.[31]

While Demetrios was fighting in Babylonia a new development took place in Syria. In Seleukeia-in-Pieria Kleopatra Thea, whatever assurances she had given Demetrios before he left for the east, had become vulnerable. Every city in Syria had its pro-Tryphon and pro-Demetrios factions, and Seleukeia was evidently no exception. Kleopatra was also dependent on the garrison commander and his troops. At some point in 139 she apparently came to the conclusion that this was not enough. She turned to Demetrios' brother Antiochos for help.

Antiochos had lived at Side in Pamphylia for a time, whence his nickname Sidetes. He had later moved to Rhodes, possibly to remove himself from the proximity of Tryphon, who had contacts with pirates who operated out of Rough Kilikia, next door to Side. At some point in 139 he arrived in Syria, landing at Seleukeia-in-Pieria, then married Kleopatra Thea, and so made himself king. He was about 20-years-old. Demetrios, be it noted, was still active in and campaigning in Babylonia until the middle of 138. The events have been rationalized as Antiochos' arrival following on Demetrios' capture, but the dates of coins and the entries in the *Astronomical Diaries* demonstrate a clear overlap of about a year.

Kleopatra could get no help from Demetrios while he was in Babylonia. Quite apart from the fact that he was fighting Mithradates it would take him at least a month to march to Syria. Antiochos, on the other hand, was close, and could arrive quickly and by sea – virtually secretly. Coins issued at Antioch, Seleukeia-in-Pieria, and at Tyre clearly show that Antiochos was installed as king during 139 – and that therefore he had married Kleopatra Thea to attain that position. It is not recorded, but it is quite possible, that Antiochos arrived with some mercenary reinforcements; it does not seem likely that his mere presence would have seriously altered the situation in Seleukeia.[32]

The reaction of Demetrios to all this is not known. He continued fighting in Babylonia until his capture in mid-138, by which time his wife and his brother had been married for a year. By that time he may have known that Tryphon had been defeated by Antiochos in Syria. His capture did not end the Babylonian fighting. The satrap Kabneskir III, installed by Mithradates in Elymais, had apparently been unsuccessful in controlling that province, and from late 138 to 133 the Susa mint produced coins in the name of a man called Tigraios, who had possibly succeeded in defeating a Parthian attack. In southern Babylonia Hyspaosines, the great survivor, at last became directly involved in the war, but against the Elymaeans, and so presumably technically on the Parthian side, and so in defending his lands against the old enemy.

The original ease of the Parthian conquest of Babylonia had been, as such speedy conquests usually are, superficial, and had only raised the local people to a later resistance. The result was a long and no doubt destructive campaign of reconquest. But the real damage was done, by the conquest of that land and the capture of the king, to the Seleukid kingdom.

Chapter 7

The New Seleukid Kingdom (139–131 BC)

upport for Tryphon had depended above all on antipathy towards Demetrios, but this was a factor which was really confined to some of the cities of Syria. So, even with the removal of Demetrios II from Syria, Tryphon was unable to extend his power any further, for in the two years that Demetrios spent fighting in the east, Tryphon made no progress. He could hold what he had seized, exerting his military strength and his political control, but the rest was beyond his grasp. The arrival of Antiochos VII spelled the end for his venture. From his initial base in Seleukeia-in-Pieria Antiochos gained control of Antioch almost at once, as the coins indicate.[1] This had been one of the cities which had been most ill-treated by Demetrios, so its rapid accession to Antiochos indicated clearly that he would be able to expand his authority throughout Syria relatively easily.

During the Seleukid year 175 (that is, 138–137 BC), Tryphon minted coins at Byblos, at Ptolemais-Ake, and at Ashkelon. Antiochos had gained control of Tyre in the previous year (176 SE: 139–138 BC) and now minted at Sidon, Tarsos in Kilikia, and Damascus.[2] There is no real pattern in this, nor is there any record of these cities being captured: it seems probable that Antiochos was being persuasive rather than violent. Of course he had to defeat Tryphon in battle, which he did at some unknown place in northern Syria. The campaign culminated in Antiochos' army besieging Tryphon at Dor on the Palestinian coast.[3] Tryphon also held Apamaea.

In order to reach Dor from Seleukeia–in-Pieria, Antiochos had to march 500km. On the way he passed three cities which give indications as to his reception and his methods. The obvious route south was along the Phoenician coast, where Sidon had held to the cause of Demetrios ever since his arrival. Byblos, on the other hand, further north, had coined for Antiochos VI in 142, and for Tryphon in 140 and 138; Orthosia north of Byblos, is said to have stayed with Tryphon until the end.[4] Tyre had switched to Antiochos VI and Tryphon, coining for them in 143–141 and 139–138, and Ashkelon further south did so in 141 and 139–138.[5]

So to reach Dor, presumably in pursuit of Tryphon, Antiochos had to pass by several hostile cities, or through friendly ones, and his journey must have been fairly slow. At Dor he had to lay siege to the city, a task for which he also needed ships. *I Maccabees* notes that he had a fleet of ships which blockaded the port, though only intermittently.[6] The excavations in the city have produced evidence for the siege: a lead sling bullet inscribed with the optimistic slogan 'Tryphon victory' and dated from Dor in Tryphon's 'year 5'.[7]

The fleet would need to be of a substantial size to blockade even so relatively small a city as Dor. Antiochos must have arrived at Seleukeia in ships, though whether he could keep them in his service once he was king is not known. He will have inherited some ships at Seleukeia, and he could certainly call up ships from Tyre and Sidon and from the Kilikian cities. There is also a suggestion that Arados provided ships. Arados resumed coining its own coins in 138–137, and put an engraving of a ship on the reverse. For a port this is hardly surprising, but the date indicates that the coining privilege was conceded by Antiochos. Arados had long manifested a desire for autonomy or even independence. Providing ships to the king in return for an increase in its autonomy would be a good bargain for Antiochos.[8]

Another indication of Antiochos' progress, and his methods, is in the negotiations with Judaea. Even before besieging Dor he contacted Simon the ruler in Judaea, whose brother Jonathan had been killed by Tryphon three or four years before.[9] Simon had manoeuvred his principality into effective independence as a result, but he was clearly obligated to assist the enemy of his brother's murderer. A version of the negotiations is contained in *I Maccabees*.[10] Antiochos' envoy, Athenobios, went up to Jerusalem, where he demanded the return of Gazara and Joppa, and the payment of a thousand talents. Simon claimed the two places as ancestral possessions, but also offered a hundred talents, which rather undermined his claim. Athenobios left, supposedly 'in a rage', but probably merely to report to Antiochos.

Josephos does not report any such negotiations, and instead says that Simon and Antiochos made a 'friendly alliance'.[11] Further, *I Maccabees* claims that Antiochos rejected Simon's offer of military help while Josephos says that Simon provided money and supplies to the besiegers at Dor. These are not, of course, necessarily contradictory, since it was only the men that Antiochos refused. Some sort of *modus vivendi* seems to have been reached, probably because both were interested in removing Tryphon, but it can scarcely be called an alliance. There were advantages to both in such an agreement. Antiochos gained supplies, and also gained protection against an attack out of Judaea, while Simon had someone else doing the fighting. The evidence from Arados and Judaea therefore shows that Antiochos was willing to make such agreements with the local Syrian states; he was being flexible and pragmatic, and of course he was reserving his position. This is presumably the approach he had used with other places in Syria during his campaign.

Antiochos, as the Seleukid king, was no doubt not entirely pleased to have been repelled by Simon, even if he got supplies from Judaea, but he did succeed in finally bringing Tryphon to destruction. Within a fairly short time, and certainly before the end of the Seleukid year 175 (138–137 BC), he had won the war. Tryphon escaped from Dor by sea, a sign that Antiochos' blockade was not very effective. He landed at Orthosia in north Phoenicia, and moved to his original base at Apamaea. This was his final throw, and it failed. He was captured and executed.[12]

The removal of Tryphon left Antiochos in control of all Syria. However, years of war had left the land in need of a respite, and the central government control had clearly been loosened. Its restoration was necessary. Judaea was one example. Conflict developed when the governor of Koile Syria appointed by Antiochos pressed on Judaea in search of the agreement which had not been concluded earlier. This was a man called 'Kendebaios' by the Jewish sources (though this seems to be his city of origin, Kendebe in Lykia). No doubt on Antiochos' instructions he aimed to recover the lands gained by Judaea outside the Judaean upland, in particular Joppa and Gazara, which Athenobios had earlier demanded. The two sources on the conflict describe almost different wars which followed. Josephos speaks of fighting in the passes leading from the coastal lowlands to the Judaean plateau, the type of fighting in which Simon had excelled in the campaign against Tryphon.[13] *I Maccabees*, however, having briefly noted Kendebaios' harassing tactics, which might be a version of Josephos' fighting in the passes, goes on to describe a Judaean invasion of the lowlands and a victory over the Seleukid army at Kidron.[14]

It is possible to reconcile this discrepancy by making Josephos omit the battle for some reason, and by enlarging the Maccabees' account of the guerrilla preliminaries from Josephos. But it is difficult to see why Josephos should omit such a signal victory for his people in open battle against clearly stronger forces. His purpose was to describe Judaean history for the Romans, after all, and it was military victories which particularly impressed Roman opinion. A different solution is needed. The preliminary guerrilla campaign for control of the routes up from the coastal lowlands is common to both accounts and may be accepted. The battle is the problem.

Looked at more closely there are curiosities in the account in *Maccabees*. The Judaean army was commanded by Simon's sons Hyrkanos and Judas, of whom the first was later to be Simon's successor. Hyrkanos' part in the battle is much greater than Judas', who was wounded. Hyrkanos also used unusual tactics, in placing his cavalry in the centre of his army with the infantry on the wings, the very reverse of normal Hellenistic battle tactics. After their defeat the Seleukid forces are said to have taken refuge in Kidron, a fort earlier built by Kendebaios, and in towers in the territory of the city of Ashdod, while Hyrkanos burnt the city.

This last item may be the clue. Simon's brother Jonathan had won a victory in the same area (also using unusual tactics) against an earlier commander, Apollonios. He had then captured and burnt Ashdod. Combined with the clear exaltation of the actions of Hyrkanos in the Maccabees account, it seems probable that the Kidron battle was an exaggeration of a small fight in the campaign of ambushes. The purpose of the author of *I Maccabees* in composing his account of events was partly to glorify Hyrkanos, under whose rule it was written. The author, not wholly conversant with battle tactics, described an unprecedented military manoeuvre, gave the command to Hyrkanos, and borrowed the burning of Ashdod from the earlier victory of Jonathan.[15] The battle of Kidron cannot be accepted, therefore, and may be deleted from the record.

There is no doubt that there was fighting, and that the Judaean plateau was successfully defended. Similarly, the lands to the north and west which had been acquired by Simon and his predecessors remained under Judaean control, as did Joppa and Gazara. If Kendebaios' aim was to recover these places, as Athenobios had demanded, he failed, though he may have been successful in deterring Judaean raids into the lowlands. (It could be that the fight at Kidron – clearly a Judaean invasion of Seleukid territory – was actually a Kendebaian victory; it would not be the only Judaean defeat turned into a victory by the Maccabees author.)

The dating of all this is not clear. Antiochos is said to have appointed Kendebaios when he left Dor to chase after the fleeing Tryphon, that is, in 138. There is no indication of how long the subsequent fighting in Palestine lasted, but it probably simply continued in a desultory fashion for the rest of Simon's life. Josephos claims that the last period of Simon's life was peaceful, but this looks to be a purely conventional terminus to his account of Simon's life and reign.[16] And since he had handed over command of the force to his sons, it was in a sense accurate.

Antiochos was not directly involved in affairs in Palestine between 138 and 134, apparently leaving matters to Kendebaios. Given that the situation in

Palestine was obviously unsatisfactory, he was presumably busy elsewhere, but it is difficult to specify what he was doing. Whatever it was, it was more important than the minor war being conducted in the south. Justin says he subdued the cities which had rebelled against his brother.[17] This may indicate that more fighting in northern Syria was needed even after Tryphon's defeat and death, or it may be code for a less violent campaign of subjugation and persuasion. It certainly seems that he had plenty to do, and that, whatever methods he used, they were successful in convincing the Syrian cities to support him.

However, this did not include several of the less urbanized regions. Judaea was clearly determined on some sort of independence, and other regions were moving in that direction during Antiochos' reign, as Arados' bargain with him had shown. In the north, Kommagene later dated its dynasty's origin to 163 or 162, when Ptolemaios the founder became governor of the sub-province. In about 130 he was succeeded as governor by his son Samos, who later made himself king.[18] Ptolemaios does not seem ever to have been more than a governor, but his length of time in office, and his ability to pass on his position to his son shows that he and his province were at least semi-independent of the kingdom by the time of Antiochos' reign, and that the family aimed at enlarging his sphere of authority. Presumably his support for Antiochos had secured Ptolemaios' position. (Coins continued to be produced, probably at Samosata, but of decreasing legibility; they could no longer be taken as even copies of Seleukid coins, but their metal content no doubt ensured their acceptability in the local area.)[19]

Next door, across the Euphrates River, the city of Edessa came under the rule of a man who founded a monarchy at some point between 137 and 132.[20] The names of the kings were all Arab, though Edessa itself was a Macedonian city founded two centuries earlier on the site of an age-old Syrian city. Presumably the Arab dynasty which became established in the city was based originally in the surrounding lands – the Seleukid sub-province of Osrhoene – and presumably also this meant that Seleukid royal authority had largely vanished from the lands east of the Euphrates. Given the preoccupation of all the Seleukid kings and pretenders with control of Syria during the past ten years this would not be surprising. Demetrios II marched through Mesopotamia on his way east in 141, and coined vigorously at Nisibis to the east of Edessa.[21] The subsequent dating of the origin of the Edessan dynasty to the 130s does not mean that they were independent at that time, only that the first of the dynasty was exercising some power in the region at that time. It would seem likely that one of the kings gained control of Edessa in the confusion following Antiochos VII's Parthian war. The combination at Edessa of king and city proved successful, and the dynasty lasted for almost four centuries.

This puts the Judaean situation into a better context than simply accepting the unlikely heroics and divine inspiration described by Josephos and *I Maccabees*. Antiochos, hampered by the general weakness and disintegration of the kingdom he had acquired, was unable, at least at first, to impose his authority on these peripheral regions. On the other hand, he was clearly hoping to, and aiming to, expand his territory and authority, given any opportunity. In 134 events in Judaea supplied one such opportunity.

In February 134 BC Simon was murdered at a banquet at Dok, a castle overlooking Jericho, by his son-in-law Ptolemaios. The deed triggered a political crisis in Judaea which lasted for several months. During that crisis Simon's two eldest sons and his widow were also killed by Ptolemaios, who had held them hostage, but the third son, Hyrkanos, eventually succeeded in driving Ptolemaios out of Dok and of the kingdom. The murderer took refuge with the ruler of the city of Philadelphia across the Jordan, Zenon Kotylas.[22]

On the surface this is an almost classic example of a *coup d'etat* mounted from within the ruling group of the state. But Ptolemaios' first action after accomplishing the assassination, even before gaining the acquiescence of the army, or securing his hold on Jerusalem, the only city in the state, was to send the news of what he had done to 'the king', that is, to Antiochos VII.[23] The significance of this move by Ptolemaios is that he recognized that Antiochos was the suzerain of Judaea, and that he would require Antiochos' approval, or at least his acquiescence, for his coup.

Simon had been in control of Judaea since 142, and had built up his institutional authority within Judaea. He was high priest and *ethnarchos* or *hegemon*, offices to which he had been elected by 'an assembly of priests, people, rulers of the nation, and elders of the land' in Jerusalem.[24] This was not a process necessarily regarded as valid by any outside political authority, but it did give him a clear authority within Judaea, which reinforced that which he had inherited as heir of his brothers, who had held such offices before him. The power and authority of the hereditary principle was well respected. Simon had further reinforced his power by having the offices declared to be his 'in perpetuity', which also implied that they were heritable.[25] He was also *strategos*, a governing office to which he had been appointed by the Seleukid king, though he had scarcely exercised it, and it cannot have survived Antiochos' arrival as king. He thus held hereditary, religious, elective, and military offices, all concentrated in himself. Nevertheless, Ptolemaios' message to Antiochos shows that, despite his many titles and despite his election, Simon held power in Judaea as much by grace of the Seleukid king as by hereditary and elective right. Their relations during the siege of Dor had been a mark of his subordination, as the demands which Athenobios had presented showed; and Simon's counter-offer, though it was rejected, was a clear recognition of his inferior position. The desultory fighting since then showed that neither side was satisfied with the situation.

Simon had taken advantage of the Seleukid dynastic disputes in the 140s to secure the removal of the Seleukid garrison which had held the Akra in Jerusalem (the acropolis of the city);[26] he had also taken control of the fortress of Gazara and of the sea port of Joppa, and these were incorporated into Judaea[27] – it was the return of these places which Antiochos had demanded through Athenobios, and which Kendebaios had been trying to secure; they had, in fact, been the gift of Tryphon, the usurper, none of whose actions Antiochos could accept as valid, so Antiochos clearly felt he had the right to require their return.

The point of the contest between Simon and Antiochos, however, was that this was part of a continuing process of negotiation, which was being conducted carefully enough on each side to avoid provoking the other to a major military effort. It is significant that Simon's internal authority as *hegemon* of Judaea or as high priest was not being challenged by the king, and Simon was not challenging the rights of the king over Judaea. The two sides were really not very far from reaching an agreement. Hence the continuing low level of the fighting.

This was the situation when Ptolemaios sent off his message to the king with the news of his murder of Simon. He also despatched men to kill the remaining son of Simon, Hyrkanos, who was in post as commander at Gazara facing the threat of Kendebaios. But a man escaped from Dok, Ptolemaios' castle, and warned Hyrkanos. He captured the assassins, and then moved rapidly to seize control of Jerusalem.[28] Ptolemaios was thus foiled.

Ptolemaios and Hyrkanos had identified different and conflicting sources of power in Judaea: Ptolemaios relied on the king for decisive support; Hyrkanos had seen that it was, in fact, an internal Judaean matter, and by seizing Jerusalem he was able also to claim the high priesthood by hereditary right, a right which the king had earlier in effect recognized by not challenging Simon's occupation of the office. This in turn provided Hyrkanos with the authority to command at least a major part of the Judaean army. He had commanded part of it, of course, in the campaign against Kendebaios and he already commanded the garrison at Gazara.

Ptolemaios' forces – he clearly commanded a respectable fraction of the Judaean army, and one element of his coup had been to promise wealth to the military officers – were not sufficient to ensure the capture of Jerusalem, but they were enough to prevent Hyrkanos from achieving a clean sweep right at the start. For the next several months, the dispute between them centred on Hyrkanos' siege of Ptolemaios at Dok, above Jericho.[29]

The stalemate seems to have lasted into the autumn, though the dating is difficult. Simon was murdered, according to *I Maccabees*, in Shebat 177 SE, which is January–February 134 BC.[30] Josephos' account implies a lengthy siege of Dok lasting some months. Hyrkanos' mother and brothers were in Ptolemaios' hands, and this explains the stalemate, while Dok was also well fortified.[31] This long stand-off provided Antiochos with all the time he needed to decide on his response. Possibly he hoped that Kendebaios could sort the problem out, but we must presume that Hyrkanos was able to fend him off at the same time as blockading Dok.

Eventually Antiochos decided to take advantage of the internal Judaean dispute – just as Simon had taken advantage of the Seleukid civil war – and his response was, as before, partly military and partly diplomatic. The man he had been negotiating with, Simon, had been killed, the man who had done the killing, Ptolemaios, was losing the subsequent civil war, and the winner, Hyrkanos, had seized the office of high priest, to which Antiochos could claim the right of appointment, or at least the right of confirmation in office.[32] Further, the civil war showed that authority in Judaea was divided and uncertain; it was the clear responsibility of the king as suzerain, to sort the matter out. Plus, of course, the opportunity now existed to reduce the Jewish state in size and to a proper obedience.

However, Antiochos did not intervene directly in the civil war, though he clearly could have done. It was only when Hyrkanos had won, when Ptolemaios killed his hostages and then escaped across the Jordan to take refuge in Philadelphia that Antiochos moved. When he did so, however, it was with overwhelming force. His army, without any fighting of any significance – at least none is mentioned in our sources – closed in on Jerusalem and formed a siege. The ease of his invasion incidentally demonstrates that Kendebaios' activities had been aimed at pressure rather than at conquest.

The account of the siege in Josephos[33] is not a credible description of what actually happened, but rather a compilation based on the literary assumptions about what might be expected to happen in a siege.[34] In fact little actually happened. The one concrete indication of the length of time involved implies a siege lasting a year, from before November (the 'setting of the Pleiades') to October of the next year (the 'feast of Tabernacles'),[35] which seems fairly unlikely.[36] Antiochos, in fact, was still not necessarily aiming at conquest in this campaign, instead he was aiming at a return to the political position as it had existed before the Seleukid collapse which had begun nearly twenty years before. That is, he aimed to impose the same conditions as had been proposed by Athenobios four years before.

In the end, after an unknown period of time under siege, Hyrkanos surrendered on these terms. Josephos dresses it up in a story of Antiochos' gifts to the city on the Feast of Tabernacles, but this is clearly a local invention, as is the implication of a siege lasting almost a year. Hyrkanos, in fact, did not resist for very long, and probably could not, given that Judaea was no doubt very short of supplies after the previous civil war. He asked for terms, and Antiochos offered what he had demanded of Simon earlier: either payment of tribute for Gazara and Joppa and other places, or their surrender, and the return of the Seleukid garrison to the Akra in Jerusalem. Hyrkanos replied by refusing the Akra garrison and in its place he proposed a payment of 500 talents.[37] The payment of tribute was thus not to be for Joppa and the other places, but to avoid the imposition of the Akra garrison. Details of the negotiations are not known, but it would seem that the result was that tribute was paid, and the garrison was not imposed. Instead the city walls of Jerusalem were pulled down; this would leave the city open to attack, and so obviate the need for the garrison, and Antiochos saw to the dismantlement before he withdrew. (It would also save Antiochos the cost of the garrison.)

Two other items are not mentioned: Hyrkanos' political position was regularized, for once he and Antiochos had an agreement, it became in the king's interest to see that Hyrkanos stayed in power. He had already been elected high priest – or so the theory went: in fact he had seized the position, but in hereditary terms he was the rightful heir. He had also acted as civil governor. These posts were positions in the king's gift, and if Hyrkanos held them after the siege, Antiochos must have confirmed him in them as part of the treaty. It was not part of the purpose of Hyrkanos to imply any dependence on the Seleukid king, however, so this element was subsequently ignored by the Jewish sources. Yet the slighting of the walls of Jerusalem was decisive, since the city was the only place of any real military strength in the Judaean state. Without a fortified base, Hyrkanos was wholly at the mercy of the king's power. He showed he understood this by refortifying the city as soon as he got the chance.

The second item which is not mentioned is that Hyrkanos did surrender Joppa and Gazara, as well as a place called Pegai. Hyrkanos complained later that the Seleukids were holding these places, indicating that he had given them up, but that he was not reconciled to their loss.[38] Josephos carefully fudges his account to make the overall defeat appear less serious than it was, but Hyrkanos had to suffer the disarming of his main (only) city, payment of tribute, and the loss of two major posts, including access to the sea. Judaea was reduced once more to the upland plateau, and was once again clearly a subordinate of the Seleukid kingdom. A little later Hyrkanos was summoned by Antiochos to take part in the Seleukid military expedition against Parthia.[39] His obedience demonstrates Hyrkanos' subordination.

In addition there is a new element: Hyrkanos handed over hostages.[40] There is no indication of the reason, but hostages in such a situation were usually delivered to ensure the performance of the terms which could not be executed at once. One was the payment of the indemnity, of which only 300 talents were handed over at first, with the other 200 due later; another was the transfer of Joppa, Gazara, and Pegai. The full peace terms therefore were: destruction of the walls of Jerusalem, payment of the indemnity, delivery of the lowland cities to Seleukid control, all guaranteed by handing over hostages; in return Hyrkanos got an official appointment to the offices of high priest and *strategos*. Such terms could only have been imposed as a result of Hyrkanos' comprehensive defeat.

The result of this crisis in Judaea was therefore the return of Judaea to Seleukid control, as a subordinate principality governed by a member of the Hasmonaean family (the Maccabees), with the local title of high priest, and the Seleukid office of *strategos*. During the three following years, 132–129, coins of the Seleukid king were minted in Jerusalem, inscribed as from King Antiochos Euergetes, with the Seleukid emblem of the anchor on one side and on the other a lily, the emblem of Jerusalem. These coins would seem to be produced as part of the tribute Hyrkanos continued to pay while Antiochos lived.[41]

The geographical adjustments to the boundary of Hyrkanos' state (or province, in the Seleukid view) pushed Judaea back into the hills. The loss of Joppa severed the only Judaean connection with the Mediterranean; the loss of Gazara and Pegai (the site of the later Antipatris[42]), pushed Jewish power out of the fertile lowland between the hills and the coastlands, and the loss of these territories also removed the Judaean connection with the main routeway through the lowland, the 'Way of the Sea'. Being pushed back into the hills meant a severe reduction in Judaean power and resources, and within those hills the destruction of the walls of Jerusalem was almost as severe a blow. Jerusalem was, in effect, the only defensible site in the whole province. Without its walls, behind which the Judaean army and population could shelter, Judaea's military significance was much reduced. The Jewish army could usually be defeated without much difficulty by the Seleukid royal army. The only recourse was to avoid battle and to retreat to the city. A reliance on guerrilla tactics to harass the enemy left the whole of the Judaean countryside open to occupation and destruction by the enemy forces, but a siege of Jerusalem was always a difficult problem for an attacker since supplying the besiegers in a relatively poor territory like the Judaean hills was expensive and very manpower-consuming. So without the central fortress to pin down the main force of the enemy, there was no point in fighting in the first place.

Antiochos VII's success in Judaea was impressive, but it left the enemy in existence. This seems to fit with the toleration of other semi-independent principalities, such as Kommagene in the north. The story of the Judaean campaign also reveals the existence of the principality of Zenon Kotylas, 'tyrant' of Philadelphia. His son Theodoros inherited his position, so that between them they ruled in Philadelphia and the area around that city for at least the next fifty years.[43] Zenon probably emerged as a local ruler when the Seleukid collapse after c.150 left the Transjordanian area exposed to Judaean raids, and without the hope of rescue by the preoccupied Seleukid forces. Yet after Antiochos VII's success in Judaea in 134, which removed the threat of Judaean raids, Zenon was left in place, though whether on Seleukid terms is not known. Even if Antiochos VII imposed a subordinate status on Zenon, he now ruled an independent or semi-independent principality.

To the south and east of Judaea and Philadelphia was the kingdom of the Nabataeans, consolidated out of a set of related Arab clans. In 168 a man called Aretas gave refuge to a fleeing Jewish high priest; he is described as a 'tyrant', which must signify that he was regarded as a local strong man, but also independent.[44] By about 100 BC there was a king of the Nabataeans in place, another Aretas, conventionally called Aretas II.[45] By that time he was a formidable local political power, suggesting that he had been in power for some time. If the two Aretai were related, they were probably grandfather and grandson.[46]

The 'tyrant' Aretas of 168 may be the same as a king of that name referred to in an early but undated inscription.[47] Earlier encounters with the Nabataeans by Demetrios Poliorketes in 312 and by the Ptolemaic official Zenon in 259, provide no indication at those times of a Nabataean kingship, and this therefore seems most likely to have been a development of the second century.[48] The crisis in Judaea, and Judaean aggressiveness from 168 onwards, is the best context for a defensive consolidation of peoples under one military commander, in Nabataea as it was in Philadelphia.

The various Nabataean groups were shepherds and traders, inhabiting the lands east of the Dead Sea, southwards into North Arabia, and northwards into the lands east of the Greek cities as far as the hills of the Hauran. The Hauran is an upland area which captures rain from the west, which would suit the Nabataeans well enough as would the nearby Gaulan area (noted earlier as a traditional meeting place of nomad tribes). The Nabataeans were settling in there in the third century BC, and they developed into skilled farmers of semi-arid lands.[49] Hemmed in by the desert to the east and the Greeks and Jews to the west and north, the development of a kingship would be a sensible defensive gesture when the violence of the Jewish uprising began in the 160s. Nabataean wealth, as opposed to their subsistence, was derived from long distance trade; they were thus vulnerable to raids on their bases and caravans by better armed and more highly organized neighbours. There is no indication at all that the Nabataeans were in any way subordinate to the Seleukid king at any time.

The southern part of Syria in the 130s was thus only just under Seleukid control, and had a set of independent and semi-independent minor states on its inland boundary, just as it had in the north. Direct Seleukid rule was confined mainly to a strip of the coastland. The lands which had shifted into independence or developed independent monarchies were nevertheless much the poorer and less important regions. Nabataea did not have any notable urban centres – for Petra was hardly a city – and in Judaea only Jerusalem could be counted as urban, and that was now unfortified. Similarly in other areas; Kommagene was largely rural, though not entirely; Osrhoene (the name of the new kingdom which included Edessa) contained only one, or perhaps two urban centres, Edessa and Karrhai. Philadelphia was a city, but it was fairly small and was set amid a wide and arid landscape exploited mainly by nomads.

The areas which had remained loyal to the Seleukid monarchy were, by contrast, largely urbanized, and very much wealthier. In the south the Palestinian coast was lined with a dozen cities from Ptolemais-Ake to Gaza, the Vale of Jezreel contained the cities of Samaria and Skythopolis, and there were more Greek cities east of the Jordan. These last were mainly small and weak, clearly vulnerable to an enemy such as Judaea; one of them, Gerasa, eventually came under the rule of Zenon and Theodoros of Philadelphia, but others could for the present look to the governor of the coastlands, Koile Syria, for protection. The south, Palestine, was thus in the 130s a complex politico-geographical region, with the cities and kingdoms intertwined.

The rest of Syria was superficially rather less politically complicated, and had, once Antiochos VII was accepted everywhere, suffered much less change.

The centre of royal power in the north was the land which Seleukos I had sowed thickly with new cities. The four great cities of Antioch, Seleukeia-in-Pieria, Laodiceia-ad-Mare and Apamaea occupied about half of the area; half a dozen other, smaller, cities occupied the drier and less fertile space to the north and east of Antioch – Nikopolis, Beroia, Kyrrhos, Chalkis, Hierapolis, Seleukeia-Zeugma, Doliche, Europos – as far as the Euphrates.[50] North Syria was thus a region with a strong concentration of Greeks and Macedonians, whose ancestors had populated the new cities and who owned the lands round about. But in turn these surrounding rural areas were inhabited by descendants of the Semitic populations who had occupied the land for millennia before Alexander's conquest. It was thus a region which could produce large armed forces from the Greco-Macedonians of the cities, armed and trained in the Macedonian manner, for service under royal command, and it had become one of the great economic centres of the kingdom.

The importance of this area must be emphasized. The weight of historical source material for this period comes from Palestine, but this must not detract from the fact that geographically, politically, and economically it was north Syria which was the most important region left to the Seleukids after the loss of Babylonia and Media. And in north Syria it was those dozen cities founded by Seleukos I which were the political elements which counted most. They were of all sizes from the giant city of Antioch, by now one of the largest cities in the Hellenistic-Roman world, down to the relatively small Doliche and Kyrrhos and Europos. Seleukeia and Laodikeia were great seaports, Apamaea a great military centre. Among the smaller cities, Seleukeia-Zeugma controlled the most important crossing of the Euphrates, and Hierapolis housed the great temple of Atargatis, a city with a strong Syrian basis and the recipient of royal favour, but only superficially Hellenized.

These cities are reassuringly solid and permanent, but some change was working at a lower social and political level. The Judaean uprising, for all its religious content and motivation, was also a rural and Semitic rebellion against urban and Macedonian rule and domination. The Jews were a relatively numerous, geographically concentrated, and self-conscious group, hence their eventual success. The Nabataeans were also a clearly self-conscious and distinct group, but were also living on the periphery of the Greco-Macedonian area, and the same could be said of Kommagene. The Phoenician cities, led by Arados in this, were putting slogans in their own Semitic script on their coins. Much of this emerged once the whole of Syria was united by Antiochos III's conquest of the south, and in the main it was in the old Ptolemaic-Seleukid borderland region which had been thinly populated during the repeated wars between the kings in the third century, but once the frontier was eradicated, settlement increased, and it was evidently Syrians rather than Greeks and Macedonians who were the new settlers.

So here and in other peripheral areas the new Semitic presence developed. It did not emerge in a political sense in the centre and north of Syria for a generation after Antiochos VII (except in the Phoenician cities) but a self-conscious groundwork was certainly being produced in this reign and before. How much of this was a reflection of the successful revolt of a Semitic people in Judaea is not something we can find any direct evidence for, but common sense suggests that the victories of the Jews will have contributed substantially to the rising consciousness of being Aramaic or Syriac; and it seems that, as with the Jews, at base the Semitic revival was based in religion. The civil wars may not have caused much change to the superficial view in north Syria, but it was happening nonetheless.

There were more cities in Kilikia, another geographically distinct area, hemmed in by the Taurus Mountains to the north and the sea to the south, and separated off from north Syria by the Amanus range. It had been a part of the Seleukid monarchy since the time of the founder, Seleukos I, but some of its cities were much older, claiming to have been founded back in the Homeric period, while others were of Seleukid foundation. They were all concentrated in the lowlands, while the mountain areas had been left to the descendants of the original inhabitants. So Tarsos, Adana, Mopsuhestia were old cities with some traditions of independence, while Alexandria-ad-Issum, Epiphaneia, Aigai, Seleukeia-on-the-Kalykadnos, were later foundations.

The evidence for Antiochos VII's power in Kilikia is mainly numismatic. Coins in his name were minted mainly at the city of Tarsos, but also in Soloi, Seleukeia-on-the-Kalykadnos, and Mallos.[51] The number of coins from these last three mints was not large, and it has been suggested that the issues were symbolic more than economic; that is, the coins were issued as pledges of the cities' loyalty to the king, and to demonstrate to those who would use the coins just who the king was.[52] Symbolic or not, these issues show that Antiochos had a firm grip on the lowlands of Kilikia, an important territory with several cities and ports, productive of soldiers and wealth.

The inland area of Kilikia, the foothills of the Taurus and the mountain areas were fairly thinly populated – even now the hills are largely forested – but any ruler of the lowlands had to maintain a serious grip on the Kilikian Gates, the narrow pass behind Tarsos, and on Seleukeia-on-the-Kalykadnos, which blocked the other main route from and into Asia Minor. At least one castle of the Seleukid period has been located, embellished with a relief of an elephant, an exotic beast for such a place.[53] A large production of coinage in Tarsos suggests a substantial expenditure by the Seleukid government in the two cities, perhaps the result of the need to pay an important garrison stationed to supervise the passes.[54] The lands beyond the mountains were outside Seleukid control, as perhaps were much of the mountains themselves, which made them dangerous and always a region which required watching.

These cities were supervised by an attentive royal government. Each had an *epistates*, appointed by the king but living in the city, as its link with the court, though in no way could he be called the city's governor. Internally they were all self-governing, with the standard set of Greek civic governmental institutions – *boule*, *agoranomos*, priests, and so on. But there had been no signs of any independent action by any of these cities at any point in their history, no hint that their citizens looked to anything other than a comfortable dependence on royal protection. All were dominated by *acropoleis* which were occupied by royal troops, and all acquiesced in that condition without protest.[55] The lack of political initiative by the cities was not total, of course – Antioch had taken a major corporate part in the crisis of the year 145, and Arados (not a Greek city, of course) had powerfully and frequently asserted an autonomy, and just as often had it removed – but any such activity of this sort occurred only in times of crisis, and only in terms of the royal government and the person of the king. The cities' general acquiescence to royal authority provided the king with a substantial political weight, for it was from these cities that he recruited his army, the ultimate source of his power.

Connecting this Greco-Macedonian plantation of cities in north Syria with Palestine was the mountainous area of Phoenicia. Two parallel ranges, Lebanon and Antilebanon, separated three elongated lowland areas. Along the coast was a string of ancient Phoenician cities, from Arados in the north through Tripolis, Orthosia, Byblos, Berytos and Sidon, to Tyre; the reaction of these cities to events was always idiosyncratic. Inland, between the mountain ranges, was the Bekaa Valley, a frontier area separating Seleukid and Ptolemaic power during the third century, but which had slowly become settled and cultivated in the second.[56] In the centre of the valley was the temple town of Baalbek, called by the Greeks Heliopolis, but the political centre of the valley lay to the south of that, at Chalkis, a former Ptolemaic fortress.[57] The valley northwards of Baalbek was thinly settled, being generally less fertile than the southern part, but south of Baalbek a denser settlement had developed in the past half century, and Chalkis could be reckoned almost as a city by the 130s.

East of the Antilebanon range the land was in the rain shadow of the mountains, and was and is desert, though a road ran along the mountain foot. The Barada River breaks through the Antilebanon range from the Bekaa, flowing eastwards and then forms a large oasis, the Ghuta, within which is the city of Damascus. South of the Ghuta was a rugged area of black basalt and solidified lava, its sections called Batanea, Trachonitis, and other names, then the better-watered Hauran, the Nabataeans, and the cities of the future Decapolis, and Palestine.

These cities, Syrian, Kilikian, Phoenician, Palestinian, were under Antiochos VII's control, and were the source of his strength, the human reservoir of his army. These were the places which Antiochos had aimed to control first of all. Their acceptance of his rule had provided the political authority and military manpower with which to reduce the various dissidents, from Tryphon to Hyrkanos, to order. But that authority was very largely based on the Greek and Macedonian manpower of those cities – that is, the men descended from the Greeks and Macedonians who had settled into those cities, or men whose claim to Greekness was generally accepted. The loyalty of these men was generally automatically given to the Seleukid king, partly because of inherited factors, but perhaps mainly because they were conscious of the presence all around them of the great mass of the population, non-Greek speakers all, descendants of the Semitic population which had been present when Alexander conquered the land.

This ethnic factor was one of the major elements in the Jewish revolt in Palestine which had begun in 166, but that revolt had also persuaded the coastal cities of Palestine to cleave all the stronger to the Seleukid cause. The early relations of the Jewish rebels and the Nabataeans had been friendly, for both of them confronted the political, linguistic, cultural, and social aggressiveness of the Greeks and Macedonians.[58] This initial friendship did not last, but both groups were still defiantly non-Greek, even anti-Greek, emphasizing their own Semitic languages, for example. A third non-Greek group whose possible enmity must also be taken into account by a Seleukid king was the Phoenicians, increasingly self-conscious.

The most persistent, if underlying, manifestation of continuing Semitic identity had been the prosperity of the temples which had existed in Syria even before the Macedonian conquest. Even in Alexander's time, the temple of Atargatis at Bambyke, which Seleukos I Hellenized as Hierapolis, issued coins proclaiming the high priest of the temple as a king.[59] There were similar, if not quite so assertive, temples all through the land, Melqart at Tyre, Baal at Baalbek in the Bekaa, Dusares at Si in the Hauran, Dagon at Gaza, Hadad in Damascus, the temples at Olba and Hierapolis-Kastabala in Kilikia, and, of course, Yahweh at Jerusalem. All these and others provided foci for local loyalties, and many of them emerged as political centres in the next half century after Antiochos VII. The local rulers who emerged usually claimed the title of high priest, as did the Hasmonaeans in Judaea. Only where organized civil life already existed, as at Tyre and Gaza, did the office of high priest remain one of minor political significance. In other, less urbanized areas, it was usually the high priests who emerged as ruling princes.

Syria was thus divided into many geographical regions by its hills and mountains, rivers and deserts; it was divided socially among Greeks and non-Greeks; the Greeks were divided between numerous cities, and the non-Greeks were divided into speakers of several Semitic languages or dialects, Aramaic, Phoenician, Syriac, Nabataean, Palmyrenian, Arabic, Hebrew (if it was still a spoken language), and further divided into the worshippers at a variety of temples. And, of course, there was the perennial division between rich and poor, where the rich tended to be Greek-speaking and the poor generally spoke one of the Semitic languages – unless you were a rich Phoenician, or a rich Judaean or Nabataean, or a poor Greek in one of the cities.

This was the land which Antiochos VII succeeded in recovering for his house. What had been in disintegration in 138 had been stitched back together by the late 130s. The speed of his work does suggest that the disintegration had been little more than superficial – or perhaps reversing the idea, that it was the reunification which was superficial – there were clearly many possible sources of division in the country. In some cases, outside the urbanized areas, he had to settle for less than total control. Had he insisted on full conquest of these separated lands he would have had to fight harder and longer. In turn his forbearance might suggest that his means were limited, or of a recognition of the determination of the separated communities to remain as separate as they could.

So the new geopolitical condition of the Seleukid kingdom consisted of the urbanized areas of Syria from the Taurus Mountains to the Sinai Desert, which was fringed by the semi-independent or independent minor states along the northern and eastern borders. This was the work of Antiochos VII, to reconstruct a new political base for the kingdom he had inherited. This was also to be the stage on which Seleukid history was to be acted out over the next eighty years. It was a populous and wealthy land, and would have formed a good and sufficient kingdom for any ruler, and would have provided him with enough problems to keep any king busy throughout his reign.

But Antiochos was not just a Syrian king. He was a Seleukid king, whose brother was a captive in enemy hands. We do not have any idea of what Antiochos hoped to do with his kingship, but one thing he was compelled to do was to march east to contest control of Babylonia and Iran with the Parthians. That he did not do this for several years might indicate his unwillingness to undertake such an adventure, but it is more likely a sign of the need to sort matters out in Syria first. But in the end he had to march east.

Chapter 8

Defeat (131–129 BC)

T he king of the Parthians, whom Antiochos prepared to attack in 131, had succeeded in driving out the authority of the Seleukid king from Iran and much of Babylonia – and even, more spectacularly, had captured the king himself – and yet had not succeeded in imposing his own full authority in his place. The incomplete nature of the conquest had opened the way for local rulers to develop their authority and investigate the extent of their autonomy. There were, of course, several kingdoms already in existence which were now neighbours to, and perhaps subordinate to, the Parthians, but new kingdoms now also emerged.

These were largely in Babylonia, where the density of the population and the existence of many cities provided a firm demographic and institutional foundation for new states. When they become known in the written sources, they usually have names ending in '-ene'. This marks them out as originally sub-provinces of the Seleukid state (and perhaps of the Persian Empire earlier); in the west Kommagene and Osrhoene are examples. In Babylonia two of these states emerged in the 130s, one at the mouths of the great rivers, based at the city of Antioch-on-the-Erythraean Sea, which from its fortification, became called Charax (fortress), and eventually the kingdom was called Charakene; its earlier Seleukid name had been Mesene.[1]

The other new kingdom in the region was in the valley of the Tigris, north of Babylon, an area called Adiabene.[2] Charakene developed into a kingdom under its active and long-standing governor-become-king Hyspaosines, who took the title of king about 140 or 138 – that is, in the wake of the Parthian conquests; Adiabene is not recorded to be a separate kingdom until sometime later, but it seems probable that it was effectively independent by the 130s, if only because no supervising empire had the energy to impose itself.[3] It was a region through which Demetrios II will have marched on his way to Babylonia. One city, close to Alexander the Great's great victory at Gaugamela, had been founded as Demetrias–on-the-Tigris, either by Demetrios I or his son; the city's coins featured Tyche ('Fortune') as the city's emblem.[4]

Mithradates of Parthia died soon after this victory over Demetrios. This is possibly recorded by the Babylonian Diarist, who notes that someone – the name is missing – is said to have had a stroke. The date was August 138.[5] His successor, his son Phraates II, was initially too young to rule, and the regency was held by his mother, Ri-in-nu.[6]

She might have faced a challenge from Bagasis, Mithradates' governor in Babylonia. The Babylonian Diarist refers to him as 'the brother of the king' in 133 (so meaning Phraates), so, since Bagasis had been governor of Media for some years and was thus already adult, Mithradates had clearly chosen a much younger son as his heir (and the son of a possibly Babylonian mother). Bagasis obviously remained loyal to his brother – an object lesson to the Seleukids in the future which they ignored. His loyalty will have provided welcome support to Ri-in-nu, and a new viceroy, Pilinissu of Akkad, operated in Babylonia.[7]

Under the circumstances a degree of looseness in the Parthian government and some disorganization in the kingdom is only to be expected. Demetrios was kept a captive, and, presumably after some cogitation as to what to do with him, was assigned a residence in Hyrkania, guards, and a new wife, Rhodogune, sister of Phraates. No doubt this last was a result of news from Syria of Kleopatra Thea's acquisition of a new husband.

This is generally assumed to be a gesture of consolation by Mithradates for Demetrios' adversity – 'out of the goodness of his heart', claims Justin.[8] (It could also have been a gesture of contempt – he had been branded a drunkard in Parthian propaganda.) However, it has a good deal more significance than that. First, it may not have been Mithradates' decision, since he died less than a year after Demetrios' defeat and capture; even if it was his decision, as Justin implies, the succession of a new king to the Seleukid throne had clearly changed matters.

The obvious thing to do with a captured king was to negotiate peace with him, then release him, or perhaps supervise his implementation of the terms of peace. The death of Mithradates will have disrupted that process (assuming it was begun), and the accession of a minor further delayed matters. The news of the marriage of Kleopatra Thea and Antiochos VII also changed Demetrios' value. With Antiochos as king in Syria, where he was busy suppressing Tryphon's rising, and thus establishing his authority, he was gathering to himself the prestige of a victorious king, so Demetrios' usefulness was changing daily. In one sense his value was diminishing, for he no longer had the capacity to agree to peace terms; in another sense he had become particularly valuable as a potential disruptive force for Syria.

So the captive king was not simply a man to negotiate with, or to keep, but one to use. His marriage to the Parthian princess Rhodogune was a political act, designed to tie Demetrios to the Parthians, and Justin makes the point that it was intended that he was to be used against Antiochos at some point.[9] Demetrios' recalcitrance – there is no hint of peace negotiations, and he managed to escape twice, each time being recaptured – rather suggested that this scheme would not work; in addition, any agreement he made could be repudiated once he was freed, as being concluded under duress, for example.[10]

On the other hand, Demetrios' continued determination to return to his kingdom also suggested that if he did so his arrival would cause difficulties for Antiochos, so he was still useful as a Damoklean threat to the latter. No doubt Demetrios knew this (as would Kleopatra Thea and Antiochos as well) and that the only way to react was to cut himself free rather than accept the obligations implied if he was freed by a Parthian decision or concession.

In the meantime he had two children by Rhodogune. On the analogy of Alexander Balas, these children could well be used later as claimants to the Seleukid throne. (In his escape attempts Demetrios did not take his wife and children with him, which is not to say he would have rejected them if his escape had succeeded.) If one child was born in the first year of Demetrios' captivity, he would be old enough to be used as a claimant by the 120s. This is never explicitly stated in any source, but it is all inherent in the situation – and that Demetrios fathered these children was clearly well known.

King Phraates faced his own set of difficulties once he had achieved full control of the kingdom. The main local source, the Babylonian Diarist, does not survive for the years 136–134, but in 133 it reports fighting in Elymais.[11] This may be connected with a notice in Strabo of a Parthian raid to seize the treasure of the temple of 'Athene and Artemis' in Elymais.[12] At the same time, the Diarist records that Hyspaosines of Charakene raided a city and harbour (not named), operating as 'a friend of the Elamite enemy'. Other notices throughout the year and into 132 attest continued fighting, including a massacre of Elamites in Susa. One consequence seems to have been the replacement of Pilinissu as governor of Babylonia by 'Te'udisisu', which seems to be a Babylonian version of the Greek name Theodosios. In Media Phraates' brother Bagasis was viceroy at least until 133. The whole emphasizes the wide authority of the governors and the continuing enmity of the subordinate kingdoms.[13]

This was the situation into which Antiochos VII ventured by his expedition to the east. The enemy was divided at least in Babylonia, and he could count on the residual loyalty of a large part of the Greco-Macedonian population of the area – presumably he had received information on the situation. Once he had enforced his control of Syria it was clearly worth attempting an eastern reconquest.[14] The situation in his immediate political neighbourhood was also favourable. The Ptolemaic kingdom had dissolved into civil war during 132, a war which looked very much as though it would last for some time, and would certainly leave the kingdom weakened, whoever won in the end. (Also, Ptolemy VIII, one of the participants in the civil war, had shown no interest in returning to Syria; indeed it may have been at his orders that the region had been evacuated by the Ptolemaic forces in 145.) In Asia Minor the death of the last legitimate Attalid king (Attalos III) in 133 had brought in Roman power, but again the change had produced a war of succession between the Romans and a son of Attalos III, Andronikos, who claimed the kingship as a bastard son of that king – just as Alexander Balas had; but Roman encouragement was distinctly absent this time, where gains for themselves were in hazard. Antiochos VII, having lived in Rhodes and in Side, a city which was a neighbour of Attalos' kingdom, would fully appreciate the position.

Internationally, therefore, this was the most favourable occasion for an eastern expedition since Antiochos IV's time, and Antiochos VII seized the chance. There was no point in doing anything by halves, so in 131 Antiochos assembled the full force of the lands he ruled – 80,000 soldiers, so it was later claimed, though this seems an exaggeration.[15] This included a contingent attending from Judaea, and commanded by Hyrkanos, and no doubt there were other subordinate kingdoms – Kommagene, Arados, the Arab ruler of Osrhoene – who also supplied forces and commanded them.[16] It was presumably safer for these rulers to be taken on the expedition with Antiochos rather than to leave them at home, possibly plotting or even rebelling – and their troops could be useful, if only as cannon fodder or garrisons; the Judaean force seems to have been used in the latter capacity.

Antiochos' route was across the Euphrates at Seleukeia-Zeugma and then through Mesopotamia to the Tigris Valley, the same route used by almost all armies invading Babylonia from Syria, including Alexander the Great and Demetrios II. The march through Mesopotamia would take at least a month. It is about 400km from Zeugma to the Tigris, a march which took Alexander's army about that length of time in 331, and probably also that of Demetrios ten years before.

Like Alexander, Antiochos was met near the site of the battlefield of Arbela by a Parthian army. It was commanded by Indates, who is recorded by Josephos as 'the Parthian *strategos*', which might mean he was a governor or only an army commander. At the Lykos River (the Greater Zab), in Adiabene, this first battle was a victory for Antiochos. The fight took place about June 131. Hyrkanos is said to have requested no march the next day so his men could celebrate the Jewish Passover, but the whole army would surely be given a rest after the battle, so this story cannot be used to date the battle – even if it can be accepted as true, and not just another Josephan invention.[17] It seems highly unlikely that Antiochos would pay much attention to such a request.

This victory opened the way for Antiochos into Babylonia. Justin claims that Antiochos had to win two more battles, though it is not clear when or where these were fought, but then the whole region fell to him without further fighting.[18] Antiochos advanced with some caution, it seems, and stayed in Babylonia for the winter of 131/130.[19] This would seem to imply that his occupation of the centre of Babylonia was too late to allow him to get through the Zagros passes before they were closed for the winter. Coins in his name were minted at Seleukeia-on-the-Tigris, at Uruk in southern Babylonia, at Susa, and at Ekbatana.[20] It was presumably during this approach march that the city rose against Parthian rule and killed Enius, who appears to have been either the governor of the city or, less likely, the governor-general of Babylonia.[21] The governor/king of Charakene, Hyspaosines, submitted to Antiochos, and may well have been appointed satrap of Babylon – that is, governor-general of the whole region.[22] Other local kings joined him, according to Justin, though he is unspecific as to their locations.[23]

In the spring of 130 Antiochos took his army on an invasion of Media. During 130 and 129 his coins were minted at Susa, which means that he had received the submission of Elymais, whose last known king, Tigraios, had been removed in 133, after the latest fighting, by the Parthians.[24] The defection of the sub-kingdoms – which certainly included Charakene, Adiabene, and Elymais, probably included Atropatene and possibly Persis – was no doubt accompanied by the surrender of the cities of western Media as Antiochos' army advanced and the Parthian forces withdrew to their home country. So comprehensive was Antiochos' victory that Phraates asked for terms. Antiochos required the release of his brother, acceptance of the Seleukid recovery of Babylonia and Media, and that Phraates pay tribute for his own kingdom.[25]

These terms were precisely similar to those imposed on Hyrkanos of Judaea: the recovery of recently lost lands, and an acceptance of the enemy's subordinate political status, enforced by the payment of tribute. Phraates, driven back into his ancestral kingdom from all his father's conquests, can have expected no less, but he seems to have rejected the terms – and had he accepted, it seems unlikely that he would have continued as king for very long. And, after the recent

Parthian successes, it is likely that war would have been soon resumed. That is, Antiochos's terms were inadequate; he would have needed to fight again, and this time aim to destroy the Parthian state in its entirety.

The Seleukid army wintered in 130–129 in Media, spread among the several towns and cities of that region.[26] This was obviously necessary as a means of keeping a grip on the conquered territories, and at the same time helped to ease the logistical problems involved in feeding the soldiers. Yet it was also dangerous, since each garrison was only a fragment of the whole army – even 80,000 soldiers would be spread thin to garrison all Babylonia and Media, and there were probably many less than that. There is no reason to doubt that the people so occupied were annoyed, but it seems unlikely that the Seleukid soldiers were any more oppressive or greedy than the Parthians they had replaced. This is often taken as the main reason for the collapse of Antiochos' position in the spring of 129.[27] There were, however, better reasons.

Phraates responded to his losses and the failure of the peace negotiations with four measures. First, he recruited up his army and hired mercenaries from the Saka nomads beyond his eastern border.[28] Then he released the imprisoned Demetrios, sending him back towards Syria, presumably expecting that his arrival at the heart of Seleukid power would cause trouble for Antiochos, though he cannot have been certain of this, after Demetrios' behaviour in his imprisonment.[29] Demetrios' release had been demanded by Antiochos, so it must be presumed that Antiochos would welcome him. There is no reason to assume that the brothers were fratricidal; Kleopatra Thea, however, would have a problem. As a means of sowing trouble in Antiochos' rear this had little chance of success. It is perhaps a measure of Phraates' desperation that this tactic was tried.

More useful was a direct attack aimed at the sections of the Seleukid field army in their garrisons, while at the same time, Phraates contacted and activated his friends in the recently lost territories.[30] There were Parthian loyalists and sympathizers in the reconquered lands who were the people who had already agitated against the requisitions which the Seleukid army necessarily made. (It would be useful to know who these were. The general assumption is that the Greco-Macedonian population remained loyal to the Seleukids, but there are plenty of examples of men with Greek names serving the Parthian kings – Theodosios in Babylonia, for one. The native Median population might favour the Parthians, or they might not.) Finally because Antiochos' army was dispersed into winter quarters, the king himself had only a small force, his personal guard presumably, with him. Antiochos' own winter location was known as a result of the negotiations.[31] Phraates could bring a larger force into action than any of the individual Seleukid detachments, and when Antiochos went to the assistance of one of the detachments Phraates succeeded in ambushing him. Antiochos was killed. This was always the most effective means of victory: kill the commander (or, in the case of Demetrios, capture him) and the force he commanded would collapse. (Did Phraates contact the potentially disloyal subordinate kings, such as Hyrkanos? This was, after all, the tactic repeatedly employed by Judah Maccabee, with some success – though it is unlikely that the Parthians needed any tutoring in military tactics.) If the commander was the king, this was even better, for his kingdom would then be reduced to confusion as well as his army. Sure enough, Antiochos' death was followed by a widespread pro-Parthian rising, particularly in Media, but also in Babylonia. The Seleukid army was supposedly annihilated.[32]

A good deal of detail which is supplied by our sources about this campaign was clearly conjured up later to explain the defeat, with historians selecting assumptions based on other such defeats, or on their imaginations. The size of the original Seleukid army is unlikely to have been as much as 80,000 soldiers, or anywhere near it, and still less would there have been 300,000 camp-followers carried along with it. However, if these numbers are recognized to be inflated, it is nevertheless a sign that Antiochos had collected as large an army from Syria as he could for the campaign. It was so large, though, that other details, such as the idea that the conduct of the army alienated the population by its demands and oppressions, is rendered a little more credible.[33] But Babylonia, in particular, and even the Median cities, were countries which were rich enough to cope with an army for one or two winters without too much strain, though their recent histories might have reduced their resources somewhat. In Babylonia also, even the presence of the new and numerous garrison did not prevent Arab raids.[34] The real Seleukid defeat came when the Parthian king identified Antiochos as the key to the situation and appreciated his physical isolation. When Demetrios II had been captured in 138 the Seleukid campaign had also collapsed, so Phraates was only doing in 129 what his father had done nine years before. And the new Seleukid ruler fell into the same trap.

The immediate collapse of the Seleukid army in both 138 and 129 is thus a vivid indication of the absolute and disastrous centrality of the king to the Seleukid system of government and military command. The Parthians had appreciated this when they kept Demetrios II prisoner, just as they did when, having released him in order to make trouble for his brother, they made strenuous efforts to retake him when Antiochos VII was killed.[35]

The Seleukid army was severely damaged by the defeat, and Diodoros has a purple passage purporting to describe the universal grief in Syria – or rather Antioch – when the news of the defeat arrived. He implies that every man in the army died, but this is not the case.[36] Certainly Phraates captured a large number of men, and he took them farther east to use them against his enemies there. Not surprisingly they joined the invaders, and Phraates died in the subsequent defeat.[37] What became of the Greek soldiers after that is not stated, but some at least will have managed to return home, either in small units bristling with weapons, or singly.

Others had done so already. The contingent of the original army commanded by Hyrkanos from Judaea certainly escaped from Babylonia on hearing of Antiochos' death, and no casualties are reported, though presumably some had been incurred.[38] (Hyrkanos is said to have begun to employ mercenaries, which may have been the force he took east.) If Hyrkanos' contingent was in Babylonia it will not have been affected at once by the defeat in Media, and Hyrkanos seems to have set out for home rapidly, in effect deserting his companions. The Seleukid general, Athenaios, is said to have tried to take refuge in the countryside only to be killed when he was recognized, or he may have starved to death.[39] And if the Judaean contingent could get away, apparently unscathed, others could, particularly those who had been stationed in Babylonia and so had less distance to march to safety. If Athenaios was only killed when he was recognized, other soldiers, not tainted by his reputation or his rank, could continue their flight to reach safety more anonymously, and perhaps could get help locally. The grief of Antioch at the loss of men, described by Diodoros, may well have been genuine, but it has clearly grown in the telling.

Nevertheless, however the claimed grief is toned down, and the absolute destruction is argued away, the casualty list must have been huge. The numbers are not even to be guessed at, since we do not know the size of the army in the first place, but the defeat, the distribution of the forces, and the distance from Syria of many of the troops must imply that at least half of the men did not return home. Grief was certainly and justifiably widespread. Antiochos had made a major effort to collect as large an army as Syria could produce, so that the destruction was all the more serious. This was a matter, also, of the serious reduction of Syrian power. Antiochos had fashioned a new Seleukid kingdom, based wholly in Syria, which had been capable of sending an army as far as Parthia, but the losses meant that this would no longer be possible. This was Antiochos' final achievement, to confine the Seleukid state to Syria.

Captured along with the soldiers was Antiochos' son Seleukos, who cannot have been more than 7 or 8 years old at the time.[40] Justin also claims that a daughter of Demetrios II was captured, and that she was taken into Phraates' harem.[41] This last may or may not be true, but if so, it is probably a similar move to that of providing Demetrios with a Parthian princess to beguile his captivity – if the girl gave birth to a son, he could be used to, at the least, disrupt the Seleukid succession in the same way as Alexander Balas, and even possibly seize the throne. This is certainly how Phraates used his new male captive, for Seleukos was maintained at Phraates' court, so being recognized as Seleukid king, or at least as a pretender to it, in succession to his father, while the released Demetrios II was chased in order to recapture him. Had he been retaken, Seleukos would have seemed the more useful, and no doubt Demetrios would have died. But Demetrios proved to be too fast this time, and got away.[42]

The obvious danger to Syria after the debacle in the east was that Phraates, with Seleukos in his train, would move westwards, first to recover his lost lands, and then to invade the remaining Seleukid territories, perhaps putting Seleukos forward as his candidate for king in Syria. He may have succeeded in occupying Media, which is where the bulk of Antiochos' army presumably was when it surrendered or scattered or fled, but matters were different in Babylonia.

Before Phraates could reach Babylon he had to turn back to cope with trouble in his eastern territories, caused by Saka nomads. He had failed to pay the wages of a group of Saka mercenaries hired for the emergency of Antiochos' attack but who had not been actually used in the fighting, and they were taking out their resentment at the absence of their pay by ravaging the land.[43] This fighting lasted for ten years or more, and drew in Sakas from outside the Parthian kingdom. It eventually resulted in the settlement of a Saka group in the old province of Drangiana, which thus became Sakastene (and now Seistan).[44] Phraates and his army were clearly required in the east. In Babylonia Phraates appointed a new satrap, Himeros (or Euhemeros, probably another Greek) and presumably gave him some troops.[45] 'Arsakes', that is, Phraates, was recorded as king in Babylonia during 128–127, but for how long is not clear; by 127–126 Hyspaosines of Charax had asserted control at least as far as Babylon. In what capacity he acted is not clear; he could have been acting as king and so independent; he could, if he had been appointed satrap by Antiochos, as has been suggested, have been acting as a Seleukid official. The chaos in Syria prevented any worthwhile contact, but if such forces as that of Hyrkanos had stayed in Babylonia, the outcome might have been different. Hyspaosines held out for some time, but 'Arsakes' was counted as king the year after he took Babylon, that is, 126–125.[46]

Phraates was killed in battle in the east fighting against the unpaid Sakas and their allies, when his Greek captured soldiers changed sides to join the Sakas in the midst of the fighting.[47] He was succeeded by an uncle, Artabanus I, and then in 124–123 by Artabanus' son, Mithradates II. All during this period of upheaval, Himeros, having driven out Hyspaosines, ruled in Babylon and Seleukeia, gaining an evil reputation among the Greeks in the process.[48] But these areas had rebelled against the Parthians, and had then supported Hyspaosines, so a period of tough government is only to be expected, especially since Hyspaosines continued as king in Charakene to the south – that is, the Parthians controlled only central Babylonia after 125. The difficulty Himeros had in governing, combined with the relative ease of Hyspaosines' brief conquest, suggests that there was a clear opportunity for a Seleukid recovery in Babylonia, especially since the main Parthian forces were inextricably involved in the east. But the situation in Syria, as we will see in the next chapter, was not conducive to a distant expedition.

Mithradates II, who acceded to the Parthian kingship in 124 or 123, after Artabanus' death, had therefore much to do, including re-imposing Parthian suzerainty on the several small kingdoms of the Babylonian region, and on those in Iran, and on the city of Seleukeia, which had rebelled against the rule of its Parthian satrap.[49] What with the fighting on the eastern frontier and the need to re-impose Parthian authority within the empire, it is evident that there was no danger of a Parthian attack on Syria for at least ten years or more after Antiochos' defeat.

The campaign of Antiochos VII in the east emphasizes a number of problems facing the Seleukid kingdom. The Parthians proved to be a much more resilient and cunning foe than perhaps had been expected. And yet the Seleukid kingdom, even though controlling only Syria, had been able to produce an army powerful enough to conquer Babylonia and most of Iran, assisted by the institutional weakness of the Parthian state and its internal looseness. But the war was lost because the Parthian king had worked at and exploited the corresponding weakness of the Seleukid state, its absolute dependence on the person of the king. So whereas Parthia tended to fall apart into its constituent parts when struck a heavy blow, the Seleukid kingdom collapsed when its king was taken out, captured or killed. As a result both were to be preoccupied with internal recovery for a decade, but for the Seleukids there was now the greater problem of a superfluity of possible kings. This, as had already been seen more than once in the past, was a recipe for another civil war.

Chapter 9

Dynastic Conflict (129–121 BC)

T here was a formidable range of potential Seleukid kings – and a queen – when Demetrios II returned to Syria. There was Demetrios himself, who naturally reclaimed the kingship of which he had been deprived for a decade. There was his wife, Kleopatra Thea, who had acted as a monarch in disposing of the kingship to Demetrios' brother, and who had ruled in Syria twice, for two years each time, while her successive husbands were campaigning in the east. There were the children of Demetrios II and Kleopatra Thea – Seleukos and Antiochos – and those of Antiochos VII and Kleopatra Thea – two Antiochoi and a Seleukos. Of these last, Seleukos was in Parthian captivity; also probably held by the Parthians was Laodike, the daughter of Demetrios and Kleopatra, now said to be married to Phraates II. The daughters of Antiochos and Kleopatra, also both called Laodike, were also alive. Then there were at least two children born to Rhodogune in her marriage with Demetrios II, whose names are not known, and in future any children born to Phraates and Laodike. In addition there proved to be another element, not known to anyone as yet.

Demetrios II reached Antioch during the Seleukid year 183, which is 130–129 BC. Since it was in the spring of that year that he had been released, he presumably arrived in Syria in the late spring of 129. (He had been released before Antiochos was killed, which happened while his army was still in winter quarters, which were probably intended to break up about March.) We do not have the precise timings and dates provided earlier by the Babylonian Diarist, whose tablets are missing at this point, but the coins issued by several cities are dated and can provide clues as to the sequence of events. Once again the historians have dealt with Syrian and Babylonian events separately, whereas the coins show a timing overlap.

Antiochos VII was killed in the spring of 129, according to the accounts in Justin and Diodoros.[1] By then Demetrios had been set free, and escaped from his Parthian handlers about the same time. It took some time for the news of Antiochos' death to spread, and to be verified, and the mint at Seleukeia-on-the-Tigris coined for him into the next Seleukid year, 184.[2] By that time Sidon, Tyre and Ptolemais-Ake were already coining for Demetrios II, and indeed Tyre and Damascus had done so in 183, having begun by coining in Antiochos' name earlier in that year.[3] So Demetrios reached Syria in time for mints to design and produce new coins in his name before the end of 183 SE, while Seleukeia-on-the-Tigris had still produced coins for Antiochos into 184. It would therefore seem that Demetrios had been released by Phraates well before his brother's death, as is only to be expected, and had made his best speed back to Syria.

It is surprising, given that conclusion, that no coins in Demetrios' name were produced by the mints of the great north Syrian cities, in particular Antioch. This was, of course, the government centre, where Kleopatra Thea was in control. The conclusion, based on the absence of these coins, must be that Demetrios had some difficulty in recovering his position as king. To do this he had to displace Kleopatra Thea from the head of that government, probably at first being uncertain of the fate of Antiochos.

It is very likely that by this time Kleopatra had developed a loyal following at the court, while Demetrios is unlikely to have been able to call on many adherents after a decade's absence. He had presumably returned with those who had accompanied him in his exile, such as Kallimandros, who had helped him in at least one escape attempt, but he will have been quite out of touch with the conditions and personnel of the government in Syria.[4] The Parthian plot to cause disruption thus succeeded. Antiochos VII was dead, but Demetrios was not accepted everywhere, and memories in Syria had not improved his reputation. He surely struggled to be an effective ruler.

There has been a theory, now abandoned by its original proponents, that Kleopatra Thea put forward her eldest son (by Demetrios) as king in Antioch in 128. It is based on a small group of coins produced at Antioch, which shows Antiochos VIII as a child. The theory therefore was that he had been proclaimed king on the news of Antiochos VII's death, but that Demetrios then turned up. This idea is now discredited, since Demetrios arrived in Syria before the news of Antiochos' death. But even a theory shown to be wrong is useful, for it highlights the confusion there must have been in Antioch in the later months of 129 and early 128. Furthermore, it remains a fact that no dated coins of Demetrios II were issued from the Antioch mint in 128 (nor indeed at any time during his second reign), and the child–coins must still be accounted for.[5]

During Antiochos VII's campaign in the east Kleopatra Thea had acted in his name in Syria, and she had done the same earlier during Demetrios' own eastern campaign. In that first instance she had been under great pressure from Tryphon, and her invitation to Antiochos to take over in 139 shows her political savvy. The sudden return of Demetrios was perhaps less than welcome since he would now take up the governmental reins from her. She was a Ptolemy originally and it may have been family memories of murder – but these were hardly absent from the Seleukid family either – which persuaded her to send her younger son, another Antiochos (IX), by Antiochos VII away. He was probably only about 7 years old, and was sent to Kyzikos under the care of one of her eunuchs, Krateros, and so became known as Antiochos Kyzikenos.[6] She retained her sons by Demetrios, Seleukos and Antiochos, her eldest son by Antiochos VII, and her daughters, with her in Antioch.

The absence of coins of Demetrios II from the Antioch mint, the despatch of the child Antiochos to Kyzikos, and the presence of Kleopatra Thea in Antioch suggests what was certainly clear later, that there was a personal distaste between Demetrios and Kleopatra. The uncertainty over the fate of Antiochos VII lasted for some time – was he dead, captured, on the run? – but it seems that Kleopatra in Antioch was excluding Demetrios from the city during that time of uncertainty. Authority was thus obviously divided.

Phraates had changed his mind about freeing Demetrios after Antiochos was killed. He may have felt that by treating him well, and by making him his brother-in-law, he had gained influence over Demetrios. Rhodogune and their children were certainly still in his hands, and might be a potential point of pressure. Now he prepared to return the body of Antiochos for burial in the dynastic burial ground either at Antioch or Seleukeia-in-Pieria, a gesture which was clearly intended to sow further disruption.[7] Justin comments that Phraates 'had designs on the throne of Syria', to which as the husband of a Seleukid princess, and uncle of the children of Rhodogune, he could lay a more or less plausible claim.[8] These various actions and marriages of Rhodogune and of Phraates himself to Laodike were clearly politically calculated. This was another factor Demetrios had to take into account. As it happened Phraates had enough to do for the present, and was unable to launch his expected attack westwards, then his campaign and death in the east prevented him from pursuing any western plans. The claim, however, could be resurrected by his successors at need.[9]

The condition of Syria when Demetrios returned was not perhaps as bad as when he had left it twelve years before, thanks to his brother's work, for there was at least no civil war this time – though the simmering dispute between him and Kleopatra was dangerous. But the destruction of Antiochos' army in the east (and of Demetrios' own army before that), even if not anywhere near as total as is implied, can only have weakened the kingdom substantially. But then Demetrios also stepped into the ongoing crisis in the Ptolemaic kingdom and as a result it spilled over to engulf him.

In 132–131 Kleopatra II had carried out a coup at Alexandria to oust her brother Ptolemy VIII from control of the kingdom. Ptolemy, a man all too familiar with the ups and downs of politics, withdrew to Cyprus, and then returned to recover his throne by conquering Egypt, and for a time he did so by ignoring Alexandria. By 129 he had recovered most of the country, though Kleopatra II still held out in Alexandria, a position she could probably hold on to for some time. However, Ptolemy had acquired a second wife, Kleopatra III, his niece, and he had killed his and Kleopatra II's son, presumably so she could not be able to rule through him; she responded by ruling alone, in her own name, even starting a new dating era to emphasize this. Kleopatra II was the mother of Ptolemy's new wife by her marriage to Ptolemy VI, and she was also the mother of Kleopatra Thea.[10]

Kleopatra II finally escaped from Alexandria, but went to Antioch, bringing with her the Ptolemaic treasury. The coincidence of her and Demetrios' arrival was perhaps not accidental. She appealed to him, her son-in-law, to restore her to her Egyptian throne, an expedition which was no doubt to be funded by the treasure she had brought. She also, according to Justin, promised him the Egyptian throne.[11]

The appeal to Demetrios soon after his return, but not to Kleopatra Thea while she was in charge in Syria, provokes speculation. Was Kleopatra Thea estranged from her mother? This would not be surprising, since they had not seen each other for almost twenty years. Or was it that Kleopatra Thea did not have the authority to indulge in any military activity? She certainly demonstrated later a ruthless and unscrupulous nature, so Antiochos VII might have bound her around with strictly limited powers. (In this she was equalled by her mother's murderousness and ruthlessness; perhaps they were too alike in temperament to be amiable colleagues, or to trust each other.) Demetrios, on the other hand, needed a foreign policy success to re-establish his authority in Syria, which a victorious war against the old Ptolemaic enemy might well provide. He also gained control of Kleopatra II's treasure. This would usefully replenish that of the Seleukids, which was no doubt much depleted by the war against Parthia. An Egyptian expedition also put him in command of an army, and so separated him from the court, which was now full of Antiochos' and Kleopatra's men.

Demetrios accepted the charge from his mother-in-law. But it is necessary to consider why he did so in some detail. As the recently restored king of a much weakened kingdom, his expedition to conquer Egypt would hardly be easy – and his military reputation was hardly of the best. But it may well be that he saw an unusual opportunity. The clue here is in Justin's report that Kleopatra II offered to make Demetrios king in Egypt.

Demetrios had had experience of ruling, of both victory and defeat, and of Parthia, and in captivity he had the time to reflect on all this. Twice he had attempted to escape from his imprisonment, only to be recaptured each time. He had not, therefore, as the Parthians had hoped, no doubt, when they gave him a wife, simply waited supinely for his release, which could only be as a potential Parthian puppet. These escapes, and his successful evasion of the Parthian pursuit when he was finally set free, are highly significant. They fit with his two great adventures: his abandonment of the war against Tryphon to go and fight the Parthians, and his abandonment of Syria and its restrictive politics to go to conquer Egypt; evidently he had a dislike of being constrained, of being subject to restrictions. This probably originated with his teenage experience of being controlled by the Cretan mercenary general, Lasthenes.

In the years of his imprisonment the overall situation of the Greek states of the eastern Mediterranean had altered seriously for the worse. The Seleukid kingdom had lost its eastern territories, so that the boundary of the Greek world had receded from eastern Iran to the upper Tigris Valley – and the Greek kingdoms in Baktria were also falling before the assault of the nomads. The Attalid kingdom had been replaced by a Roman province, which had taken over the richest areas and left the rest as more or less autonomous mini-states in central Asia Minor; the Romans had had to fight a serious war to gain control, and it must have been clear to all those who were in touch with Roman affairs that Rome's purpose was to mulct the wealth of the region for its own purposes. Roman foreign policy – if such a concept could be said to have existed – had shifted in the past generation from destroying any perceived challenge – such as Macedon or Carthage – to exploiting the regions within its reach for its own benefit.

The boundary of the autonomous Greek world had thus receded in the west as it had in the east, from the eastern Aegean to the Taurus Mountains, symbolized by the organization of a new Roman road, the Via Aquillia, which ran from the Hellespont to Side, close to the western boundary of the Seleukid lands, and was completed in 129.[12] This might have seemed a most unpleasantly threatening development from the Syrian point of view. And now the Ptolemaic kingdom had collapsed into a dynastic civil war; this had included native Egyptian rebellions and much confusion in the countryside. Fighting there was still going on when Demetrios was restored to Syria.[13] The Seleukid manpower losses in the east were yet another part of the Greek catastrophe, but the fact remained that the Seleukid heartland of Syria/Kilikia was now the only substantial and stable Greek state between Roman Asia and Parthian Media when Demetrios returned to Antioch.

Demetrios, therefore, returned to a reunited kingdom, controlling all from Kilikia to Sinai. It was weakened by the apparent antagonism of Kleopatra Thea and by the temporary paralysis this produced, and by the losses in the east, to be sure; there were also the same semi-independent lands and border states as before, but it was a state which was by no means powerless. Demetrios was able to take an expedition against Egypt in response to Kleopatra II's appeal, so there was still a considerable military force available for the king. The Egyptian treasure would fund the recruitment of mercenaries. A considerable capability was still there. It is, however, not reasonable to see this expedition as a romantic, or quixotic, or family-loyalty, gesture. Kleopatra II's offer to make Demetrios king in Egypt means that it was Demetrios' purpose in this extraordinarily timed expedition to bring the two surviving Hellenistic kingdoms into a closer relationship, possibly to unite them under himself.

This was not the first time such a project had been considered. It is possible that Antiochos IV in 170–168 might have intended something of the sort, perhaps by establishing Seleukid suzerainty over the Ptolemaic kings. Ptolemy VI had briefly been made king in Syria in 145, but he withdrew from the position after a short time, no doubt having appreciated the difficulties – the Parthian invasion of Iran had already begun. But in 129–128 Demetrios could see that the union of Egypt and the Seleukid state, which was now restricted to Syria, would produce a much less cumbersome state than Ptolemy VI had faced. And it was the only way the Hellenistic world could survive. Between Rome and the Parthians the great Hellenistic monarchies were the last truly independent powers of any appreciable size. Their union would be clearly advantageous, and would form a single power capable of facing both Rome and Parthia.

Having reached the conclusion that he should respond to his mother-in-law's appeal, Demetrios had several problems. He could easily drum up an army, as he showed by starting on the expedition almost at once, but the precise mechanism by which he would become king in Egypt was hardly obvious. Kleopatra II's personal history, however, suggests what would have been intended. She had children by her two husbands: by Ptolemy VI she had Kleopatra Thea and Kleopatra III (her two sons were dead); by Ptolemy VIII she had Ptolemy Memphites through whom she had probably been hoping to rule, but the boy had been killed by his father. Thus Demetrios was her son-in-law and the husband of the eldest and therefore most eligible Ptolemaic princess, as well as being the Seleukid king. Marriage to a Ptolemaic princess had long been recognized as a prime factor in establishing a claim to the Egyptian throne, which was why most Ptolemaic princesses were married in the family – Ptolemy VIII was married simultaneously to Kleopatra II, his sister, and to Kleopatra III, his niece, which prevented them from being married to anyone else.

The elimination of Ptolemy VIII Physkon would cause few people any grief, and once that was achieved his wife, Kleopatra III, would be a widow. A marriage of Demetrios II and Kleopatra III would certainly put Demetrios in power in Alexandria as well as at Antioch, and possibly Kleopatra II would then rule in Egypt as his viceroy. Equally possibly Demetrios might seize power in Alexandria himself. The advantages of a union between the two kingdoms could well become obvious to all, at a time when the twin menaces of the Roman Republic and the Parthian kingdom had become ever clearer. In personal terms, however, rather too many people were seeking the same power; it was obviously liable to turn messy.

(The better option for Demetrios, if he was determined to go to war and not settle affairs in Syria first, would have been to return east with his forces, and recover control at least of Babylonia. This could probably have been done, as was suggested in the previous chapter, at any time between 128 and 123, while the Parthian kingdom was under attack from the east and the Babylonian area was being fought over. But the treasure was Kleopatra II's, and so her aims were paramount. Had Demetrios been as ruthless as all the royals around him, he might simply have seized the treasure, sent Kleopatra II back to Egypt, and marched east. But it seems he was not so ruthless, and the last chance of holding Babylonia was lost.)

The success of the Egyptian scheme, barely thought out as it was, was dependent on speed of execution, for there were many vested interests and ambitions ranged against it, not least the fact that Ptolemy VIII was in control of much of the Egyptian countryside and he had to be Demetrios' first and main target. Demetrios and his army marched as far as Pelusion, at the eastern corner of the Nile delta, but by then Antioch had taken advantage of his absence and of his forces' absence, to revolt. Justin claims that the leader was a man called Tryphon, which may be a mistake for the earlier revolt leader, or it may be a pseudonym, or another Tryphon was the leader.[14] In Josephos' account the rebels sent to Ptolemy for him to send them a Seleukid to be their king.[15] Perhaps they felt that one of the several possible claimants among the children of Kleopatra Thea would be produced – but this seems an unlikely request for the Antiochenes to make, and may well be a misunderstanding by Josephos, or later anti-Seleukid black propaganda.

Given that Kleopatra Thea was in the city the revolt would most likely be her doing, and it is at this point that the curious coins of the child Antiochos VIII might fit. If he did actually receive a request, Ptolemy VIII reacted remarkably quickly, though the news that Kleopatra II had gone to Antioch will no doubt have warned him that she was seeking Seleukid help. He conjured up a pretender to the Seleukid kingship, who took the name Alexander. The speed with which this lad was produced suggests that Ptolemy had selected and trained him already, and held him in reserve. He is said to have been the son of an Egyptian merchant, Protarchos, though this is quite possibly more black propaganda.[16] The name he took was, of course, deliberately reminiscent of Alexander Balas, and his coins show that he claimed to be Balas' son; in other stories he was called Antiochos VII's adopted son, or the son of an unnamed Seleukid family member.[17] This variety of claims exposes the pretence – though his own coin-claims are the most important. And if it was rumoured, or was known, in Antioch that a son of Balas or a son of Antiochos had been given refuge in Egypt, this might explain the curious request for a true Seleukid from Ptolemy. But most likely all the stories were inventions.

Alexander's claim was generally regarded as false, even by some of his supporters, and he was awarded the popular nickname 'Zabeinas', 'the bought one' from Aramaic, as a sign that he was seen as having been bought by Demetrios' enemies. He was nevertheless able to gather support from many of those who disliked or distrusted Demetrios. He arrived with enough forces loaned by Ptolemy Physkon to be able to take over at Antioch, and this was sufficient to allow him to call himself king (reinforced by his spectacular display of grief on receiving the corpse of Antiochos VII (his adoptive father on this occasion), sent home by Phraates, who thus continued to further the disruption he always aimed for in Seleukid Syria.[18]) Alexander was then able to spread his power over other areas in Syria and Kilikia.

Events at Antioch, however, can be sorted out more precisely from the account in Justin. The problem began in the city, whose citizens were roused to anti-Demetrios action by 'Tryphon', whose name, adopted or not, might well remind them of their earlier opposition to this king. The rising he stimulated spread to Apamaea (also associated with Tryphon) 'and all the other cities'.[19] This last claim is clearly wrong, since several of these 'other cities' continued to accept Demetrios, as is shown by their continued coining for him until his death. Justin is thus clear that the rebellion in Syria happened before Alexander Zabeinas appeared.

So it was a separate action by Ptolemy to sponsor Alexander. He had supposedly been asked by, as Josephos puts it, 'the Syrians and the soldiers', though this is probably only what Ptolemy claimed.[20] But here two groups who were operating against Demetrios are identified – though which Syrians and just which soldiers they were is not obvious. However, despite the deliberate confusion being caused, it is clear that there were certainly substantial parties in Syria who opposed Demetrios, either as king or as the expeditionary leader against Egypt.

Then there was Kleopatra Thea, who had been left, for the third time in her life, as head of the Seleukid government while her husband went off with the army on an expedition. It was surely obvious to her that Demetrios was liable to fail, for quite apart from the resistance to be expected from Ptolemy VIII, his unpopularity in Syria was evident from the start, and clearly left his regime, such as it was, vulnerable.

She must have known the truth about Alexander's pretensions. At the same time she had spent years of her life fighting the original Tryphon, and she would hardly accept this new one without betraying her earlier actions. Of the two groups of anti-Demetrian activists, therefore, Alexander was perhaps marginally less unacceptable to her. When he arrived, she had to make a decision. She could accept him. She was the widow of Alexander Balas, one of the men the new pretender claimed as his father; she was the widow of Antiochos VII, another of his claimed fathers (though anyone who could believe that a grown man was the son of a king who had just died at the age of less than thirty would be discouragingly gullible). If anyone knew the truth about the new Alexander it was presumably Kleopatra Thea, but she must have felt deeply insulted by his pretensions. She could decry him, but this would mean she had to throw her support to Demetrios or to the new Tryphon, and it seems she could do neither.

We do not know what her decision was at the time, but she sent another son (the later Antiochos VIII) for refuge to Athens, ostensibly for his education, but actually to protect him from his stepfather, and from Alexander.[21] On the other hand, the other children were probably with her, including the eldest son, Seleukos, who was about 16 years old by now.

While all this was going on in north Syria, Demetrios and his army reached the Egyptian frontier fortress of Pelusion on their march. It was there that the news of the rising in Antioch reached him, followed by news of the landing of Alexander, and the reactions of Kleopatra Thea. At Pelusion the army found that the fortress was strongly held – Ptolemy VIII must have reinforced it as soon as rumours of Demetrios' approach arrived – and that the troops had to camp in the desert. They did not stay long, though it was probably more than a few days. The political collapse in their rear, the prospect of a long and likely fruitless siege before them, a likely shortage of food and water in the desert, and an unpopular commander, broke the troops' nerve. They rebelled, or rather mutinied, and compelled Demetrios to return to Syria.[22]

The result of all these manoeuvres and confusions, not surprisingly, was a new dynastic civil war in Syria, in which each city and territory had once again to decide for itself which claimant to support. Some places, of course, would find the decision made for them, where a garrison existed; such seems to have been the case at Ptolemais–Ake, where Kleopatra Thea took refuge, and where she was clearly in control, as later events show. Antioch had welcomed Alexander, and there his coins were produced as early as 128; Apamaea also accepted him.[23] It seems, therefore, that the rising in Antioch was subsumed within the acceptance of Alexander; Tryphon disappears.

No doubt the presence of Alexander's garrisons in those cities then precluded further discussion. Demetrios held Phoenicia, where his coins were minted at Tyre and Sidon, Ptolemais–Ake, and Damascus.[24] If Kleopatra Thea was already in Ptolemais–Ake by 128–127 or 127–126 she was holding the city for Demetrios, for it was his coins which were being minted there. But we only know she was in the city later (and if coins were to be produced only Demetrios' name would be possible). Demetrios seems also to have held Seleukeia-in-Pieria, where his coins were minted in 127–126.[25] Some places changed hands, either by conquest or by a coup, though since the evidence is generally only numismatic, only the change at Berytos, at Damascus, and Ashkelon is known.[26] In one case, at the city of Laodikeia-ad-Mare, a coup was mounted against Alexander by three men whose Macedonian names imply that they were citizens, and probably important men. Alexander replied by attacking the city, which then reverted to his control quickly enough.[27]

Alexander does not seem to have been without ability. He had arrived with some Ptolemaic forces, but Ptolemy VIII could hardly have spared many troops when he had to control the upheavals in Egypt, defend Pelusion, and besiege Alexandria. Possibly he had loaned some Ptolemaic commanders to Alexander, and some mercenaries, and he was then expected to recruit Syrians. (Ptolemy VIII, of course, did not really care how Alexander fared, so long as he lasted long enough to distract Demetrios from his invasion of Egypt.) Alexander certainly raised a worthwhile army, for he is credited with various victories, at Antioch, at Laodikeia, and later at Damascus.

In other words, the situation was confused, with no clear royal authority. Demetrios was discredited, Alexander a joke, Kleopatra Thea diminished. The simultaneous weakening of Seleukid power by the casualties of the Parthian defeat and the subsequent rebellions and usurpations against Demetrios II now alerted those who wished to escape Seleukid authority or rule altogether, and several made shifts into independence at this time. It is, however, noticeable that all of them were distinctly cautious in what they actually did. Hyrkanos of Judaea was inevitably one of these. His agreement with Antiochos VII having expired with the latter's death, he now certainly acted as an independent ruler, by contrast with his obedience in the Parthian expedition. He ceased to mint coins in the name of the Seleukid king, and made it clear very quickly that he repudiated Seleukid authority.

Josephos reports that, before the intrusion of Kleopatra II into his affairs, Demetrios was intending to campaign against Hyrkanos; no doubt the king aimed to re-impose the conditions of the treaty made with his brother.[28] Once Demetrios was distracted, however, Hyrkanos was able to go on campaign himself. But when he did so, he used his army, not to recover the lost lands to the west, such as Gazara and Pegai, but in a campaign to the east of the Jordan, and he was careful not to be too provocative. He did not mint coins in his own name, and his military operations were in quite carefully selected areas, where opposition was minimal. Josephos claims that he 'marched against the cities of Syria', but in fact he did no such thing.[29] He first crossed the Jordan to lay siege to the town of Medaba. This town seems to have been independent, having been abandoned by any Seleukid authority, and, though it was fairly close to Philadelphia, the 'tyrant' Zenon Kotylas made no attempt to intervene in this war. It took Hyrkanos' army six months to take Medaba, and Hyrkanos then went on to capture Samoga, a small place nearby.[30] Hyrkanos was beginning the process of constructing a Judaean mini-empire, and was choosing the very softest targets for his attacks. The performance of his army suggests that only such targets were within his grasp.

This action was not directed against any Seleukid area, nor against Zenon's principality of Philadelphia, though Medaba lay just south of the latter. The six months' campaign will have taken the whole campaigning season of 128 (while Demetrios was marching to Pelusion and Alexander was arriving in Antioch, and Phraates was fighting and dying against the Sakas) but having taken so long to capture a small town, it was clear that the Judaean army was hardly a serious threat to any other military power. On the other hand, it was clearly a well calculated move, and Hyrkanos continued to profit from the confusion in the Seleukid realm. He was able to attack the Samaritans around Mount Gerizim, though his action was no more than an armed raid to sack their temple. He could have justified this as part of his duties as high priest in suppressing a schismatic sect, if any of the competing Seleukids had questioned his action, though such an explanation would probably have made little or no sense to anyone but a Jew. There is no sign that any territory was retained; it was a move concerned above all with internal Jewish politics.[31]

Hyrkanos next conducted a campaign to the south of Judaea, into Idumaea, in which he captured the towns of Marisa and Adora and compelled the Idumaeans to succumb to forced conversion to Judaism – or presumably, leave their homeland.[32] This produced another extension of Judaean lands. This expedition is treated much more definitively by Josephos, contrasting with the cursory way he had discussed both the Medaba and the Mount Gerizim expeditions. All of these expeditions were very noticeably directed away from any Seleukid territory. The raid on Medaba and the Idumaean expeditions were intended, it seems, to establish wider defences for the Judaean homeland and so to deter the sort of raids the Idumaeans had mounted into the settled Judaean lands in the past. Control of Idumaea would make any attack from the south, such as those which had resulted in the Seleukid conquest of Judaea in the 160s, much more difficult. In addition Hyrkanos enforced the 'conversion' of the Idumaeans, a process which will have included a good deal of killing, much brutality, and will have driven many people into exile; it did, however, leave a population loyal to Judaea rather than to its enemies.

Hyrkanos' actions were thus very cautious, even ambiguous. He was acting in a way which could be seen as that of an independent monarch at home but, just in case Seleukid suzerainty was re-imposed, he could argue that he was extending Seleukid territory into lands which were outside the kingdom. These actions kept him and his army fully occupied and exercised his forces, and they gave him a perfect excuse for not complying with any summons by any of the Seleukid contenders for help in the civil war. It was a very well calculated, ambiguous policy, perfectly attuned to the situation.

Just as Hyrkanos could feel free to take advantage of Seleukid preoccupations with the kingship to attack his weaker neighbours, so that preoccupation left other bordering and independent states undisturbed, though neither Kommagene nor Osrhoene, the Nabataeans nor Philadelphia were even as minimally aggressive as Judaea. The Nabataeans, however, may well have been expanding into areas east of the Jordan, and at some point Philadelphia took control of its northern neighbour, Gerasa. The timing of any of these moves is unknown, but none of them attracted Seleukid attention for another three or four decades.

Other independently-minded groups in Syria were equally cautious and limited in their actions, and were just as unwilling to tackle any of the Seleukid powers head-on. The island-city of Arados now finally succeeded in shaking loose the Seleukid shackles, but did so without any Seleukid interference, either for or against, in part by being as carefully limited in its actions as Hyrkanos, but just as brutal. For Arados, a small, heavily populated, offshore island, being independent required having political control over the nearby coastal lands, its *peraia*, as a source of food supplies, and in order to eliminate mainland competitors.

In 128 two of the settlements there, Marathos and Simyra, were destroyed as political entities, and their lands were parcelled out among Aradian citizens.[33] This sort of thing had been tried by Arados before, though not so drastically or so brutally; in 128, for the first time, the city succeeded in achieving its goals, but this time it limited its aims to acquiring direct control of only a part of the *peraia*. It did not attempt to secure control of the northern extension, around the town of Gabala. This success was only due to the continuing weakness of the Seleukid state, of course; earlier attempts by Arados had also coincided with the times of such weakness. After 128, only time would tell if this latest attempt would be successful. For Arados the longer the Seleukid conflict went on the more likely it was that their mainland conquest would seem to be permanent. The danger would come, if and when the conflict over the kingship was resolved.

The rest of the cities of Syria, in contrast to the persistence shown by Arados, had always been notable for their lack of any obvious desire to claim independence, other than that permitted or recognized by the Seleukid government. They all had a limited autonomy under the supervision of a Seleukid official, the *epistates*, but Arados wanted full independence. Arados' ruthlessness in 128 – the fate of the original inhabitants of Marathos and Simyra was presumably enslavement and sale, for those who did not get away in time – is an indication both of the city's determination to make itself fully independent, an aim it had maintained for over a century and a half, but also of the desperation of the Seleukid condition. Three kings within a year in Antioch, overwhelming defeat in the east, civil war, a usurper on the throne in Antioch with Ptolemaic backing, a twice-rejected Seleukid king, the only possible Seleukid successors no more than children – all this had brought the kingdom low, and very quickly. Arados clearly felt the moment was ripe. What is striking is that few other cities followed Arados' lead.

The unpleasant savagery of the Aradian conquest of the mainland *peraia* is reminiscent of the forced conversion of the Idumaeans by the Judaeans. Despite the self-consciously Semitic aspect of these states that rejected the Macedonian Seleukid rulers, the victims were almost entirely, in all likelihood, their fellow Semites. This fits with the Judaean Maccabees' origins as terrorists who were ostensibly resisting Seleukid pressure on their religions, but had turned mainly on their fellow Jews whom they regarded as less than rigorous, and compelled them to conform to their interpretations. Both Arados and Judaea decided that only a 'pure' Semitic country was acceptable.

Of the several Seleukid, near-Seleukid, or non-Seleukid contenders for power in the kingdom, Demetrios fell first. In 187 SE (126–125 BC) he suffered a defeat at the hands of Alexander II Zabeinas near Damascus. Demetrios fled to the west, while Alexander took over in the city, and the coinage shows a change of king in that very year.[33] Demetrios went to ask for refuge at Ptolemais-Ake, but Kleopatra Thea shut him out of the city (hence the presumed personal antipathy between them far earlier). He acquired a ship and sailed north to Tyre, which had minted coins for him all through the fighting (and was now the only city still doing so). He apparently intended to seek refuge in the sanctuary of Melqart there, but as he landed he was killed on the orders of the city's governor.[34]

Tyre had minted coins in Demetrios' name since he had returned from captivity,[35] so the governor – presumably in fact the *epistates* – was a man who had claimed to be loyal to Demetrios in the first place, and so Demetrios had had good reason to seek a refuge there.[36] Kleopatra Thea was also blamed for Demetrios' death in late sources, but unless this was a pre-concerted plot, her responsibility is unlikely.[37] Demetrios' voyage to Tyre was not something she could have expected, and he was killed as soon as he landed, which implies a very swift decision by the governor, who had presumably made an earlier determination to rebel. Kleopatra could scarcely have given him instructions in time, and Demetrios' arrival had no doubt taken him by surprise. The sequel is apparent in the city's coins, and this may or may not have been part of the murderer's programme: the next coins name no king; that is, after Demetrios' death, the city assumed full independence.[38] Tyre therefore followed Arados' lead, but perhaps only accidentally. It was the only Syrian city which emulated Arados at this time, but it may be noted that it did so only three years later, and seems to have done so by chance – had Demetrios not turned up to be killed, Tyre would presumably not have seized its independence just then.

In a way Demetrios' death should have handed the kingship to Alexander, the victor in the fight near Damascus, and the only king left standing, but he never seems to have been taken seriously as king except as a temporary opponent of Demetrios. Despite his military victory, and the fact that he had come to control most of Syria, the removal of Demetrios simply cleared the air, and destroyed the basis of Alexander's kingship. Ptolemy VIII at once withdrew any support for him, for Demetrios' death meant that the threat to him from Syria had gone; soon after he became reconciled with Kleopatra II, a process which took time to negotiate, but which was under way by 126.[39]

With the death of Demetrios, it was up to Kleopatra Thea, who controlled the children of both Demetrios II and Antiochos VII, to organize the succession. The eldest boy was Seleukos V, and he was briefly king in 126, but when he attempted to exert an authority independent of his mother she had him killed. The reasons given are either that he intended to take revenge for his father's death, presumably against his mother, or that he claimed the throne without her permission, thereby assuming that it was his by hereditary right.[40] Both reasons are plausible, even likely, and, given the challenge he obviously presented to her power, she could only kill him or be killed herself.

Kleopatra now issued coins in her own name, at first at Ptolemais-Ake, and promoted her next son, Antiochos VIII, the son of Demetrios II, who had been sent to Athens for refuge, as the new king. It will have taken some time for him to return to Syria, during which time she will have been able to establish her grip on power. Once he had arrived and been enthroned coins were issued showing both of their heads on the obverse.[41] These unsavoury antics no doubt slowed the reduction in support for Alexander Zabeinas, and the coins of Kleopatra Thea and Antiochos VIII were only minted at Ptolemais-Ake for three years. It is worth noting that Kleopatra was now apparently favouring the direct hereditary succession. She had not disputed Seleukos V's accession, and when he died, the next son followed. Meanwhile her eldest son by Antiochos VII was still in exile at Kyzikos.[42]

Between 126, the year of Demetrios' death, and 124, it looks as though the dynastic war was finely balanced between Alexander, who, by the evidence of the dated coins, certainly controlled Antioch, Damascus, and Ashkelon, but also in all probability the Kilikian towns, Seleukeia-in-Pieria, Berytos, and Apamaea, while the only mint operating for Kleopatra Thea and Antiochos VIII was Ptolemais-Ake.[43] But by 124 Ptolemy VIII and the two Egyptian Kleopatras had become fully reconciled, at least in a political sense. This settlement was only worked out slowly, the first element appearing in 126.[44] In the process, Ptolemy VIII withdrew his support for Alexander on Syria and entered into negotiations with Kleopatra Thea. She exacted a price. The new King Antiochos VIII Grypos was to marry the eldest of three daughters of Ptolemy VIII and Kleopatra III, Tryphaina.[45] This was only the second time such an eligible princess was given in marriage outside the family – and Kleopatra Thea was the first. Ptolemy had two more daughters, Kleopatra IV and Selene, but it would seem that Kleopatra Thea was almost as interested in the Ptolemaic succession as the Seleukid. She had certainly broken with her husband Demetrios in the end, but only after his defeat by Alexander, by which time the Egyptian claim was effectively dead. It may well be that she had not been opposed to his Egyptian expedition after all.

The marriage of Antiochos VIII and Tryphaina took place in 124–123, probably soon after he returned to Syria from Athens to become king.[46] This indicated to all that Ptolemaic assistance, if any was required, would now go to Antiochos VIII, and indeed Justin claims that much help was provided.[47] Certainly Antiochos – or rather presumably military commanders operating in his name, for the king was only 16 or 17 – succeeded in defeating Alexander, who retreated to Antioch. He attempted to recruit his treasury from the citizens, who were reluctant to contribute to a clearly losing cause, so he turned to the temples – a Seleukid tradition – first taking a statue of Victory – or was this a superstitious attempt to use the statue as a mascot? Caught trying to remove the great gold statue of Zeus from the city's main temple he and his men were chased out of the city. He was refused refuge in Seleukeia-in-Pieria (just as Demetrios had been turned away from Ptolemais-Ake) and was finally captured making his way south, at Poseidion on the coast. He was brought to the camp of Antiochos VIII and there killed. His death – either execution or suicide – took place only two days after the attempted theft of the statue, so Antiochos' army was close to Antioch by then, which would make the citizens even less keen to openly support the cause of the usurper any more.[48]

By the time, in 123, that Alexander had been defeated and killed, other parts of the Greek east had also settled into a condition of peace. The quarrel in Egypt had ended in 126 and Ptolemy VIII and his wives were more or less reconciled; in Asia Minor, by the same date, the war between Rome and Aristonikos had ended in the latter's defeat and the Roman reorganization of the former Attalid kingdom had been completed. The west was therefore quiet by 126.

The result in the Seleukid region was that the two main antagonists, Parthia and the Seleukid kingdom, had effectively ignored each other since the return of Demetrios to Syria. Both had had to fight their individual battles, with the result that Babylonia, after much disturbance had been retained by Parthia, while Syria had, by 123, become a single kingdom again. But in all this both Parthia and the Seleukids had shed territories into independent and subordinate kingdoms. The precise systems were somewhat different in the two cases: the Parthian sub-kingdoms appear to have quickly subsided into obedience in exchange for being allowed their autonomy and even Hyspaosines continued as king in Charakene as a Parthian vassal. In Syria, though, secessionists had to assert their full independence, as now with Kommagene and Judaea, while Tyre and Arados had also asserted their effective independence.

It was in this situation that Hyrkanos of Judaea sent an embassy of three men to Rome, seeking diplomatic recognition, and with specific requests. Josephos says that Alexander Zabeinas had been friendly towards Hyrkanos, so that Alexander's elimination brought danger; Josephos also suggests that Antiochos VIII threatened to attack Judaea (though his timing is unclear).[49] These comments are not necessarily accurate. He had said earlier that Demetrios II aimed to attack in 128, but he had hardly had time to do so, and it may simply be Jewish paranoia at work – seeing that Demetrios mustered an army (to attack Egypt) Hyrkanos had immediately assumed that Judaea was the target. This was a normal reaction in Judaea, and was only very rarely justified. Similarly there is actually no other indication except Josephos' comments that Demetrios II, Alexander, or Antiochos VIII paid any heed to Judaea.

Hyrkanos' embassy resulted in a polite Roman reply which is quoted by Josephos.[50] It is dated by the praetor in office, 'Fannius, son of Marcus', who must be C. Fannius M. f., who was consul in 122, and whose praetorship was probably in 125 – just the point at which Alexander's cause was beginning to collapse.[51] It appears that the envoys asked for the 'renewal' of the Roman alliance, and for the restoration of those places which they had lost to Antiochos VII in 134: Joppa, Gazara, and Pegai.

This request in fact confirms both the loss of these places and the lack of aggressiveness of Hyrkanos' policy since his return from the east. Even in the conditions of dynastic civil war and confusion he had not felt strong enough to move into Seleukid territory. The Senate was willing to agree that the return of the three places should happen, but was not, as usual, willing to do anything to ensure it. The embassy had no practical effect, though Josephos implies, by his placing of the record of the embassy as he does, that it helped to deter Antiochos VIII – who was in fact busy with Alexander for another two years. The implication, and indeed the whole suggestion of a threat to Judaea, is not acceptable.

The defection of Tyre and Arados left the cities of the central part of the Phoenician coast – Tripolis, Byblos, Orthosia, Berytos, and Sidon – technically loyal to the Seleukids. The coinage of Sidon, however, gives out an ambiguous signal. Coins of Demetrios II were minted in Sidon in 127–126, and for Kleopatra Thea and Antiochos VIII in 122–121, though none in the years between. But then for ten years two parallel series were produced, one for the dynasty every year except one, and one for the city in four separate years. On those coins the city claimed the status of 'holy and *asylos*', which is normal, but also '*nauarchos*' ('supreme at sea') into the bargain. The first of these was usually a royal grant – Ptolemais-Ake bore the title also – but the second was just local boasting (unless it indicates that the city had a locally significant navy). The continuing royal coinages show that at least some royal authority remained in the city, but the city coinages suggest also that the city had a greater autonomy than earlier.[52] It may be that this ambiguity reflects the situation of many people and communities better than the clearer decisions achieved by Tyre and Arados.

Kommagene, along the southern slopes of the Taurus, had been at least semi-detached for a generation and more. The governor Ptolemaios' son Samos at some point took the title of king. When this happened is not known, but the dynasty used an era commencing in 163 BC, and there is a coin of King Samos of the year 33, which, if that era was used, would be 130.[53] Samos' own son was king by about 96.[54] The difficulty is that the era is calculated from another coin very much later in date, and the coin of Samos may thus refer either to the era (in which case it is dated to 130 BC) or to the years of his reign – and both the start and end of his reign are indeterminate (130 is only an estimate, therefore). But the coin does prove that he took the royal title, and that he succeeded his father (who in turn is attested independently in the reign of Demetrios I). A mint in Kommagene continued to produce coins in the name of Demetrios I, becoming steadily more debased and illegible. Four stages can be detected, which could well reflect the first four Kommagenian rulers.[55]

The area which Samos controlled was relatively small, but it included as his main centre the town of Samosata (possibly named, or more likely renamed, for him). This is a place which was built on top of a huge mound of preceding city ruins and debris. Once it was properly fortified, it formed a major power centre which was almost invulnerable. (It took Mark Antony and the Roman army a major effort to take it in the 30s BC.) Samos was even less aggressive than Hyrkanos of Judaea, and his initial ambition can only have been to establish his authority locally and have his independence recognized. Caution in the face of the Seleukid troubles would be sensible, given that access from Syria to the southern areas of his lands was relatively straightforward. By taking over his father's position by inheritance, Samos was proclaiming his independence; his taking the title of king may have come later, but was only confirmation of a condition he had already acquired. Since he later passed that title and kingdom on to his own son Mithradates, he had established that independence from the start, assisted, no doubt, by the Seleukid confusion in the 120s. This is a much more decisive action than any taken at this time by Hyrkanos, but it is similar to the actions of Arados and Tyre, and less aggressive than any of them.

All this necessarily happened in the 120s because by the end of that decade the Seleukid confusion had died down. Antiochos VIII had been born in 141 or thereabouts, so he was only about 15 years old when his father Demetrios II was killed. Having made the boy king by killing his elder brother, Kleopatra Thea must have known that he would eventually move to take power to himself, just as Seleukos had. However, either Kleopatra maintained a much firmer grip on this son, or Antiochos was much more cautious than his brother, but their joint rule lasted for five years. During that time their area of control spread out from Ptolemais-Ake. Their coins were minted at Antioch from 123–122 and at Sidon, Ashkelon, and Damascus amongst other places in the next year, 122.[56] That is, they were recognized and accepted throughout Syria and Kilikia during 122. The methods used were probably a mixture of force – as with the army which was close to Antioch when Alexander fled the city – and persuasion, and an element of resignation by those who submitted. There is little doubt that most of the Syrian communities were only too pleased to find a stable government facing no dynastic challenges in control once more.

If Antiochos VIII's actions were deliberate and calculated his timing was certainly good. In 121, when he was 20 years old, and when it was clear that the Seleukid kingdom now exercised full control over the Syrian region, he turned on his mother. She died by poison, and the event is portrayed as spontaneous self-defence by Antiochos rather than a calculated assassination. She is supposed to have realized his growing need to be independent of her, and his fear of being subject to the fate of his brother, and had prepared a cup of poison for him when he returned from a hunt; he realized her intent and compelled her to drink it herself.[57] This may even be true, but the transfer of responsibility for her death from him to her might also be a propaganda story for public consumption, and he certainly waited until she had succeeded in producing a kingdom which he could rule without challenge.

That kingdom now consisted of the North Syrian region from the sea to the Euphrates. Beyond the river it is not clear whether the Osrhoenian king acknowledged Seleukid suzerainty; if not Antiochos VIII's authority stopped at the river. The Kilikian region had been under his control when Alexander was removed. To the south, however, neither Arados nor Tyre were under his control, and the coinage system operating at Sidon implied that that city was seriously contemplating joining those two Phoenician cities in independence.

The Palestinian coast was Seleukid, but the land from the edge of the Judaean hills as far as the desert was composed of independent states – Judaea, the Nabataeans, Philadelphia-Gerasa. It was a much mutilated kingdom Antiochos inherited from his mother, but at least he did not have to fight anyone.

The adventure of Antiochos VII was the immediate cause of the Seleukid collapse, since the casualties the army suffered – including himself – weakened the kingdom decisively. The equally rash adventure of Demetrios II, and the reactions it caused brought the collapse of the Seleukid position in Syria, assisted by Ptolemy VIII's interference. But neither adventure was unreasonable, and if either had succeeded, they would be counted as masterstrokes.

The reunification of Syria at the end of the 120s can be attributed to the policy of Kleopatra Thea. She had been unable to prevent Demetrios II from attacking Egypt, and it may well be that she had liked the idea, but after his failure and death she had been the main engine in working to bring about the reunification. Neither Seleukos V nor Antiochos VIII would probably have been able to accomplish this, being far too young, though the latter perhaps gained much of the public credit simply by being with the army at the time Alexander was killed. The coincidence of the death of Kleopatra Thea and the end of the civil warfare is strongly suggestive that Antiochos waited deliberately until she had finished the main work before he struck. At least that implies a certain political nous, if of the unscrupulous and unconstructive sort. Kleopatra's reputation has not been of the best, thanks to her killing of Seleukos V and the accusation of complicity in the death of Demetrios II, but her responsibility for the Seleukid recovery between 126 and 123 seems clear, and it is time she was given the credit for it.

Chapter 10

The Kingdom Failing (121–108 BC)

The several states which had seceded from the Seleukid Empire, and those in the Parthian kingdom which were autonomous, were all, like the Parthian kingdom itself, powerfully affected by their Seleukid parentage. They inherited, whether they wished it or not, the culture, above all the political culture, of the Seleukids. They were all, without exception, kingdoms; their kings adopted similar titles and acquired or took or were given nicknames or honorifics very often copied from Seleukid titles. And although the internal political systems of these minor states are mainly invisible to us, their administrative systems were copied from their parents – men who were friends (*philoi*) of the king were employed variously in many roles, provinces where the territory was big enough were formed – and their very names derived from Seleukid nomenclature. As the Seleukid kingdom disintegrated it produced a whole series of minor Seleukid-similar states.

After 121 and the death of Kleopatra Thea the dynastic conflict in Syria ceased for seven years, but that does not mean that Antiochos VIII Grypos was free of concerns about his tenure of the kingship. Within the kingdom no further moves by cities or regions into independence were made during this period of peace, so far as we know: the distraction of the death of the Seleukid king, and the governmental confusion so produced, was clearly required for such a move to be successful. In normal conditions of peace, or even merely with a competent king ruling, there was clearly neither incentive nor the possibility for minor political states or single cities to break away. The ambiguity of Sidon's apparent intentions was clearly in suspense, resolved neither for loyalty nor for separation – which in effect meant that loyalty won out in practice.

At the same time none of the states which had already become detached in the 120s was suppressed. Kommagene, Osrhoene, Arados, Judaea and Tyre all continued to act as independent states, and were not forcibly reincorporated. The reason for this abstention by the king may be the inactivity or laziness of Antiochos VIII, or the general exhaustion of the Seleukid state, or possibly a series of agreements to respect their autonomy. It has to be said, however, that the sources for Antiochos VIII's early reign are minimal. This may mean that little which the historians thought worth recording happened, and since they were usually attracted to disputes and wars it suggests a period of peace.

By this time, of course, the Parthians had ended their eastern war. In about 123 or so it is possible that Mithradates II was able to impose his suzerainty on Adiabene.[1] Osrhoene's independence, certain by 128 if not earlier, cut off Syria (just beginning its new civil war) from the rest of Mesopotamia, and King Artabanus had gained final control of Babylon by 126: Parthian expansion north along the Tigris is very likely to have followed, especially since all that was needed by whoever ruled in Adiabene was a submission to the Parthian king. The sub-kingdoms strung along the southern Parthian border – Charakene, Elymais, Persis – continued in some sort of autonomy under their own kings. Hyspaosines was certainly able to pass his throne on to his very young son a few years later, and Persis has a series of kings during this period. One must assume, however, that Mithradates II, one of the most able of the Parthian kings, insisted on the submission of these sub-kings. It is uncertain how far west Parthian power encroached, but from Adiabene there was only the steppe-land of Mesopotamia and a few cities such as Nisibis to separate their lands from the Seleukid boundary at the Euphrates. Osrhoene controlled the western part of Mesopotamia, but between that kingdom and Adiabene sovereignty is not known. However, Parthia had a strong tendency for its power to flow into ungoverned lands, and it would not be long before it was Osrhoene's eastern neighbour.

Syria was now in effect, the Seleukid kingdom, along with Kilikia. It was a land which had been, one assumes, fairly badly damaged by the previous fighting, as well as by the casualties of the Parthian war. (We do not have any precise evidence for this, but it seems reasonable to assume it.) But it appears to have been able to recover quickly. This is what might be expected from a population which was essentially agricultural and commercial. Antiochos VIII held games at Daphne on a lavish scale, giving generous gifts, though the date is not known.[2] Poseidonios is the main source for this period (though his work survives only in fragments), and he was a native of Apamaea, and lived through these years; it may be presumed that he was reporting accurately. He makes a point of noting the wealth of the land, though he uses the fact to claim that the population had become decadent.[3]

For the breakaway sections of the kingdom as restored by Antiochos VII in the 130s were geographically very small – the kingdoms of Kommagene and Judaea were only confirming in independence what had been their autonomy earlier. These may be discounted in the reckoning, leaving only Arados and Tyre as completely new detachments. If a name for Kleopatra Thea's policy in the later 120s had been needed, it could well have been 'restoration', a recovery of this new Seleukid kingdom which Antiochos VII had formed, with as little diminution as possible. In this she had largely succeeded, presumably allowing the independence of Tyre and Arados to avoid having to indulge in more warfare. And in the process she had returned the kingship to the 'rightful' king, the eldest son of Demetrios II.

She had also contrived a reserve king in her son by Antiochos VII, in exile in Kyzikos, and by the Ptolemaic marriages she had arranged for the two boys, she had set up a situation in which future policy options might have been developed. The grandiose scheme of Demetrios II to unite Syria with Egypt had failed, but the intermarriages of the Seleukid and Ptolemaic dynasties could well produce a situation in the future in which the possibility of a union of the two might return. On the other hand, this could also lead to continual interference – by the Ptolemies in Syria, by the Seleukids in Egypt. And of course the actual course of events was very different from any such intentions.

Antiochos VIII Grypos' own pacific inclinations may have been one of the reasons for not campaigning to reduce the new independent detachments to submission. His reputation among later historians was as an indolent, pleasure-seeking man.[4] No doubt the interpretation put forward by Poseidonios, but it may also have been his deliberate policy to allow Syria a term of peace in which to recover from the previous strains and disasters – a policy quite probably originally established by his mother. The fact that he had her killed did not necessarily require that he reject her policy. He would presumably remember the disaster an early activism had earned his father, Demetrios II. Whatever the reason, for ten years those autonomous areas were left alone. The result, of course, was that their autonomy became accepted and entrenched, and solidified in full independence.

There was, however, a better reason than a mere personal enjoyment of the pleasures of life for Grypos' apparent paralysis, a reason which has echoes from earlier Seleukid history. The real problem for Grypos was his half-brother Antichos Kyzikenos. Kleopatra Thea had sent him to Kyzikos for his safety when Demetrios II returned to Syria, and it is evident that the enmity Demetrios may have felt for his brother's son – though this is the only 'evidence' for such an attitude – was fully developed in the two half-brothers. It is said that Grypos made an attempt to poison Kyzikenos while he was still at Kyzikos,[5] and there are hints that Kyzikenos was also making preparations to attack him in Syria.[6] It is clear from these comments, and from later events, that whatever detestation Grypos had for Kyzikenos, it was fully reciprocated.

All the ancient sources compress the events between 121 and 114 into a sentence or two, but Josephos is clear that Kyzikenos made his preparations to invade first, and that it was then that Grypos tried to poison him. (On the other hand, the story of Kleopatra Thea's death by poison administered by Grypos might have attached such a method to him, not necessarily with any foundation in fact: one would like to know the source of Appian's information on the matter.)

A note in Livy in the summary of his missing book 62 remarks that there were disturbances in Syria.[7] This book covers the years 118–115, exactly the period for which the other sources are absent or very thin. But there is no mention in any of these summaries of any of the fighting between the brothers which began in 114, so it could be that Livy was simply getting this matter out of the way, and so getting his chronology wrong. This is another and a particularly clear indication of the general lack of Roman interest in Syria and the Seleukids.

The conflict between the brothers provided a repetition of the paralysing situation which had pinned Alexander Balas down in Syria in the early 140s, when Demetrios II was preparing to attack. Then advantage was taken by the Parthians in their conquest of Iran; this time it was both the Parthians and the separated Syrians who benefitted.

Of course, it may have been the intention all along of the Seleukid government of Syria to recover control of the separated lands and cities, but, if so, the king delayed for far too long, and was unable to involve himself in a new war while still under threat from Kyzikenos – as soon as Grypos was involved in a war Kyzikenos would intervene. If Grypos attempted to suppress the independent detached states he might well find that those who were contemplating following them might come out against him, not wanting such an option to be closed off; no doubt they would be encouraged by messages from Kyzikenos. And this in turn suggests that Grypos was fully aware that Kyzikenos had considerable support among the Syrian population. The more the possibilities are considered, the more politically delicate the whole Syrian condition appears.

Finally in 114–113 Kyzikenos made his move, and challenged his half-brother in arms. It is not known where Kyzikenos got the support he needed for an invasion. He may have been able to count on some internal support, but he would also need an initial armed force to be a convincing challenger to the sitting king. The course of the war is reflected mainly in the numismatic record, and also in detached glimpses in the written record.[8] It is usual to try to fit these fragments together to make a reasonably coherent account, but there really are too many gaps for any such account to carry any real conviction, though the numismatic record does provide an outline for a time.

The coins produced in the city mints show that Kyzikenos carried through an almost completely successful initial campaign of conquest, but Grypos then recovered, and from then on they grappled with each other without ever seeming to be able to achieve a clear result in the contest.[9] Josephos has a vivid image to describe the situation: 'Both of them were in the position of athletes whose strength is exhausted, but who are ashamed to yield, and so continue to prolong the contest by periods of inactivity and rest.'[10] The overall result after a year or so was that Grypos held most of the kingdom but Kyzikenos could never be fully beaten and driven out.

The coins suggest that Antiochos VIII Grypos, having controlled Antioch since his elimination of Alexander II in 123–122, lost the city in the first rush of Antiochos IX Kyzikenos' attack in 114–113. Within a year this had been reversed and Grypos held the city for perhaps two more years. Kyzikenos retook it during 110/109, but held it only briefly; from 109–108 Grypos was in control until his death in 97–96. This sequence is in fact the latest theory, replacing one in which an extra reign at Antioch for both men was postulated (which in turn replaced an even earlier theory). The dates are also uncertain in detail, but probably they are no more than a year out in any one case.[11]

It is really only at Antioch where the coinage is susceptible to such a detailed chronological analysis. Part of that analysis, however, includes a statistical calculation which purports to determine the use of the dies for producing the coins. The theory is that the frequency of the changes of the dies gives an idea of the length of the king's reign, based on some assumptions about the quantity and regularity of the production of coins – under more or less normal circumstances. However, there are as great uncertainties in the results for this theory as there are in the vagueness and contradictions of the written evidence; both have to be treated with considerable caution and scepticism.[12]

The awkward details do not hide the fact that the initial bout of warfare between the rivals gradually subsided to a stalemate. By 108–107 most of the successes for each man had been achieved, and from then on for a decade little changed in the overall balance. On the other hand, the productive mints declined in number, and most of the coins produced were now undated, so that from 107–106 we have only one or two sets of dated coins to base conclusions on – until 104–103 at Ashkelon, and from that year on at Damascus.[13] This is of little use in estimating the fortunes of the rivals in Syria as a whole, and there may well have been many more changes than are at present understood.

The source of Kyzikenos' early support is never stated, but suggestions have included both the Parthians and the Ptolemies. The theory of Parthian support relies on their capture of the town of Dura-Europos on the Euphrates, upstream from the great Babylonian cities, which event is dated to 113 BC; the coins of Grypos from the town were found to have been countermarked by Mithradates II.[14] This would certainly suggest the town's capture, but the date must in fact be much less definitive, and none of this can be taken as a sign of an alliance between Mithradates and Kyzikenos. The Parthian advance is in fact consistent with their slow moves along the two rivers, to Adiabene in about 125 or so, and to Dura-Europos perhaps ten years later. So this is not evidence of Parthian assistance to Kyzikenos; further, it would be a valuable propaganda weapon for Grypos if such an alliance was discovered (the son of Antiochos VII in alliance with his father's killers), and it could hardly be kept secret. I conclude no such alliance existed.

The Ptolemaic connection is much firmer and inherently more likely. Grypos was, of course, married to Tryphaina, the eldest daughter of Ptolemy VIII and Kleopatra III. During 116 both Ptolemy and his mother and rival Kleopatra II died. This left Kleopatra III in control, and she made her younger son Ptolemy X Alexander king in Egypt; the elder son, Ptolemy IX Soter Lathyros had already been installed as king in Cyprus, but he was dissatisfied with this. Next year (115) Lathyros was compelled to divorce his wife, his sister Kleopatra IV, and to marry the youngest of the three sisters, Selene.[15] Kleopatra IV, once her sister Tryphaina had gone to Syria to marry Grypos, was the eldest Ptolemaic female in Egypt, except for Kleopatra III herself; clearly the latter could not allow the eldest Ptolemaic male to be married to the eldest Ptolemaic female; together their joint royal charisma would be too great a threat to her own position.

Selene, meanwhile, had been promised to Kyzikenos in Kleopatra Thea's scheme, but the marriage had evidently not taken place – Kyzikenos was only born in the mid-130s, and so was only just adult when he began his war in Syria. With the death of Kleopatra Thea the arrangement seems to have failed.

In 114, while Antiochos Kyzikenos was in control of Antioch, and seemed to be winning his war, the newly divorced Kleopatra IV arrived in Syria from Cyprus, with an army and a treasure, and proposed herself as Kyzikenos' wife.[16] (This was, of course, a partial repetition of Kleopatra II's move to Syria in 128 to recruit Demetrios II for her war in Egypt.) The fact that Kleopatra IV went to Syria and then met and married Kyzikenos shows that the latter had already begun his war; but this does not exclude a previous agreement between them, and the possibility of previous assistance to Kyzikenos; he arrived in Syria with his own forces, which Kleopatra's army now reinforced, but it looks very much that it was the prospect of her support in soldiers and treasure, together with the prospect of support from inside Syria, which brought on the war. (Kyzikenos was already married, to an unknown woman.) The dowry was convincing, but did not stop Grypos driving both newly-weds out of Antioch soon after. Kleopatra IV was captured, and, at the insistence of her sister Tryphaina, killed.[17] This may have been partly a personal act of hatred, though it is more likely that Tryphaina was politically enraged by Kleopatra's support for her husband's rival. A year later Tryphaina made the mistake of being captured by Kyzikenos' army; he had her killed in revenge.[18] It may well have been this personal element which helped prolong the war for another decade and a half.

Kleopatra IV's forces must have made a certain difference, perhaps resulting in Kyzikenos' swift but brief early success, for it was in 112 that he conquered most of Syria. It was probably in this period that Grypos was temporarily driven from the kingdom and took refuge for a time at Aspendos in Pamphylia, an episode known but not securely dated.[19] His recovery of much of Syria over the next years may or may not have been assisted by support from Kleopatra III in Egypt, but a recovery certainly took place.

This contest in Syria would seem to provide the ideal conditions in which independently minded Syrian communities were able to achieve their aims. In fact no new moves for independence happened, at least not for some time. Partly this must be due to the fact that each of the competing Seleukid kings was relatively well armed, at least in comparison with the political seceders, and were very likely to take umbrage at moves into independence, but also because for two or three years the contest swung so wildly from one brother to the other that it seemed that a final victory for one or the other was imminent.

Given the partial and fragmentary nature of the sources, it is not possible to do more than provide an indication of what resulted from all this. The only relatively continuous written account is by Josephos – Diodoros is fragmentary, Justin a condensation, Appian minimal – but the drawbacks of his account are as substantial as ever in his record of Seleukid affairs. The account is late (two centuries after the events), and he was writing a Jewish history, not a Seleukid, and so he concentrated on events in Palestine, and can be careless with other regions. A certain corrective is available from the other written sources, Justin and Appian particularly, and to a degree from the geographer Strabo, but none of these is any more interested in Syrian history as a whole and for itself than is Josephos; numismatics provides a certain chronological precision, but is very narrowly focused on a few places, and tends to fade away disconcertingly; archaeology, by contrast, is chronologically imprecise and in Syria has mainly been directed at periods other than the Hellenistic. In short, the sources provide both uncertain guidance and major problems.

The dynastic Syrian war had been going on for three years before the first Syrian community made a move into independence. This was, not surprisingly, Sidon. The city's coin evidence, as already mentioned in the last chapter, shows alternating issues of royal and municipal coinages, and implies an ambivalence in the period 122–121 to 114–113 about whether to cleave to the king or to go for independence, like Tyre, its rival, or Arados. Indecision maybe, but it also shows that there was a rising trend of local consciousness. Its two neighbours had already seized their independence, and there were surely men in Sidon who wished to emulate them, though perhaps not so violently as either.

The revival of civil warfare from 114–113 eventually forced a decision on the city, and no doubt increased the numbers of those who felt that the monarchs were less than competent. The city fell to Kyzikenos in the first part of his campaign, and his coins were produced in the city in 114–113, 113–112 and 111–110. However, during the latter year the city adopted a new dating era.[20] That is to say, despite being effectively under Antiochos IX's control for the previous three years, the city then rejected him and then chose to become fully independent rather than submit once more to Grypos. (It may be assumed that the city council chose a moment when Kyzikenos was absent and his forces either absent or very low in numbers for their *coup d'etat*.) The distraction of the civil war was surely the occasion for this decision, and perhaps the demands made by Kyzikenos as his cause became more difficult to sustain contributed to the decision. But the apparent ambivalence in the city over the previous decade indicated that this was not an easy decision to reach. No doubt the threat of a royal reaction (by either, or both, kings) was strong. Nevertheless the decision stuck: Sidon produced no more royal coins; the city's independence dates from 111 BC.

Sidon clearly took its independence decision carefully and deliberately and took a long time to make it. Together with Arados and Tyre it controlled the coastal route through Phoenicia, though it seems clear that armies were still able to march along that road simply by passing the cities, for it is unlikely that any of the cities could actually prevent an army's passage, though they could certainly deny themselves to any armed force from behind their walls or, in Arados' case, on its offshore island. The royal armies were, of course, usually intent on a different target; the lands around the cities would suffer, but not the urban centres. The obstacles formed by those coastal cities however, put a greater importance on the route through the Bekaa Valley, and on the control of Damascus, which became a newly important route centre; control of this city could also provide control of access to Palestine from the north, or, of course, vice versa.

It was in this area that there emerged at about this time a people called the Ituraeans. They inhabited the Lebanese mountains, both the Lebanon and the Antilebanon, and in the late second century, if not before, they were infiltrating out from the mountains into the surrounding lower countries. By 104 they were encountered by Judaean forces in the area of Galilee, which implies that they had already occupied the lands around Mount Hermon, and that they had been in Galilee for some years.[21] Twenty years later they were strong enough to threaten Damascus, both from the north, where they occupied a series of places along the Antilebanon range,[22] and from the south, from their lands in Batanaea, Trachonitis, and Auranitis (the Hauran), though when these areas were occupied is not clear.[23] Archaeological evidence also suggests that they were numerous in Gaulanitis (Golan),[24] and they have been identified as the makers of a distinctive type of pottery found in all these areas.[25] (This expansion pattern was repeated much later by the Druzes, who began in the southern Bekaa and spread into the southern lands from Batanaea to Gaulanitis.)

Like other newly emerging Semitic groups in Syria at this time the Ituraeans appear to have begun with only a minimal political organization so that a fully organized Ituraean principality is not mentioned in any source until the 80s BC. The later Ituraean rulers used an era starting in 115 BC,[26] which was a most unlikely date for striking out for independence, for this was a time when the Seleukid government was united and fully competent and not likely to permit any movements of separation; one must assume that (like the similar cases of a preliminary date at Osrhoene and Kommagene – and indeed in Parthia), it was back-calculated from some later time, and quite possibly inaccurately. The most notable of their princes is always referred to as 'Ptolemy son of Menneas', which suggests that Menneas was politically important; an era beginning with his assumption of some sort of local authority, but which authority was barely visible from outside, would seem likely.

One of the offices which the Ituraean ruler held was that of high priest at the temple at Baalbek, and the analogy which suggests itself is with other religious-cum-political leaders in Syria.[27] High priests had been central to the insurrection in Judaea, and was the crucial title of every Hasmonaean ruler from Jonathan Maccabee onwards. Ptolemy son of Menneas was similarly high priest at Baalbek. Others such as the kings of Edessa/Osrhoene were also local high priests. These offices are central to understanding what happened at this time in Syria.

The acquisition of independence was essentially a reaction by Semitic groups to the decline in power of the formerly dominant Greco-Macedonian Seleukid kings. The high priests of the various local cults – at Jerusalem, Baalbek, Emesa, Edessa, and elsewhere – were, by the late second century BC, the only men with any independent authority in the whole Syrian region who were not members of the ruling set of Greeks and Macedonians. It is normal to identify these groups – Jews, Arabs, Ituraeans, Phoenicians, Aramaeans – according to the language they spoke, but they seem to have identified themselves more by allegiances to a particular cultic centre – Jews at Jerusalem is the best known case, but there are many others – and that these cult centres became the political centres of the separating states, while the high priests eventually graduated to kings and princes.

Yet there is one study of popular religion in Syria which has convincingly demonstrated that by this time the popular religion was generally very similar throughout the land, so much so that there was really only one Syrian god with different local names.[28] The original local exclusiveness of the pre-Persian periods, where local gods were the manifestations of the politically independent states which had developed in the Iron Age, had faded with the successive subjugations and destructions of Syria by Assyrians, Babylonians, Persians and Macedonians. Throughout Syria there had emerged essentially a single supreme god, sometimes with a local name – Hadad, Dusares, Yahweh – though Baal Shamin was a widespread term, or even just 'baal'.[29] (It seems likely that it was a local version of this which was being practised in Judaea until the Maccabean terrorist campaign forced the Jews into a more exclusive Yahweh-worship centred on the Jerusalem temple.)

The existence of this single all-Syrian deity is an indication of one of the methods of survival used by the self-consciously Semitic peoples of Syria in the face of the political powerlessness they had suffered since the Assyrian conquest, and of the powerful secular attractions of Hellenism. This had been particularly dramatized in the conflict in Judaea in the 160s, which led to the Jewish insurrection, but it was inherent in the situation throughout Syria in the Persian period and after – the sudden claim of the high priest of Bambyke to royal status in 332–331 is a case in point, and Alexander's siege of Tyre was in a way a Tyrian defence of their city god – for Alexander's demand for access to the city had been in order to sacrifice to Melqart, code for a takeover of the city itself.

This Syrian-wide god in its local manifestations had, of course, been adopted by the European settlers, who attempted to make it over in their own image. Thus they called Melqart of Tyre Herakles, and Damascus' Hadad was Zeus, as was, for a time, Judaean Yahweh. But Hellenic ideas had virtually no influence on the Syrian deity, except externally in such superficial aspects as the architecture of the god's house. The description given in the second century AD by Lucian of Samosata of the temple of Bambyke–Hierapolis and of the goddess Atargatis – after five centuries of Greek and Roman influence – is of a Greek-type temple, but a wholly Syrian goddess.[30] The same may be said also of the temple of Yahweh in Jerusalem, with its Holy of Holies, so incomprehensible to the Greeks and Romans; when the temple was rebuilt by Herod, it was strongly Hellenic in architectural inspiration, yet the worship remained as before.

This survivability by the Syrian god, using stripped-down versions of the old Syrian religious beliefs, the old Semitic languages, and the old Syrian rituals, required also the survival of the god's own worshippers, since it was the worshippers who kept the god going. And as soon as the cracks and fissures in the Macedonian carapace which covered Syria had been widened sufficiently by foreign defeat and internal dissension, the Syrian gods and goddesses and their worshippers emerged politically once more; and the obvious leaders and organizers of this emergence were the high priests. Indeed these high priests had never abandoned their political role, for, like the high priests at Jerusalem, they were the obvious intermediaries between the king's government and their local communities, a role in the cities which was normally taken by the royally-appointed *epistates*. And, if the Judaean high priests are an example, these high priests were also formally confirmed in office by the king, though they succeeded to their office by hereditary right. The king's control was thus somewhat indirect and certainly very limited in the areas of the high priests' expertise.

The assertion of identity and independence among the Semitic groups, generally located in the countryside, inevitably produced a reaction among the cities where the Greco-Macedonian population was concentrated, but also in those areas where Semitic populations were already politically organized. It was not acceptable to any of the cities, for example, to have their rural territories infiltrated by hillmen; the Greek cities of lowland Palestine resisted the Hasmonaeans from the Judaean hills; Damascus resisted Ituraean approaches suggesting union (as, indeed, did the Phoenician cities later). The threat from the Aramaean countryside pushed the cities into even greater loyalty to the Seleukid kings (another good reason for them not to make a break for independence). Both Damascus and Ptolemais-Ake can be seen as seriously threatened by Semitic hillmen and as being conspicuously loyal to the king, more so than any other city in the south; one obvious explanation for this is that they were the strongest of the cities of their region but that they were, at the same time, seriously under threat by outsiders. Their real problem, however, was the dynastic dispute, which rendered their loyalty difficult to focus.

The apparent dispute, or perhaps uncertainty, within Sidon as to whether to move into independence or stick with the Seleukid king, as suggested by the part-civic, part-royal coinage of the city, seems to have been repeated elsewhere. At Tripolis, another Phoenician city, a coinage, inscribed variously 'of the Tripolitans' and 'Tripolis, holy and autonomous' was produced in 112–111, and yet a coinage in Kyzikenos' name was also produced in the same year.[31] This is a combination, as at Sidon, which rather implies a certain indecision in the city, or perhaps the installation of a garrison of Kyzikenos' soldiers (for whom the royal coinage would provide pay). The city was certainly a base for Kyzikenos later, in 108–107, when he is said to have gone there from the south, and at that time the city produced coins for him again.[32] In 110–109 Kyzikenos lost control of Antioch, for the last time, as it happened.[33] This may have been the event which brought him north to Tripolis, despite the struggle he was then involved in with Hyrkanos of Judaea at Samaria. But he did not recover Antioch, which did not produce his coins again until 97–96, after Grypos died.

Tripolis did not coin again at all until 105–104, but then its coins imply that it had become independent, and it ceased to produce any royal coins.[34] The city later began a new era in 64 BC, when it was liberated by Pompeius; before that it had produced an occasional coinage dated by a different era, whose highest date is a 'year 41'. Counting back from 64, this takes us to 105, in which year Kyzikenos may still have controlled the city, though he may have left it earlier.[35] But it would be normal practice for a newly independent city to celebrate with a new coin issue, which would also serve to inform others of its new status, hence perhaps the issue of 105–104. It would seem, therefore, that the city seized its independence in or about that year, either by expelling Kyzikenos, or by waiting until he left, and then shutting the city gates behind him. The coins of 105–104 were thus quite possibly the city's advertisement of this action, a statement of its independence.

The hesitancy and indecision which are implied by the vagaries of the coinages produced at both Sidon and Tripolis are wholly understandable. The Seleukid kings may not have been able to prevail against each other, but either of them could usually deal with a single city whose citizens were divided among themselves as to what was the best thing to do; partisans could easily be found to introduce a king's forces into a city – this had been Kleopatra Thea's problem at

Seleukeia-in-Pieria in 139, when the issue was the challenge of a non-Seleukid pretender; choosing between Grypos and Kyzikenos would be much easier. It seems likely that most Syrians did not care which of them was king, though most still felt they wished to be part of the kingdom. But the kings could rarely tie up their armies into a siege, or even a blockade if it might last long, since this would leave the rest of Syria open for his rival to mop up other places. This was the main defence of those cities which had broken away; if one king emerged victorious it might be his first task to recover control throughout Syria.

The indecisiveness of the Seleukid conflict, however, can only have induced weariness and exasperation in cities subjected to repeated occupations by different kings, and to the extraordinary demands made by kings at war. It seems that the first city outside Phoenicia to act on this resentment was Seleukeia-in-Pieria.

An inscription from Paphos in Cyprus records the grant of autonomy to the city of Seleukeia-in-Pieria by 'King Antiochos',[36] which would seem to be Grypos.[37] It takes the form of a letter by 'King Antiochos' to King Ptolemy Alexander, informing him of the grant of autonomy to the city, and is precisely dated to 29 Gorpiaios of the year 203 SE, which is 6 September 109 BC. Some time earlier the city of Tarsos in Kilikia had stopped coining for Antiochos Grypos and switched to Kyzikenos, and it was about this time that Grypos regained control of Antioch from Kyzikenos. It therefore looks very much as though Grypos' grant was a pre-emptive move to enlist Seleukeia to his support in a crisis – the text in fact refers to 'the [most critical] circumstances which have [overtaken us]', or, in another translation, 'the most desperate times we have experienced'. This might be a general reference to the civil war and the murder of his wife Tryphaina (though that had happened two years before) or, perhaps more likely, it could be a specific reference to Grypos' particular difficulties in the summer of 109, whatever they might be. (It also might be an example of the exaggerated rhetoric adopted by both sides during a civil war.) Another part of the stone contains a copy of part of the letter of grant to the city. The only additional piece of information in it is that Antiochos had also informed the Roman Senate of the grant.

There are two sides to this transaction, the city and its citizens, and the king (whichever king it was), but there is also the more general point that this is the great city of Seleukeia-in-Pieria. This grant appears to be good evidence for a desire among the Seleukeians for more control over their own affairs than they had before. Grypos' grant to Seleukeia may thus have been his way of retaining some influence in the city, and so denying it to his rival; that is, this was the price the city extracted for supporting him; yet he must have known that such a grant of independence, once given, could not be removed, and so the city would act increasingly in its own interests, and rarely in his. Nor would it necessarily keep the Seleukeians out of Kyzikenos' hands, for he might simply ignore the grant as being a device of his rival, and therefore a manoeuvre in the civil war – which of course it probably was.

Grypos' purpose was evidently a short-term matter. His affairs were, as he explained in his letter, in a crisis and this was a means of lessening the forces arrayed against him, though exactly how this worked is not easy to see. (It is possible that the city was in his enemy's hands at the time, and so this grant was a move to take the city from him.) It is, whatever the precise position he was in, an indication of the weapons being employed by both sides in this war. Grypos, of course, was the legitimately diademed king, and so was in a stronger position to give such grants than his upstart rival, but that he had to do so suggests that the fighting, as the coin evidence also indicates, was for a long time finely balanced. But, let us make no mistake, such a measure was desperate indeed, for it was a case of the king mutilating his own kingdom.

For this was not a grant of autonomy to a minor city, or even to an important Phoenician city – this was a grant of autonomy, in effect in the circumstances, independence, to the original royal city of Syria, the city the founder had designed as his government centre, the city in which at least two of the king's ancestors, including the founder Seleukos I himself, were buried. It was also a major port, so that the customs duties imposed would no longer flow into the royal treasury, and it was the main naval port of the kingdom, though to be sure it was not much of a naval power. But the main point is ideological. Grypos was fighting both to maintain his own power, but also to emphasize the legitimacy of his occupation of the kingship, so to give away the royal city of Seleukeia into independence was to show that he was no more concerned at maintaining the integrity of the kingdom than his rival. It was a gesture of despair, and one of negligence and uncaring.

This event, if any one event can be said to have done so, marks the approaching end of the Seleukid kingdom. The detached cities and provinces of the past few years since the death of Antiochos VII had been fairly minor. Judaea and Kommagene had been virtually independent even in Antiochos' time; Arados, Tyre, Sidon, and Tripolis were all physically small territories, if important cities, and could be dominated from inland simply because they relied on trade for their lives. But Seleukeia was a city in a different league altogether, and if it was to be independent, no city could be said to be a necessary part of the kingdom; and if it was to be safe in the midst of the civil war because of this grant, its independence would be a target for any other endangered city.

Seleukeia took its independence seriously. It issued its own silver coins – not just bronze as many cities did – dated by the era of its autonomy, for the next twenty years.[38] However, the first of the coin issues is dated to the fourth year, 105–104, and it is possible that the city had some initial difficulties. It would need to accumulate a treasury, for example, before issuing coins, and no doubt Grypos had ensured that he left little of value in the place before issuing his grant.

By the time the dynastic war had more or less petered out into its stalemate (that is, about the time of the grant to Seleukeia, 109 or 108), there were three more cities, Sidon, Tripolis, and Seleukeia, which had shifted their allegiance away from both the kings and the kingdom and into an independent political condition. Yet the rest of Syria was still under the control of one or other of them and, apart from the dubious case of Dura-Europos, no invader had yet attempted to take advantage of the internal wrangling.

And yet there were clear signs that this episode of civil war had been unusually debilitating. The steady reduction in the number of mints producing coins for either king was eloquent of their failure to maintain a treasury. Contributing to this, of course, was the reduction in the kingdom's tax base as the coastal cities – all commercial, tax-paying communities – detached themselves. The Phoenician cities were predominantly commercial in their orientation and so were more than usually productive of tax monies, and were now no longer contributing to either king. Similarly Seleukeia was a major port, through which much of the trade of North Syria passed. The cities may well have been induced at times by the near presence of an army to cough up a contribution to persuade that army to go away, but this is no substitute for a regular flow of tax money – and it is cash money which fuels any military campaign. In 108 Kyzikenos' army was so reduced that it was unable to defeat even the Judaean army, which was itself unable to capture a small city except by a year-long blockade (see next chapter). And Kyzikenos could not be beaten by his rival and enemy.

Chapter 11

Destruction in the South (108–96 BC)

The slow and in many ways reluctant separation of cities and small regions from the Seleukid kingdom in the twenty years since the death of Antiochos VII moved on at an increased pace from 108. Rather as the ability to recover Parthian conquests in the 140s and after was impaired by the hypnotic fascination of the king in Syria for the actions and threats of his rival – Demetrios II, Tryphon – so the paralysing struggle for the kingship between Grypos and Kyzikenos prevented the recovery of control over these separated lands, and at the same time propelled some places out of the kingdom. Josephos claims that Grypos had been unable to attack Judaea in order to restore Antiochos VII's control and the treaty conditions because he faced an attack from his half-brother which would come while he was involved in the Judaean hills.[1] This was in fact probably a fantasy, but it applies well enough in other places – Tripolis and Sidon, for example, seem to have escaped because neither king could afford to become tied up in a siege.

The coastal cities gently removed themselves from the royal power, in Seleukeia's case by means of a grant from one of the kings. Only Arados, the first of the seceders, employed violence, and even that was not directed at the king, but at its own *peraia*; the murder of Demetrios II by the Tyrian governor might count – but both cases came at the beginning of the process. So far as we can see, neither Tripolis nor Sidon had to use force, though perhaps they did employ guile.

The possibilities of external interference were obvious. A Ptolemaic intervention may have been the origin of the dynastic war. Parthian attention was no doubt intermittently focused westwards, as in the case of the capture of isolated Dura-Europos about 113. The local minor powers could also intervene, though only one of these seems to have had serious imperialist ambitions and intentions. Judaea had already attempted to expand in every direction, west to the coast at Joppa, which expansion had been stopped by Antiochos VII, east across the Jordan to Medaba, south into Idumaea. A raid into the north had resulted in the destruction of the rival temple on Mount Gerizim, but the Samaritans, a schismatic Judaean sect, had easily recovered and were now concentrated in the Macedonian colony-city of Samaria.

The existence of the Samaritans is the excuse given by Josephos for the attack which Hyrkanos now made on that city. In theory, Hyrkanos was taking a very large gamble, for the Judaean army had no competence in siege warfare, as the long siege of the small town of Medaba had shown – and that army had not been employed for a decade and a half. Furthermore, the Judaean state was by no means stable, as is implied by Josephos' account of contentions during Hyrkanos' reign, and of the civil war which brought him to power in 134.[2] Hyrkanos also had little power to enforce his will outside the hills, and his state had only flourished during periods of Seleukid division. Hence his new adventure.

Hyrkanos made no move to expand his territory until the Seleukid dynastic war had been going on for six years, and even then the attack was directed not at Seleukid territory but once more at the Samaritans. These were Seleukid subjects, to be sure, and they lived in a Seleukid city, which had, so it claimed, been 'founded' by Alexander the Great, but it is clear that it was because they were Samaritans that he launched the attack, and not as an action against the Seleukid state.[3] This may well have nonplussed the two Seleukid kings. Hyrkanos could claim to be acting as high priest in dealing with religious dissidents, not a concept very easy for Greek minds to accept. He was therefore proclaiming a new concept of statehood, that he as high priest in Judaea was also the chief of all the Jews wherever they lived, and that he could therefore claim the right to punish dissidents even if they lived in a Greek city. Again, this would have made no sense to any Greek or Macedonian. But the main point of Hyrkanos' timing is that he waited until the Seleukid king who had power locally, Kyzikenos, was much weakened, and that he therefore fully understood that by attacking the Samaritans in Samaria he would be seen as invading Seleukid territory, whatever his arguments in support of the action. Geographically one of Hyrkanos' aims was to expand to the north to get into direct touch with Galilee, where there was a considerable Jewish element in the population. Hyrkanos was an imperialist.

He laid siege to Samaria, though this took the form of a blockade rather than direct attacks, because the Judaean army did not have the necessary expertise to conduct a more active and professional siege. The process was thus a long-drawn-out affair. The population of the city consisted of Samaritans – the objects of Hyrkanos' wrath – and Samarians, who were the descendants of the Greco-Macedonians colonists; there is, interestingly, no indication of any dissension between these two elements; it is clear that they all understood that Hyrkanos aimed at conquest, and that the attack on the 'Samaritans' was merely an excuse. The city received some help from Kyzikenos, who controlled Ptolemais-Ake and Skythopolis, to west and east respectively of the city, but

Kyzikenos was driven off, and took refuge in Skythopolis; then he returned with a new army of 6,000 men which he had borrowed from Ptolemy IX Lathyros. It is perhaps relevant to point out here that another dynastic upheaval, amongst the Ptolemies, had developed at this time. Lathyros was driven out of Alexandria by his mother, Kleopatra III, leaving behind his sister-wife Selene and their children.[4] He appears to have taken refuge for a time in Seleukeia-in-Pieria (not yet independent) and eventually took over Cyprus, when his brother Ptolemy X Alexander had been summoned to Egypt. Kleopatra III was thus moving her children around as a means of maintaining her own authority and power.[5]

Lathyros clearly had a reasonable force under his command – at least 6,000 men (more were presumably left to hold Cyprus) – and his stay at Seleukeia left him open to suggestions, particularly since his former wife Kleopatra IV had earlier assisted Kyzikenos. Kyzikenos himself was by this time clearly the weaker of the two rival Seleukids, and so was keen to regain prestige by removing the Judaean threat to Samaria. Ptolemy's force appeared to be a useful supplement. Kyzikenos, with his own and Ptolemy's army, moved into Judaea in an attempt to induce the Judaean army to break off the siege/blockade of Samaria. It did not work, and the allies once more separated, Ptolemy going to Cyprus, Kyzikenos heading north, to Tripolis.[6]

It may be asked, why in all this long siege was there no battle? Kyzikenos had twice brought an army close to the besiegers, yet there is no record of any open fight. The answer is probably that by this time armies were too precious to risk in a battle, because any battle brought casualties, and armies were small enough by now not to be risked – the impoverishment of the kings' treasuries meant it was difficult for them to recruit more men. They were probably also by this time almost exclusively composed of mercenaries – the Judaean army was probably only partly so – and mercenaries might well not be too keen to be involved in a fight against more or less equal odds. And the Judaean army was not battle ready, as its later conduct shows.

For Kyzikenos, raising the siege of Samaria was a good deal less important than recovering control of other areas of Syria. What looked to the Jews, and Josephos, like great victories over the forces of the Seleukid king may actually have been withdrawals by Kyzikenos to cope with a more important matter elsewhere. When he went north, for example, it was probably to try to prevent the loss of Antioch – clearly more important than Samaria. He actually reached Tripolis, but by then Antioch had been lost.

He left behind a substantial force to continue to harass the besiegers, commanded by two generals, Kallimandros (who may have been the man who had shared Demetrios II's imprisonment in Parthia twenty years before), and Epikrates. Thus Hyrkanos' army only had to face a detachment of Kyzikenos' forces, but its presence will certainly have held up any progress in the siege. The purpose of the Seleukid force was mainly to protect other places, notably Skythopolis, whose territories will have been subjected to foraging raids, if not worse, by the besieging army, rather than to relieve the siege at Samaria. Kallimandros was killed in the fighting, and Epikrates is said to have sold his base in Skythopolis to Hyrkanos, though what Epikrates actually did was to accept money to leave; there is no evidence that Skythopolis ever fell to Hyrkanos.[7] The implication is that a peace agreement by which Hyrkanos would not attack Skythopolis had been made – but it also meant that Samaria had been abandoned. Further, such an agreement can only have been made with the permission of Kyzikenos, which suggests that he both required the money, and the forces which the agreement would release. The security of Skythopolis, however, was guaranteed.

The other price was Samaria. From the retirement of Epikrates' force the city was doomed. Hyrkanos could be assured that there would be no more interventions in the siege. After it had lasted a year, Hyrkanos forced the city's surrender. He is said to have physically destroyed it, though archaeological evidence suggests that its destruction was much less than total.[8] The site was reoccupied soon after, in a small way, and when it was reconstituted as a formal city half a century later, the same plan and layout was used, including the same street grid.[9] Josephos' description of the events is thus considerably distorted and exaggerated.

As to Skythopolis, Judaean control of the city is usually assumed, because of the Epikrates agreement, but it is unproven and unlikely. Epikrates is said by Josephos in one of his accounts to have betrayed the city to the Jews, but in another he said that the city's territory was overrun, but not that it was captured.[10] These are not necessarily wholly contradictory, but it is odd that there are no other references to Judaean control of the city. In 103 Alexander Iannai's army was driven past the city by that of Ptolemy IX Lathyros; if it had been under Judaean control, it is unlikely that Ptolemy would have left it behind him while facing a more numerous enemy – and if it had been under Judaean control Iannai's army could have taken refuge there. A little later the city was the scene of a meeting between Kleopatra III, who had pursued Ptolemy's army, and the defeated Alexander, and she was the hostess of the meeting.[11] Again there is no implication of Jewish control of the meeting, very much the reverse. Skythopolis was and remained a Greek city. Hyrkanos' payment to Epikrates was thus presumably simply for him to go away, and was no doubt used to pay his soldiers.

There must also be some doubt over the extent of Judaean control over Samaria. Normally it would be reasonable to assume that 'conquest' meant continuing control of the site. Yet if the city was destroyed, as Josephos says, there can have been little to control. (His description of the physical destruction excludes the interpretation that 'destroyed' was code for a political dissolution of the community; he clearly thought the city was dismantled physically.) The people who repopulated the theoretically demolished site would be survivors, or immigrants, perhaps Jews from Judaea, but it is not known which. Hyrkanos may have exercised some control over the community, as he clearly had a right to do, and it certainly ceased to be an obstacle between Judaea and Galilee, but the question of its annexation to Judaea must be left undecided.

The war for Samaria will have been exhausting for the Judaean state. Not only was the land subject to invasion and a ravaging by Kyzikenos' army, but the Judaean army had been occupied in the siege and the assorted operations around it for a full year, and perhaps more. Hyrkanos was the first of the Hasmonaeans to employ professional mercenary soldiers, paid for, according to Josephos, out of the proceeds of tomb robbing – though, contradicting himself not for the first time, he also points out that the tax regime Hyrkanos implemented had filled the treasury.[12] But it took more than a small force of professional troops to conduct a siege and Hyrkanos cannot have had many mercenaries; the Judaean soldiers who were the majority of his troops had no expertise in such warfare. Further, apart from the cost of paying for his army, both mercenaries and militia, he had to pay for the army of Epikrates to leave, and this may well have emptied the treasury. It would take some time for the small, rural, uncommercial Judaean state to recover from all these exertions.

Hyrkanos had attempted to get Rome to compel the return of Joppa and the other places he had asked for in 125. This was unsuccessful. (Why he should have thought Rome would bother is never explained.) He sent a second embassy to the city, whose date is unclear, except that it took place during Hyrkanos' reign. He asked that Kyzikenos be compelled to give up the places, so the embassy took place sometime after 113, when Kyzikenos first took control in the Palestinian area, but before Hyrkanos died in 104.[13] No doubt it was, as before, prompted by the weakening of the Seleukid government because of the dynastic war, and in the hope that someone else would do the hard work.

Kyzikenos was the Seleukid who had had control of much of the south since his arrival. He had held Ptolemais-Ake all through the war (though the dated coins of Ptolemais-Ake end in 108–107).[14] However, he had controlled Ashkelon for only a year, in 113–112 in the first rush of his success;[15] he regained control of Damascus in 108–107, and probably held it until 104–103, losing it then for only a year.[16] His intervention in the siege of Samaria also shows that he was in control of the south generally at that time, including Skythopolis.

Holding Ptolemais-Ake allowed Kyzikenos to dominate all the Palestinian lowlands from the southern border of Phoenicia (where Tyre was already independent) to the confines of Ashkelon, which adhered to Grypos for most of the war. Kyzikenos' control included Joppa (hence Hyrkanos' request), Dor, and Apollonia. He clearly also controlled Skythopolis until Epikrates' treaty, but that may well have meant that the city had become independent. Earlier he had been able to take refuge in that city, and Epikrates had used it as his base. According to Hyrkanos' embassy to Rome, Kyzikenos also held 'fortresses, harbours, and territory' which Hyrkanos claimed – that is, the lowlands and the coastal towns.

The use of the plural makes it clear that more than one fortress and more than one harbour were the objects of Hyrkanos' claims. Joppa and Gazara are the obvious candidates, with the only other possible harbours being Apollonia and Strato's Tower, neither of which had, so far, been subject to Jewish claims. Indeed, the whole phrase, and the embassy itself, looks very like a fishing expedition, to see just what the Romans might provide. The answer was, quite rightly, nothing. The embassy evoked no more than polite Roman attention, fair words, and absolutely no action from the Romans.[17]

As ever, Rome was not interested in Syria or Syrian affairs. If this message was received in the year before the attack on Samaria, in 109–108, when Kyzikenos had already lost Ashkelon and Damascus, it may have seemed a good moment to strike, either before Grypos conquered his rival, or before Kyzikenos recovered. But the fight for Samaria was long and difficult and exhausting, and at the end Kyzikenos still held most of the lowlands. Neither diplomacy nor warfare had had much effect – and the only success was the destruction of a Greek city.

On the other hand, this later embassy to Rome did elicit a repetition of the Senate's recognition of Judaean claims to independence. Friendship and alliance between Rome and Judaea were 'confirmed' though Rome was not, and never had been, prepared to do anything actively to gratify its ally's wishes, any more than Judaea could or would do anything to assist Rome; after all, there was nothing Judaea could do for Rome that it could not do better itself. But by encouraging Hyrkanos with words, the Senate was taking up a hostile stance towards both Kyzikenos and the Seleukid state, even if this had no practical effect.

Grypos' recognition of Seleukeia's independence had also involved his informing Rome of the change in its status. This was probably no more than a normal distribution of information about the change, and it would be up to the city itself to broadcast the news to other states. But maybe Grypos thought this might get him some support. The Senate, however, was quite capable of sending out contradictory messages; Grypos was no doubt disappointed in any hopes, just as was Hyrkanos.

Hyrkanos' hostility to Kyzikenos also implies his alignment with Grypos' cause, in which connection there was a curious issue of coins in Grypos' name from the Jerusalem mint dated to his twentieth year, that is 106–105.[18] Only a single specimen survives, or at least only one has been published, but the issue has some significance, showing as it does the probable Judaean political alignment with the legitimate Seleukid king – an ironic development and one which is a testimony to Hyrkanos' diplomatic pragmatism. That it was issued just after Hyrkanos' conflict with Kyzikenos and at a time when Kyzikenos still controlled parts of the south, was no doubt quite deliberate.

The conquest and destruction of the city of Samaria, in part the result of the Judaean animosity towards the Samaritans, was also part of the Judaean animosity towards Greek cities generally. This had been the basis of the original Maccabean revolt, and it was a continuing element in Hyrkanos' policy. The forced conversion of the Idumaeans in the south went along with the destruction of the Greek city in the north as clear signs that Judaea was an imperialist state, prepared to murder, massacre, and mutilate in its pursuit of empire. Yet it must have become clear during the obdurate resistance of the Samarians (not just the Samaritans) that such a brutal policy was not going to produce much extension of Judaean territory very soon. There were dozens of Greek cities in the lands round Judaea, and if each took a year to capture, as had Samaria, any Jewish empire would take a long time to accomplish. On the other hand, the removal of Samaria did open the way to a different method of expansion.

To the north, beyond the ruins of Samaria, there was another Jewish population. At least one of Hyrkanos' sons, Alexander, was fostered out to be brought up there.[19] It follows that Hyrkanos was accepted by the Jewish population there as having the authority which a high priest would expect. Without the need for a military campaign it is probable that Hyrkanos' authority now extended into this territory. Until then the area had been no doubt subject to the Seleukid governor based at Ptolemais-Ake, or perhaps to a sub-governor at Philoteria on the Sea of Galilee or at Samaria, which in the 160s had been the seat of a sub-governor.[20] In the weakened state of the Seleukid government this annexation of Galilee by Judaea was clearly possible, and may have been hardly disputed by Kyzikenos, preoccupied as he necessarily was by the need to fight for North Syria.

The war in the south had therefore largely sidelined Grypos, and had developed into a war between Kyzikenos and Hyrkanos. Grypos would be quite content with such a situation, since Kyzikenos' preoccupation there would reduce his ability to make any progress in the north. And indeed by losing Antioch, being unable to acquire Seleukeia, and losing Tripolis, it seems clear that Kyzikenos was in serious difficulties in the north. It also seems that the dynastic war was separating into two different wars, north and south. Not entirely, though, as the fact that Grypos held Ashkelon and recovered Damascus occasionally show, but the contests certainly developed differently.

The latest bout of Seleukid civil warfare thus took several years to have an effect beyond the kings and their armies, but the destruction of Samaria seems – the sources are poor – to have had wider repercussions. Those areas which already had some autonomy before 114–113 – Tyre, Arados, Judaea, Philadelphia, Edessa, Kommagene – were all only thinly hellenized regions and cities. In the warfare after 114–113 the first states which left the Seleukid grip were of a similar Semitic population and culture: Sidon and Tripolis were, like Tyre, at root Phoenician. But by 109–108 the first of the Greek cities were becoming detached. In the north Seleukeia–in–Pieria was, of all the cities of Syria, perhaps the last one which might be expected to claim its independence, the name-city of the founder of the dynasty, the burial place of the kings, a major port and city, a naval base, and the place of access to the sea for the royal city of Antioch.[21] Given this background, conspicuous loyalty to the dynasty might have been expected of the citizens. Yet they took advantage of the civil warfare to gain a greater degree of autonomy than before. And within a year or so of Seleukeia's separation, in the south, the city of Samaria, a Macedonian foundation dating from the time of Alexander the Great, had been captured and destroyed; and only one of the kings had made any attempt to rescue it, and that unsuccessfully. In different ways the failure and ineffectiveness of the kings had been all too clearly demonstrated.

It is clear that more influences were operating on the varied communities of Syria than simply the civil war between the Seleukid rivals. One aspect of their reactions was ethnico-religious: it is surely no accident that the earliest seceders, from the Jews of Jerusalem to the Phoenicians of the coastal cities to the Arabs of Osrhoene, were all lands or cities mainly inhabited by Semitic peoples. The Greco-Macedonians of the great cities were, perhaps instinctively, and certainly in practice, more loyal to the kings, and it is this attitude which makes Seleukeia's action so surprising and politically destabilizing to the whole kingdom and which makes the failure of the rescue of the people of Samaria such a blow to Greek morale. Some cities were menaced by Seleukid enemies, such as Damascus by the Ituraeans, the Palestinian coastal cities by Judaea, and this probably helped them to stay loyal even where they were basically Semitic- and Samaria, a mixed Samaritan and Greek city, had been conspicuously loyal, and had gone down to destruction for its loyalty.

The long continuation of the civil war, however, gradually introduced a new outlook. The land was divided between the rival kings for a much longer period than in earlier dynastic wars.[22] The longer such a division lasted, the more it would appear a new but normal condition, so that neighbours might feel that separation had become a natural condition. From 114–113, for example the southern Palestinian coast and much of the interior was controlled by Kyzikenos, but Ashkelon by Grypos; for at least a decade, Ashkelon was isolated from its hostile neighbours and had to rely on its own resources, helped presumably by a garrison provided by Grypos; it can have had little or no contact with the government centre of Koile Syria at Ptolemais-Ake, the nearest of Grypos' cities. Similarly Ptolemais and Damascus were under rival authorities for several years during the same time; they were separated also by the Ituraeans of the mountains, and by the Jews of Galilee. Inevitably these separations interrupted, even severed, contacts for lengthy periods, and the longer they lasted, the more they would become institutionalized.

One of the results was, fairly obviously, to increase uncertainty and insecurity. In the Transjordanian lands the city of Philadelphia had become a 'tyranny', under a family of rulers, though this is actually a fairly neutral term, meaning simply rule by one man, not necessarily oppressive, in this case at first Zenon Kotylas, then his son Theodoros. This was a sensible reaction when it was impossible to gain access to 'official' Seleukid support. The failure of Kyzikenos to rescue Samaria had a similar effect in the coastlands. He rushed off to the north, to Tripolis, away from his failure to rescue the city, and he does not seem ever to have returned to the south. The great city of Ptolemais-Ake was left, no doubt with a garrison of Kyzikenos' soldiers, essentially abandoned. Ashkelon went on producing Kyzikenos' coins for several years, but there is no sign there that the king was ever present. In between, two of the coastal cities, Dor and Strato's Tower, both useful small ports, came under the rule of another 'tyrant', a man called Zoilos.

Nothing is known of Zoilos' origins. His acquisition of power over the two towns must have taken place after the departure of Kyzikenos to the north in 108 or 107, and he is recorded as being in place by 104.[23] It seems reasonable to suppose that during this short three-year period the Seleukid position in the south was in the process of collapsing. The hostility of the Judaean state was palpable, and it cannot have been unknown that Hyrkanos still aimed to secure Joppa and Gazara and so the domination of the coastal area, if not other places as well. We may thus add Zoilos' territories to those which had shifted into independence. No others seem to have done so, yet, but neither Grypos nor Kyzikenos was present in the south after about 107, and the cities which professed loyalty to them were effectively left to themselves.

Despite all this, it is difficult to see that any serious damage had yet been done to the overall unity of most of the Seleukid state in Syria. The greater part of the land still acknowledged one or other of the two kings, who both claimed to be kings of the whole. From the borders of Egypt to the Taurus and the Euphrates, much of the state was largely intact. Most of the greater cities – Antioch, Apamaea, Laodikeia, Tarsos, Damascus, Ptolemais-Ake – were all still part of the state and acknowledged one or other of the Seleukids as king, and so were most of the small settlements and the rural areas. Those areas which had broken away were either marginal, like Judaea or the Ituraeans, or easily recoverable, like Zoilos' principality, or, as with the Phoenicians, were so economically dependent on the rest of Syria that their separation from the kingdom might in some cases be no more than tentative. The separation of Seleukeia, though, was a clear sign that worse would come if the war continued – and it did.

The next major change, which came in Palestine between 104 and 101, resulted in the final wrecking of the Seleukid position in the south. It came about through a complex interaction of the Seleukid civil war with the continuing Ptolemaic dynastic dispute and the ambitions of the Hasmonaean ruling family. The Seleukid civil war was at the root of the problem, for both of the kings now concentrated on attempting to maintain their positions in the north, and abandoned the south, so ambitious neighbours filled the void.

In 104 Hyrkanos of Judaea died. His son and successor, Judah-Aristoboulos, sent an armed raid northwards, commanded by his brother Antigonos, which encountered Ituraeans in Galilee.[24] These had moved in from the north. Aristoboulos is said to have forcibly converted them to Judaism, and he may well have been concerned with asserting and defending the Hasmonaean position in Galilee. The Galilean population was certainly part-Jewish before the conquest, so the process of Judaization there was already well under way.[25] As with Hyrkanos' conquest of Samaria, Aristoboulos could, if challenged, put forward a reasonably convincing ethnic and religious argument for his actions, so long as his premises were accepted.

The Judaean state went through an unpleasant and murderous succession crisis when Hyrkanos died. Out of his five sons only two survived; one, Absalom, declined any political role, and the other, Alexander Iannai, was elevated to the high priesthood by marrying his brother's widow, Salome. He, or perhaps his predecessor Aristoboulos, adopted the title of king, and coins were issued from the Jerusalem mint inscribed 'of King Alexander'. In so far as they can be dated, it seems that the earliest of his coins call him king, but whether these coins were issued at the start of his reign is by no means clear.[26] Comparatively few of his coins make the claim to the royal title, though others depict the royal diadem. He may have claimed the royal title only some years into his reign: his main title and position was always high priest, like his predecessors: 'king' was extra and possibly directed mainly at external powers, though it soon became established in Judaea.

It was more significant that Alexander rejected the old imperialist policy of brutality, massacre, and forced conversion in favour of the more usual methods of empire building, of conquest and the imposition of tribute. He left local non-Jewish communities autonomous so long as they remained peaceful and paid their taxes. It was, like the adoption of the royal title, a policy essentially identical with that of other neighbouring kingdoms. The Judaean state was therefore now on the way to becoming a normal Hellenistic kingdom, though there were deep internal currents which harked back to the old revolutionary and imperialist brutality, and these were liable to break the surface at times of crisis.

A claim to kingship in the Hellenistic world was normally made as a result of a military victory, preferably over another king, and Alexander's assumption of the royal title may be the result of events in Palestine in 103–101. This began with an attack by Alexander on Ptolemais-Ake, which took place almost as soon as he had inherited rule from his brother. The war developed into a complicated campaign by the rival claimants to the Ptolemaic throne, Ptolemy Lathyros and Ptolemy Alexander, with Kleopatra III deeply involved as usual. The whole sequence has been elucidated by the publication of Egyptian documents and by subsequent discussion, but the crucial Seleukid dimension has been ignored, for what has not been explored is why Alexander Iannai should have attacked Ptolemais-Ake in the first place.[27]

Judaean armies had a sorry record in warfare when facing properly organized, sizable, and well-commanded Hellenistic armies, and an even worse one in siege warfare. Alexander, a warrior by choice, if all too often unsuccessful, surely knew this. The poor record of the Judaean army was one reason why his father and brother had hired mercenaries. Despite this Alexander took his army through the Great Plain north of Judaea to besiege the greatest and best-fortified city in Palestine. The reason is usually ignored, the implication being that Alexander was a warrior, and that this is what warriors do, and he was a Jewish ruler and it was therefore natural for him to attack a non-Jewish city.[28] But there were closer, easier, and more tempting targets, and he could not really hope to take Ptolemais-Ake by himself.

The situation at Ptolemais-Ake had apparently not changed for several years. Kyzikenos had coined there in 110–109, but no dated coins had been produced in the city since then, though presumably Kyzikenos still held it.[29] Kyzikenos had lost control of Antioch and Tripolis, and he held no other major Syrian city, so Ptolemais-Ake was his last major urban base. Certainly it was critical for his future. If he lost that city, he would effectively lose the war.

Meanwhile Alexander Iannai's father Hyrkanos had consistently taken the side of Grypos in the civil war. The obvious explanation for Alexander's attack on Ptolemais, therefore, is that it was another move in the Seleukid war; and it is clear from Josephos' comments that the context was that of a wider campaign. Ptolemais-Ake had as allies the city of Gaza, Zoilos of Dor and Strato's Tower, and perhaps Sidon, plus, of course, Kyzikenos himself, who was unable to assist for the present, but whose presence in the north prevented Grypos from joining in.[30]

Alexander's forces defeated the city's troops, shut them up inside, and formed a blockade. The support which the city received from Zoilos and Gaza prompted Alexander to detach some of his forces to ravage their territories, judging by their complaints.[31] Local minds must have turned to memories of the treatment of Samaria by Hyrkanos only a few years before, for it cannot have been clear yet that Alexander's policy of conquest was different from his father's.

The allies thereupon appealed to Ptolemy IX Lathyros in Cyprus, another ally of Kyzikenos. He landed a force south of Ptolemais and drove Alexander's forces away. Kyzikenos' local forces therefore, clearly succeeded at Ptolemais where they had failed at Samaria – how much of the allied army was Seleukid and how much Ptolemaic is not known. Alexander stood to fight just inside Galilee, but retreated further when Ptolemy captured and sacked the town of

Asophis.[32] Ptolemy is quoted as running the campaign; he may have taken over because his part of the allied army was the largest contingent, and perhaps the best. Alexander marched east as far as the River Jordan, a march which Ptolemy was able to follow without hindrance. Alexander got across the river, but Ptolemy also got his army over and inflicted a catastrophic defeat on the Judaean army.[33]

Ptolemy was then able first to invade and ravage Judaea and afterwards to put his army into Ptolemais-Ake, on whose behalf he had been fighting. His adventures and successes had been watched with increasing alarm in Egypt, however, and he was then in turn attacked by an army out of Egypt, commanded by Kleopatra III and her younger son Ptolemy Alexander. They were convinced that now that he had a foothold in Palestine, Ptolemy Lathyros would use it to attack them in Egypt. In this they were surely right. Alexander Iannai therefore made an alliance with Kleopatra at a meeting at Skythopolis, where Kleopatra had marched in pursuit of Lathyros.[34] It was an obvious alliance to make, both parties were enemies of Ptolemy Lathyros and of Kyzikenos. Kleopatra had just sent her daughter Selene to Grypos as his new wife as a way of emphasizing that aspect of the alliance.[35] This finally fulfilled, in very different circumstances, the original marital plan of Kleopatra Thea. Ptolemy Lathyros was thus deprived of another wife by the political whims of Kleopatra III.

Alexander's forces were clearly outclassed. They would only get in the way of Kleopatra's forces, so now he kept away from the coast. Ptolemaic campaigning went on for a year or longer. He spent that time in a ten-month siege of the town of Gadora (not Gadara), and then attacked Amathos, a castle where Theodoros, the son of Zenon, ruler of Philadelphia, kept his treasure. He took the town, then the castle, but then suffered an immediate defeat by Theodoros, losing the castle again, and presumably the treasure.[36]

By that time the fighting on the coast had died away. Zoilos had been eliminated, allegedly by Ptolemy Lathyros at Alexander's instigation,[37] and Ptolemais-Ake had been captured by Kleopatra's forces, suffering much damage in the process.[38] It then presumably reverted to Kyzikenos' control when the Ptolemaic forces left, but this can only have been a nominal control. There can hardly have been any of Kyzikenos' forces or officials left in the city by this time. Lathyros had wintered in Gaza, but then evacuated his forces back to Cyprus.[39]

When all these Ptolemaic forces had left, Alexander Iannai turned once more to the coast. The rest having eliminated each other, he was, by default, now the strongest military force in the Palestinian area. He attacked Gaza, abandoned by Lathyros, first taking Raphia and Anthedon, respectively small towns south and north of the city, by which he isolated and then laid siege to Gaza for a year, before finally capturing it.[40]

These campaigns, be it noted, were conducted by Ptolemaic armies – two of them – and by a Judaean army which launched attacks on every neighbouring state. At no time in this crisis in Palestine, where the warfare ranged from Ptolemais-Ake to Gaza and east to Philadelphia, were any Seleukid forces involved, unless the garrison of Ptolemais-Ake was involved, and unless Ptolemy Lathyros was accompanied by some of Kyzikenos' people – but none are attested. It is evident that by the end of this episode no real Seleukid authority was left in the region. This is emphasized by the sieges of Ptolemais and Gaza. At Ptolemais the question arose as to whether to admit the army of Ptolemy Lathyros. At first the general opinion was in favour, but then a local politician called Demainetos argued against it, and carried the day.[41] At Gaza similarly, the defence against Alexander's attack was led by Apollodotos, the *strategos tou Gazaion*, 'commander of the Gazaians'. After the siege had lasted a year, he was challenged for power in the city by his brother Lysimachos, who led a coup in which Apollodotos was killed. Lysimachos then brought Alexander and his Judaean army into the city. The initially peaceful occupation degenerated into a sack in which the councillors were massacred and the city was said to have been destroyed, though how extensive such destruction was is unclear.[42]

In these two instances there is no sign that the cities had any Seleukid forces present, and in the discussion at Ptolemais there was no reference to any Seleukid authority. At Gaza neither Apollodotos nor Lysimachos had any allegiance to a Seleukid king. Similarly, Kleopatra III was able to establish herself and her forces in Skythopolis, which had been Kyzikenos' city five years before. The nearest Seleukid presence was in Damascus, which at one point Ptolemy Alexander aimed to attack, but did not apparently reach.[43] The Ptolemaic purpose in campaigning in Palestine was presumably to attempt to reconstitute their old province of Koile Syria – but, like the Seleukids, they were also at the same time indulging in their own dynastic war. The result, not surprisingly, was that none of them gained anything. The fragments were mopped up by Alexander Iannai, whose army was still incapable of capturing any fortified city or of winning a battle.

The Seleukid influence in this southern region was not entirely extinguished, and in the next thirty years occasional Seleukid kings and armies arrived and campaigned there. But they never stayed long and were unwelcome when they appeared. The region had in effect ceased to be part of the Seleukid kingdom when it proved to be possible for non-Seleukid armies – Judaean and Ptolemaic

– to campaign all over the region without any Seleukid interference, that is, by, in round terms, 100 BC.

The region had thus largely become composed of independent states. The main one was now Judaea, geographically the largest, and the earliest to go for independence. But further east the tyrants of Philadelphia had expanded and gained control of Gerasa, and the Nabataean kingdom had become firmly established. The Gazans had appealed to the Nabataean king for help during the Judaean siege; they did not get any but it is a sign of the developing local animosities – as is the attack by Alexander Iannai on Amathos, a town and treasury of Theodoros of Philadelphia. But Judaea was only able to expand into the coastlands because Alexander's new policy renounced destruction, except, as at Gaza, in the face of obdurate and long-standing resistance. The south had therefore by 100 BC not only shrugged off the Seleukid state, but had become a set of independent kingdoms and cities. In large part this was because of the effective abdication of the Seleukids and their concentration on their dynastic war.

Chapter 12

Survival in the North (103–88 BC)

The evaporation of Seleukid authority in Palestine was due in the main, of course, to the fact that the two royal contenders were concentrating, in so far as their weakened strength allowed, on seeking power in North Syria, so allowing local and outside powers to intrude, and compelling loyalist cities to become independent through lack of royal support. The north was a much more important region in terms of wealth and population and therefore in terms of military resources, than was Palestine. Of the great cities of the kingdom, only one, Ptolemais-Ake, was in Palestine – and that had acted independently in the face of the Ptolemaic threat. There were, by contrast, four great cities in the north, together with a large number of lesser cities in Syria and Kilikia. Clearly the two kings had abandoned Palestine to its quarrelling neighbours because there was little there to help them. This is not to say that either of the contenders had abandoned their claims to rule in the south; Damascus, for instance, continued to be held by a succession of Seleukids for decades; no doubt, if asked, both kings would say that they would return to sort out the south when they had vanquished their opponent and gained control of the north.

It would seem that Antiochos VIII Grypos maintained control of Antioch without a break from 109–108 onwards. He also clearly held Tarsos in Kilikia from 108–107 and Ashkelon from the year before. Damascus was taken from him by Kyzikenos in 108–107, recovered by 104–103, but lost again by 102–101.[1] All this is according to the coins. With regard to other Syrian cities, however, we are mainly in the dark. It seems likely that, had Kyzikenos controlled any of them he would have minted coins in some of them – at Laodikeia, for instance, or Apamaea, where mints had existed earlier. We may tentatively assume that Grypos held most of these; his mint at Antioch would supply the needs of all North Syria without difficulty. In wider terms Grypos married Selene in 103, which also brought him some Ptolemaic forces as reinforcement, but that was the year when her mother Kleopatra III began her campaign in Palestine, so it is unlikely that she had much military strength to spare.[2] Whatever help Grypos received was enough to keep him fighting, and so to prevent any revival by

Kyzikenos. It seems clear from the limited sources at our disposal that Grypos was in control of much more territory than Kyzikenos and that he should have been able to bring the dynastic war to an end, but failed to do so.

One of the by-products of the dynastic wars among both the Ptolemies and the Seleukids was the growth of piracy in the Eastern Mediterranean. This was fuelled by the demand for slaves in Italy and Sicily, where a large part of the wealth of the Mediterranean world was now concentrated.[3] The wars prevented the kings from attending to the pirates, who were based on all coasts but especially in the region to the west of Seleukid Kilikia, the area called Rough Kilikia, which had many small ports and bays where pirates could base themselves, and mountain areas where they could retreat to if menaced. This was an area which Ptolemies and Seleukids had long contested, but the latter had in effect been forced out by a clause in the peace treaty with Rome in 188, by which time the Ptolemaic naval power had decayed. More drastic might have been the order to destroy all Seleukid warships except ten small vessels, though it is likely that the Seleukid navy was re-established a short time later – if the destruction of ships in Syria actually took place.

Whether the kings would have bothered about the piracy if they were not fighting each other is not certain, but every Seleukid king, if at peace, was more concerned with Ptolemaic policy and the Parthian menace than problems at sea. If any Eastern Mediterranean power had the opportunity to suppress pirates it was the Ptolemies, who had major naval bases in Cyprus and at Alexandria. Ptolemaic kings were, of course, as often at each others' throats as were the Seleukids – and the two were as often fighting each other as well – but they never seem to have paid any attention to piracy. (In fact, of course, the pirates were at times seen as useful, for they could be hired as mercenaries when an army was needed. In the same way that Rome tolerated them because they supplied slaves by kidnapping free people, so the kings tolerated them as a useful military and naval resource, to be tapped in an emergency and ignored in peacetime.)

In 102 Rome at last assumed some responsibility for the problem, and the propraetor M. Antonius campaigned along the south coast of Asia Minor, supposedly suppressing the pirates. He was only briefly successful, since the pirates merely disappeared until he had gone away.[4] But the Seleukid kings must have been concerned as he moved steadily eastwards towards them. This was the first time a Roman force had advanced so far to the east. It was a new threat from the west, reminiscent of Alexander Balas' hypnotic watching of Demetrios II, or of Grypos watching for Kyzikenos' attack. Antonius reached as far east as Side in Pamphylia (where the trans-Asia Minor Via Aquillia terminated), and perhaps a little further, but his force was actually quite small, and consisted mainly of ships and men contributed by ports of the Aegean and Asia Minor. He was no real threat to the Seleukids, even to the exhausted kings, though they must have been relieved when he turned away and returned to Rome, claiming success.

Grypos' support from Kleopatra III expired with her death in 101, if it had even been of any size. The two Seleukid kings were then effectively without any external support, and, being therefore dependent on their own resources, the long stalemate simply continued. Yet this was only a stalemate between these kings; other participants were unaffected except that they could take advantage of the kings' preoccupation with each other. Just as in Palestine local leaders emerged, so in the north there were those who were weary of the long continuing indecisive warfare, and abandoned the kings. Antiochos VIII Grypos was eventually abandoned by his general, a man called Herakleon, who had attempted to toughen up the discipline of the army and give it a stronger *esprit de corps* by, among other means, communal meals of a very basic content. In 97–96 Herakleon turned on Grypos and assassinated him, presumably because the king was unwilling to make the same effort as his soldiers – he had the reputation of being luxurious and lazy, though this may be merely a historian's assumption, or hostile propaganda picked up by the later historians.[5] Herakleon's military improvements, if such they were, suggest that one of the reasons that the dynastic war had continued so long was military slackness; his killing of Grypos indicated, as is only to be expected, that he learned that such slackness emanated from the top.

Herakleon's personal purpose is not known. It is assumed by modern authorities that he aimed to take the throne, but no ancient source says so, and he did not follow up the murder with a coup.[6] In fact his ultimate purpose can only have been to end the dynastic war. By eliminating one of the contenders he certainly achieved this, but only briefly. Kyzikenos swiftly seized Antioch and so seemed to have won the long contest. This may or may not have been Herakleon's intentions. Kyzikenos also married Grypos' widow Selene, which was certainly an improvement on the reciprocal murders of her sisters. (He thus finally achieved the marital plan of his mother, Kleopatra Thea, but in very different circumstances than those she may have envisaged.) This marriage may well have annoyed Ptolemy Lathyros in Cyprus, for he had been married to Selene until forcibly separated by Kleopatra III, and the forced divorce certainly angered him. Kleopatra had died at the hands of Ptolemy X Alexander in 101, and Alexander had then swiftly married Kleopatra Berenike III, the daughter of Ptolemy Lathyros and Kleopatra IV.[7] Apart from Berenike, the only other eligible Ptolemaic female was now Selene, but her marriage first to Grypos and then to Kyzikenos kept her out of Lathyros' grasp. These marriages in effect kept the dynastic disputes separate from each other.

Kyzikenos' 'victory' was almost at once challenged by two of Grypos' sons.[8] The eldest, Seleukos IV, immediately took up the banner of his father, beginning, so it seems, in the Kilikian cities, where his coins were minted at Seleukeia-on-the-Kalykadnos – a huge production – Tarsos, and Elaeusa.[9] These coins helped to finance his first army, with which he attacked and defeated Kyzikenos in 95, who was either killed in the fighting or executed after capture.[10] It is very curious that Seleukos was able to raise enough money for an army at short notice whereas his father and his uncle had clearly been strapped for cash for the previous several years. It may well be that Ptolemy Lathyros was sufficiently annoyed with Kyzikenos that he was willing to subsidize Seleukos to attack him.

The background to this suggestion is the fact that Ptolemy Lathyros had assisted another of Grypos' sons, Demetrios III, to seize power at Damascus. This was one of the few cities which Kyzikenos had been able to hold for any length of time, and the move seems to have taken place even before the arrival of Seleukos VI in Kilikia, that is, while Kyzikenos still ruled, for Demetrios' coins were being issued from the Damascus mint in 97–96.[11] So the alliance of Grypos and Ptolemy Lathyros and later with Grypos' sons, may well have continued after Grypos' murder. The dual move in the period against Kyzikenos following his seizure of Antioch came therefore from both north and south, from Kilikia and from Damascus, and the seizure of Damascus first will no doubt have distracted him from what was happening in Kilikia. It was Seleukos who succeeded in capturing Antioch and in removing Kyzikenos, and this was presumably the plan.

The result of all this was the final removal of both of the contending half-brothers at long last, and the installation of Seleukos VI at Antioch and Demetrios III at Damascus as joint kings. (It has been assumed that these two were rivals, but there is no record of them in dispute, and it is better to see them as cooperating.) Yet all was still not well, for they had other competitors. Herakleon survived, and retreated to his home city of Beroia, where he established his independent rule, thus separating off one more city from the main kingdom. His principality expanded eastwards, to include the old city of Hierapolis and a town called Heraklea.[12]

For the present, however, from 96–95 for a couple of years, there was something like peace in the kingdom. Herakleon seems to have been tolerated, or was perhaps too strong to be attacked, and Seleukos VI and Demetrios III ruled in Antioch and Damascus respectively. But in the year after Seleukos' success, 95, another Roman praetor arrived in the neighbourhood. This was L. Cornelius Sulla, who was sent to install a new king in Kappadokia. In the process he held a conference with an ambassador of the Parthian King Mithradates II. The Roman arrival in eastern Asia Minor was the result of wars with Mithradates VI of Pontos, whose repeated attacks had begun to provoke a steady Roman expansion of effort in the east. So the great western power was at last approaching Syria; there had been two expeditions in the last decade, even if Antonius was using Greek auxiliaries and Sulla was only a single praetor with his suite. At the same time, there is no still no sign that Rome took any real interest in Syrian affairs.

Sulla's conference with the Parthian envoy indicated that the two powers had now made direct contact for the first time. In that meeting on the banks of the Euphrates in Armenia, the representatives of the two states which dominated the world from Spain to the borders of India discussed affairs. It is usually alleged that Sulla, and Rome, did not realize how large and powerful Parthia really was, though this is difficult to credit. Everyone in the Near East knew how big Parthia was, and had a good idea of its military strength ever since the defeat and death of Antiochos VII thirty years before. Parthia's power will have been known to the many Romans who were living in Asia Minor, and Sulla, as an intelligent man, will have done his research before the meeting; it is not reasonable to believe that he was ignorant of the power of the kingdom he was negotiating with, any more than it is believable that the Parthian king did not realize the power of the Roman Republic. In fact, Sulla was essentially grandstanding, hoping to impress his home audience at Rome, and making sure that everyone understood his gain in prestige – and this could only be effective if the Romans generally knew that Parthia was a Great Power.

This was, of course, largely bluff, and the bluffing was conducted on both sides. Both Rome and Parthia were distinctly ramshackle states in their organization, regularly liable to collapse into civil war, or to be distracted by some distant problem. On the other hand, they were both rich, powerful, and well-armed, and both were proud. Rome's internal troubles were plain for all to see, yet her praetors were still able to operate in Asia Minor, and to claim equality with kings – though the kings may not have agreed, nor even realized what the Romans meant.[13] Parthia's internal and external troubles were even more distracting, and Mithradates II was getting old, yet one of his satraps was able to intervene in Syria shortly afterwards with some success. For Syria, Parthia was closer than Rome and perhaps more immediately dangerous.

Mithradates II had succeeded in driving back the nomad invaders from his eastern borders, and in establishing an ascendancy over the nomads, in recovering the western territories, and in dominating a series of local rulers in the several parts of the kingdom. The symbol of his success in these endeavours was the title 'king of kings' (*shahanshah*) which he took in 110–109. This was a literal description of his position, for the kingdom included many minor kings. This was clearly a success for him, but also demonstrated that the Parthian state was one which was barely held together by an exceptionally able king, and no guarantee could be forthcoming that it would later continue as a single polity.[14]

Mithradates had a celebratory relief carved in the cliff at Bisitun, alongside reliefs of Darius I the Akhaimenid and the Seleukid relief of Herakles celebrating the victory of the Seleukid satrap Kleomenes.[15] He is identified as *shahanshah* (the names are in Greek) and he is flanked by three governors, including Gotarzes the satrap of satraps, that is, the viceroy of Babylonia (rendered by the Babylonian Diarist as 'the general who is above the four generals'). This is, therefore, another indication of the lack of essential unity in the kingdom, where the king of kings, apart from presiding over a set of semi-independent kingdoms was also regarded as no more than the first among equals in a group of satraps.

Mithradates had not confined himself to moderating internal affairs. Advances had been made in the east, where this was a necessity for defensive purposes, and in the west he expanded from Babylonia to Adiabene on the Tigris, and to the Seleukid city of Dura-Europos on the Euphrates, halfway from Seleukeia-on-the-Tigris to Syria, which came under Parthian control in about 113, according to an argument based on the coins found in the excavations there.[16] However, it is not known how deliberate was this spread to the west; the emergence of Adiabene as a subordinate kingdom may have been no more than a precautionary acceptance of Parthian supremacy. But it seems that Dura-Europos was conquered in a deliberate move; its geographical situation made it a useful forward defensive post for Babylonia, and so Parthian expansion would be a sensible defensive move. (It seems likely that Dura's original foundation, by Seleukos I, had been for the same purpose.) Further west it is also possible that a king of Edessa, called Fradhasht, who had an Iranian name, was a Parthian puppet, though it seems unlikely that a Parthian thrust could have reached as far west as Edessa as early as 115 when he became king.[17] Sometime after

110 Mithradates became involved further north in Armenia. At some point he fought King Artavasdes and, having won, took Artavasdes' son Tigranes into his court as a hostage to ensure future peace.[18]

This all rather suggests that Mithradates had been conducting a series of cautious moves westwards, but moving only as occasion offered, or as a response to a threat – very much in the same way that Rome was expanding eastwards. Mithradates' predecessors, notably Phraates II, had apparently had visions of taking over the whole of the Seleukid kingdom, and Mithradates was not free of such ambitions; as well as taking the old Akhaimenid title of *shahanshah*, he proclaimed himself the descendant of the Akhaimenid Great King Artaxerxes II.[19] Combined, these sentiments imply a Parthian political programme of 'restoring' the old Middle Eastern empire of the Akhaimenids and that of the first Seleukids. Snapping up occasional cities and small kingdoms in the west would be an acceptable part of the programme, particularly as there was a constant threat of trouble on the eastern frontier. How far this 'ideology' was shared by the Parthians outside the court of Mithradates II is unknown, but it may be presumed that it did not extend very far in his time though it revived occasionally in later centuries.

This was the Parthian situation when Sulla met Mithradates' envoy Orobazos at the River Euphrates in Armenia, and made a treaty with him. Orobazos was supposedly executed later by Mithradates for allowing Sulla to claim equality, though this is only stated in Roman sources, and is likely to be a Roman invention – Rome was never likely to accept equality of status with any other power, and assumed the same with Parthia. The terms of the treaty were ratified at Rome,[20] and the Parthians thirty years later claimed that they were still in force[21] – which rather contradicts the story of Orobazos' execution. The precise terms of the agreement are not known, except in one detail, in that each side agreed to refrain from crossing the Euphrates.[22]

This was presumably a provision which applied only to that part of the river which flowed through Eastern Anatolia, the area which was in question between Sulla and Orobazos. It may in fact have been no more than a military agreement for the moment, for Sulla had clashed with some Armenians earlier, and would be annoyed to find he was fighting a much greater power. Sulla's main task had been to see to the installation of Ariobarzanes as king of Kappadokia; Mithradates' concern at the time was to ensure the installation of his protégé Tigranes on an Armenian throne; the treaty thus only concerned the boundary between these client states. Later the Parthians chose to interpret it, for their own immediate purposes, as referring to the lower course of the Euphrates in Syria as well – even though on other occasions they had disregarded it. If Orobazos really was executed by Mithradates when he brought the treaty back, it was because the terms of the treaty restricted Parthian ambitions in Asia Minor, which hardly stopped at the Euphrates. Yet by claiming its continuing validity a generation later, the Parthians obviously accepted it at the time of its negotiation.

Nor do we need to assume that either side was serious about holding to the treaty. Such documents are usually superseded by later events after a fairly short time, and are simply a means of dealing with an immediate problem, reflecting the political and military situation at the time of their making. Mithradates of Parthia could not expect to be restrained from meddling in the future in the lands west of the Euphrates, in Asia Minor or Syria, because of a treaty dealing with a pair of client states; nor, in the event, did either Rome or Parthia treat the Euphrates as their automatic limit at any time. If that river actually became their mutual boundary later, it was because of later events, not because of Sulla's treaty. And at the time of the treaty, Syria was of only marginal interest to either of the powers.

The direct rule of both Romans and Parthians was actually nowhere near the Euphrates at the time. Rome had a series of client states in Asia Minor, but did not rule directly outside its Asian province; Parthia had moved no further west than Dura-Europos. Between them was a shatter zone of small states stretching from the Black Sea to the Sahara Desert, many of them fragments of the collapsed Seleukid kingdom. Some of these were within the reach of the Parthians, others of the Romans. And in the centre were the Syrian and Egyptian kingdoms which were the only truly independent states left. At the time of the meeting in Armenia (of which there is no sign that either noticed) the two monarchies were temporarily at peace, both internally and with each other. This did not last.

Mithradates II, presumably because he wanted the region to be more peaceful in the near presence of Rome, at about this time installed his ward Tigranes as king in Armenia. This would ensure a stable government in a distant region. Mithradates took, as payment, 'seventy valleys';[23] Tigranes was no doubt intended to be another of Mithradates' client kings, but he was too ambitious to be a subordinate. Almost at once, he took over the minor Armenian kingdom of Sophene,[24] and so his western boundary therefore ran along the east bank of the Euphrates, and he faced Roman-dominated Kappadokia to his west, and Kommagene and Osrhoene to his south. The vigour of the new ruler suggested that Mithradates had another powerful subordinate or a tiger by the tail.

The period 97–95 was thus a busy time in the Syrian region. A clear-out of the old feuding Seleukid kings, a meeting of Romans and Parthians for the first time, a new Armenian king showing vigour and ambition, meant that the shake-up in the region presaged more developments. In fact, as it happened, both the Romans and the Parthians turned away and became deeply involved in other affairs, so that the Near East was left to itself for the next generation.

The key to understanding the next decade in Seleukid history seems to be to appreciate that the main element was family loyalty among the children of Antiochos Grypos. He had six children, five sons and a daughter, by his first wife, Tryphaina. (He had none by Selene.) They had all been born before 112, when Tryphaina was killed, so when Grypos himself was killed, in 97–96, the youngest was at least 16 years old, and the eldest was in his mid-twenties. Two of the sons, Seleukos VI and Demetrios III, the eldest and the fourth-born, had acted as soon as their father was dead, and succeeded in removing Kyzikenos. Two other sons, twins called Antiochos XI and Philip I, seem to have accompanied Seleukos in Kilikia and were with him in his capture of Antioch. The last son, another Antiochos XII does not appear for some time; he was apparently the youngest and was perhaps also with Seleukos.[25] The daughter, Laodike, with the attached epithets Thea Philadelphos, was married to Mithradates I of Kommagene – who succeeded his father as king in 96 – an interesting development in that this implies full Seleukid recognition of that kingdom's independence.[26] The marriage of royal daughters into Asia Minor kingdoms had a long tradition among the Seleukids; at least Laodike was not married off to a succession of brothers. But the marriage enabled later Kommagenian kings to insist on their Seleukid ancestry, clearly a matter of pride to them and a mark of distinction long after the Seleukid dynasty died out.

There was, however, also another member of the extended Seleukid family. Antiochos Kyzikenos had a son by his first wife, whose name is not known, and who was abandoned when he married Kleopatra IV. He was another Antiochos (X), and had survived his father, apparently being out of Syria at the time of his death – another Seleukid tradition – as a way of protecting the life of a son, but it was also as a means of projecting a civil war into the future. He was at least 20 years old, for his parents had parted in 114 or before.[27] The immediate result of the death of Kyzikenos was that the son arrived in Syria to claim his father's throne, though he must have been some distance away (probably in Greece, the usual place of Seleukid exile) since Seleukos VI and Demetrios III easily beat him into the country. Antiochos X therefore began at Arados, which was an independent state, but from which it was safe to prospect his chances, and whence he could send out agents to recruit for him.[28] Meanwhile the victorious Seleukos VI's behaviour at Antioch is described as violent and tyrannical, and he became thoroughly unpopular; it may well have been the only way he could stamp his authority on the city and defend his position, for he was subjected also to the intrigues of Antiochos X, for whom Antioch was a prime target.[29] Seleukos ruled, it seems, for the best part of three years in the city,[30] but in 94–93 BC Antiochos X was able to come out of Arados, gather enough support, and drive Seleukos out of Antioch and back into Kilikia.[31] Seleukos attempted to tax the city of Mopsuhestia – and no doubt other places as well – in his preparations for his return to Antioch. This provoked a riot, which resulted in his death in the burning of the palace in the city.[32]

This all took place in 93–92, according to the new interpretation of the coin evidence. The old suggestion was that Seleukos VI had reigned in Antioch for only a short time, and that Antiochos X replaced him briefly, then Seleukos returned only to be driven out and then killed in Kilikia. Antiochos X returned, again briefly, and was then driven out by Demetrios III from Damascus.[33] The durations of the various reigns have now been called into question by the statistical calculations based on coin production. The changes, however, are only juggling with the dates; the succession of the reigns of the kings at Antioch remains much the same.

One of the conclusions to be drawn from this period (from the death of Kyzikenos in 97–96) is that the loyalty of the Syrian cities to the Seleukid cause had been much weakened. Antioch was not willing to accept Seleukos VI's firm government, nor was Mopsuhestia willing to pay him higher taxes; Beroia and Hierapolis seceded readily enough under Herakleon (who founded a minor dynasty). Herakleon's charges of laziness in the king and of decadence in the population, which were reported by the historian Poseidonios and which were taken up by the later sources, may be translated into the unwillingness of the population to continue to pay their taxes to a largely incompetent but greedy set of rulers, whose only purpose was to fight a civil war which they were not winning. That is, the population was progressively resigning from the struggle.

Antiochos X, having driven out Seleukos VI, ruled in North Syria, and he consolidated his position by marrying his stepmother Selene.[34] This union, of course, has caused much mingled mirth and outrage, ancient and modern (the historians are uniformly misogynist) though why it should do so after so many sibling and uncle-niece marriages in the families of both partners is not clear. But this did not much help him politically. Demetrios III still held Damascus, which seems to have been renamed 'Demetrias' about this time. In Kilikia,

Seleukos VI's position was inherited by his younger twin brothers, Antiochos XI and Philip I, who seem to have been with him all along. They became joint kings, Antiochos apparently having some precedence.[35] Presumably taking over the command of Seleukos' old forces, they attacked and sacked Mopsuhestia to avenge him,[36] and then went on to contest North Syria with Antiochos X; in the subsequent fighting Antiochos XI was killed.[37] Philip was then joined by Demetrios III from Damascus, and together they fought Antiochos X, who was able to defend his position for a time.

Antiochos X became involved in an external war, by going to the assistance of 'Laodike, queen of the Samenians', who was fighting the Parthians.[38] The location of the Samenians is not clear, but must be supposed to be in the Syrian Desert east or south of the Euphrates, either in Syria or in Mesopotamia. Antiochos was presumably at that moment free of any fighting with his cousins, having perhaps temporarily driven them out. This helps to confirm the conclusion drawn from the quantities of coins produced, whose numbers suggest that Antiochos had a reign of three or four years at Antioch in his second term.[39] He therefore seems to have been reacting to a new Parthian advance westwards, either along the Euphrates upstream from Dura-Europos, or through the Mesopotamian steppe from the Tigris. He was thus acting as a Seleukid king in Syria should, by fighting against the encroachment from the east.

There is another version, which is relayed by Eusebios, that Antiochos was defeated by his cousins and then fled to seek refuge with the Parthians.[40] Yet another version, in Appian, has him surviving in Syria for some years, until he was driven out by the Armenian King Tigranes, which would therefore have him hiding from his enemies for up to twenty years.[41] Neither of these versions have much credibility, and it is best to accept the version of Josephos with the modification that he has rather reduced Antiochos' reign from three or four years (in his second reign) to about one.

But there is another aspect of these contradictory stories. Such stories suggest that Antiochos had captured the imaginations of the Syrians, and that they retailed stories and rumours about him – but only after his death. The story of his fleeing to the Parthians might suggest that he might return at the head of an army; the story of him hiding in Syria from his enemies also suggests that it was hoped, again, that he would return. They are versions of the King Arthur myth, and they also suggest that the Syrians had a bad conscience about him, perhaps not having given him the support he asked for. They are also the sort of stories which develop long after the subject is dead.

Antiochos X died, or at least ceased to rule, in about 89 BC, according to the coin statistical calculations. Demetrios III succeeded him at Antioch, moving up from Damascus to join Philip I. Demetrios' base at Damascus had lasted from 97–96 until Antiochos X's death. He had controlled the city and had defended it against its surrounding enemies, for it was the target of both the Ituraeans from the mountains to the west and north, and the Nabataeans from the southern desert. Demetrios was also at one point called in by a rebel Jewish faction to fight Alexander Iannai of Judaea; Alexander was beaten in a battle (as usual) near Shechem, in which his mercenary forces were destroyed, but the fact that the most rigorous anti-Hellenic Jewish faction had called in a Seleukid army to fight the Jewish high priest led to a revulsion of sentiment in Judaea in Alexander's favour. (There had been a desultory civil war for some years.[42]) Demetrios' army also suffered heavy casualties in the battle. He withdrew – 'fled', Josephos says[43] – though it is more convincing to assume he had received the news from the north of the death of Antiochos X, which permitted him to seize control of Antioch. He minted coins there, at Damascus, and at Seleukia-in-Pieria.[44]

Demetrios III therefore had now reunited all the parts of Syria which had been ruled by Seleukid kings in the past few years, though the situation of Philip (the older of the two brothers) is not clear. At least they were free of a threat from a son of Kyzikenos. Inevitably Demetrios turned at once to recover the separated territories – one of which was presumably Seleukeia-in-Pieria, since he minted coins in the city. To the east of Antioch the newest and most urgent of these separated lands was the principality of Straton, the son of Herakleon, who ruled in Beroia and two nearby towns. This is presented by Josephos as an attack by Demetrios on his brother Philip, but the fact that Philip was in Beroia when Demetrios laid siege to the city does not mean that he was Demetrios' target.[45] There is no sign of any earlier hostility between them. The assumption is always that the Seleukids fought each other, but since the deaths of Grypos and Kyzikenos, the fighting had in fact been between Antiochos X, the son of Kyzikenos, and the several sons of Grypos. At no point, until the siege of Beroia in 88, had there been any suggestion of a conflict among Grypos' sons. Seleukos VI and Demetrios III had clearly supported each other against Kyzikenos, Antiochos XI and Philip I had ruled as joint kings, at the same time as Demetrios III ruled in Damascus. When Demetrios came north in 89–88 on the death of Antiochos X, Philip had not been visible as a ruling king since the death of his twin in about 93. The clear impression is that Demetrios was the more vigorous and perhaps capable of the surviving siblings. And when Philip is noted again he was in Beroia.

Beroia was ruled by Straton. Josephos is quite explicit on this. Therefore Demetrios' attack on the city was actually directed at Straton, not Philip. How Philip came to be in the city is not known, but obvious suggestions are that he had been captured by Straton, that he had taken refuge there from Antiochos X, or that he had fled there from Demetrios. Josephos in fact says that, after the siege began, Straton 'allied' with Philip, which suggests that he had been in the city all along, but that he had not been a free agent. In fact, it is quite possible that Demetrios' attack was aimed at rescuing Philip.

Josephos, who gives the only account of this episode, is very summary, and he operated on the assumption that relations between Seleukid family members were usually conducted on the basis of hostility (part of his underlying programme of insisting that the Jews were justified in rebelling). But a fight between Demetrios and Philip would break the pattern of relations among Grypos' children and so that interpretation must be called into question. We do not know why Philip was in Beroia, or how he got there, but hostility to Demetrios (who had only just arrived in the north) is not proved, cannot be assumed, and seems highly unlikely.

However, it is obvious that, by attacking Beroia, Demetrios was aiming to restore his control over the secessionist state Straton ruled in succession to his father, and perhaps to avenge the death of his own father at Herakleon's hands. There are elements of fable about Josephos' account: Demetrios, for example, is said to have laid siege to the city with '10,000 foot and 1,000 horse', which is a familiar phrase, even a formula, implying that Josephos did not really know how many men Demetrios had. More tellingly, Straton had contacts with the local Arabs, who are presumably much the same group as had been allied with Antiochos X, though 'Laodike, queen of the Samenians' was replaced by Azizos, as the Arab chief – called a *phylarchos,* that is, a tribal leader. An alignment of Straton with the Arabs and Antiochos X against Demetrios III and Philip I seems logical, and thus with Philip I as Straton's prisoner, perhaps at Antiochos X's behest, though Straton's purpose might be more on the lines of Philip as a useful card to hold in a complicated political situation. Further, such an alliance would help explain how it was that Straton (and his father) had remained independent since Herakleon's coup in 97–96.

Straton was able to call in help from the Arab chieftain Azizos, but also from the Parthian satrap Mithradates Sinakes, whose satrapy must have been somewhere in Mesopotamia. This would therefore mark another Parthian advance. Demetrios besieged Beroia but then found himself in turn besieged by Straton's allies. Thirst forced him to surrender – an odd reason, for a river runs through Beroia; perhaps it was just Josephos' guess – and he was sent off to the Parthian King Mithradates II as a prisoner.[46] Philip I survived, was released and got the surrendered soldiers of Demetrios III released as well, which again suggests that enmity between the brothers was a later invention. He went to Antioch to assume the throne as Demetrios' successor, presumably with the support of the released Demetrian soldiers.[47] (But Philip had been king with his twin several years before, so he could be said to be resuming the kingship.) This, of course, also suggests that he and Demetrios had been allied all along, and that the alliance of Philip and Straton had been one enforced by Straton on Philip.

This small conflict had little effect on the rest of Syria. Straton's principality survived, for he could, after all, call on assistance from the Parthians and the Arabs if he was attacked again. At the same time he could now be counted as yet another of Mithradates' subordinate kingdoms, though since Mithradates died in 87, any such arrangement will have become void as Parthia sank into its own version of a combined succession war, civil war, and independence movements. In the same way, it might be argued that Philip had become a vassal of Mithradates, as a result of his being released from his (presumed) Beroian captivity. This had probably been at the insistence of Sinakes (for Straton would surely want to keep him). It would be extremely useful to know the content of the various agreements and negotiations which took place at Beroia before, during, and after the siege.

The Parthian aspect of all this needs further examination. The fact was that it was due to the Parthian satrap's intervention that Straton and Philip owed their positions. The defeat of Demetrios III was due, above all, to the Parthians. What the satrap Mithradates Sinakes had done was exactly what his king, Mithradates II, had been doing in other areas in the Tigris and Euphrates valleys for the past thirty years: establishing Parthian suzerainty over a series of submissive and minor kings and states – Charakane, Adiabene, Tigranes, Dura-Europos. Sinakes had had it in his power to remove Straton and Philip just as he had removed Demetrios, who was surely seen as the most dangerous of the three. He could have annexed the Beroian principality, and even have invaded Syria with the aim of attacking Antioch, especially since there was no king left in Syria. Since he did not do so, but permitted the two men to continue ruling, he had obviously induced them to accept his king's suzerainty. The alternative would have been to be treated like Demetrios, to incarceration in a comfortable prison in Parthia. Leaving defeated or submissive rulers in place so long as they rendered allegiance to the Parthian king was a long Parthian tradition, even, one might say, the Parthian political method.

Philip acquired a kingdom which was much reduced in extent, but above all reduced in authority. Straton was independent in Beroia and his other towns; Kommagene was ruled by his brother-in-law, clearly now as a fully independent king. Within Philip's kingdom, several of the cities had gained greater autonomy than before – Seleukeia–in–Pieria, which had submitted to Demetrios, did not need to submit to Philip. Since 92 Antioch had had the right to mint its own civic coinage, implying a more responsible city government.[48] Further, although for the moment this development is invisible in the sources, there was by this time a substantial movement of smaller communities in Syria towards independence, inspired no doubt distantly by Judaea, the Nabataeans and the Ituraeans, as well as, and perhaps more, by the Phoenician cities. The Seleukid dynastic conflict had been resolved by murder, assassination and capture by their enemies, so that just one ruler of the family survived, but the size of the kingdom was now restricted to only a part of North Syria.

Chapter 13

The End of the Seleukids (88–75 BC)

The years 88–87 formed another of those brief periods when a series of deaths and events occurred more or less simultaneously and changed the whole aspect of affairs. In the Ptolemaic kingdom Ptolemy X Alexander died and Ptolemy IX Lathyros at last returned to Egypt as king. In the Seleukid state the defeat and exile of Demetrios III reduced the remaining Seleukid territories under Philip I to a vassal state of the Parthian kingdom. But then, still during 88–87, Mithradates II of Parthia died. He had already been losing his grip on his kingdom, for he faced secession, or rebellion, by his Babylonian satrap of satraps, Gotarzes, who minted coins in Babylonia claiming the title of king. Exactly when he began this claim is not clear, but he had certainly done so by about 91.[1] He was thus already competing for the kingship of Parthia when the satrap Mithradates Sinakes intervened in Beroia – so it seems that satraps had considerable independent powers. However, it was to Mithradates II that Demetrios III was sent, according to Josephos, so it would seem that Gotarzes' power was limited to Babylonia and did not stretch north and west into the sub-kingdoms of the upper Tigris or into Sinakes' satrapy.[2]

The death of Mithradates II released all those who had been bound to him by oaths of allegiance. This included Philip I and Straton of Beroia, of course, but more importantly it also released Tigranes of Armenia, who had already expanded his kingdom by taking over Sophene, and now took advantage of the confusion in Parthia to expand again. Mithradates appears to have had no direct successor, and indeed from 86, when it seems Gotarzes also died, there may have been no Parthian king – or perhaps there were several competitors, each claiming the position.[3]

Tigranes moved into the political gap which followed these deaths by taking over – 'conquest' seems too violent a word – suzerainty over the Parthian sub-kingdoms of the Upper Tigris Valley, Gordyene and Adiabene. He also gained control of Mesopotamia, between the Tigris and the Osrhoenian kingdom, and probably established his overlordship of Osrhoene as well.[4] No doubt all of this included his recovery of the 'seventy valleys' Mithradates had seized when he installed Tigranes in Armenia. Quite reasonably, given the situation he had now achieved, Tigranes now took the title of King of Kings, or Great King, presumably doing so once both Gotazes and Mithradates II were out of the way. This was a title with much wider implications than simply claiming suzerainty over several sub-kingdoms. It implied a claim to kingship over Iran and the Iranians, a successor to the Parthian kings, to the Seleukid kings, and to the old Akhaimenid Empire. It was a dangerously ambitious claim to make, especially for a king whose patrimony was only a minor kingdom.

Tigranes was also an ally of Mithradates VI of Pontos, and had married his daughter Kleopatra.[5] The two allies had divergent geographical aims, but their alliance served to protect them from each other. During 88 – another event of that year – Mithradates successfully invaded and conquered much of the Roman territories in Asia, and then went on to attack the Roman position in Greece.[6] So, only a few years after Parthian and Roman representatives had conferred at the Euphrates, apparently bestriding the world between them, both had been driven back to Iran and Greece respectively by the reassertion of independent action by several of those in the 'shatter zone' between the great powers.

These developments relieved Philip at Antioch of any obligation he might feel towards the Parthians. The death of Mithradates II ended his personal allegiance, and the Armenian conquest of Mesopotamia eliminated any immediate Parthian threat of seeking revenge and renewal. Instead, of course, there was now a new threat, in the form of Tigranes, but he and Mithradates of Pontos were clearly fully occupied, at least for the present, with their immediate ambitions and enemies elsewhere.

Philip I sent his surviving brother Antiochos XII to take over Demetrios' rule in Damascus.[7] There Antiochos faced a complex situation in which, in contrast to Philip in the north, he was probably the weakest of the main contenders. The Ituraeans, under Ptolemaios son of Mennaeas, had long wished to gain control of Damascus; the Nabataeans had recently defeated their Judaean rivals, and must now be considered the strongest of the local Palestinian states, for Judaea, under Alexander Iannai, had collapsed into civil war as a consequence of that Nabataean defeat.[8] There were also numbers of Greco-Macedonian cities which were now independent – Philadelphia (with Gerasa), several small cities between Judaea and Nabataea in the region of the Sea of Galilee – Skythopolis, Dion, Gadara, Hippos, and others – and several more along the Mediterranean coast, which were probably independent for the moment. But none of them was seriously powerful.

Alexander Iannai is reputed a great conqueror, but the Judaean civil war blocked any real expansion he might wish to make. He had captured Gaza, of course, but had then razed it. Some of the coastal cities had fallen to him, probably including Joppa, but north of Joppa the old area of Zoilos' principality, Dor and Strato's Tower, seems to have been still out of his power.[9] Ptolemais-Ake dominated the land between Carmel and the ladder of Tyre and Western Galilee.

It may be that the much-widowed Selene, once her last husband Antiochos X had died, had taken refuge in Ptolemais-Ake. If she was not there, her whereabouts are not known; she was certainly in the city in 70–69, and it is most convenient to assume that she had arrived there earlier. She had two sons with her, another Antiochos, and a boy whose name is not known; these were presumably sons of Antiochos X. So here was a further complication for Antiochos XII in Damascus which was spared his brother in Antioch – a living claimant to the Seleukid throne of the rival royal line. It may be that Selene had attempted to promote her eldest son as king (Antiochos XIII) when her husband was killed, the evidence being a coin of uncertain interpretation, but Demetrios III had been clearly too quick for her.[10] At Ptolemais-Ake she was relatively safe, since, besides being protected by a fortified city, she would be able to call in one of the other local powers if attacked by Antiochos XII from Damascus. Selene's presence in the city meant that the Seleukid dynasty had recovered one of the main cities of Syria. Her relationship with the local city council, which had been clearly independent and perhaps actually democratic some years earlier, is not known. If she had brought some forces with her, she was no doubt in the position of a tyrant, though her basis for this would seem to be as a regent for her son. But the threat from Damascus was surely real, for a union of Ptolemais and Damascus under a Seleukid king such as Antiochos XIII, a grandson of Kyzikenos, might well produce a rallying of Hellenic sentiment among the several small cities of Palestine.

It may be assumed that Antiochos XII hoped and intended to recover the Seleukid position in the south. One of the enemies he faced was the Nabataean kingdom, whose King Obodas I had gained control over much of the land east of the Jordan, as far north as the basalt areas south of Damascus – Trachonitis, Batanaea, and Auranitis. Most if not all of the small Greek cities near the Sea of Galilee lay outside the kingdom. These places were later often members of the Decapolis, a league of cities which was formalized under Roman rule, but their cooperation may well have begun with the Seleukid collapse, as a collective defence; certainly they were left alone for some time and this would be an ideal occasion for the formation of such a league.

The Nabataeans in the Hauran were thus close neighbours of Antiochos XII in Damascus, and he fought them soon after reaching Damascus, certainly within the first year of his reign.[11] Josephos has a story that Philip tried to seize Damascus while Antiochos was off on his campaign, but it seems more likely that Philip had come south in order to ensure that the city remained under Seleukid control while Antiochos was absent.[12] If it is accepted that the brothers supported each other it can be seen that Josephos' story has twisted the facts. Given the political situation of Damascus when Antiochos campaigned against the Nabataeans, it was clearly necessary for someone to defend the city against a possible Ituraean attack, which would require reinforcements being brought to the city. The villain of the piece is said to have been Milesios, the citadel commander, who is said to have first handed over the city to Philip, and then returned it to Antiochos' control; Josephos' story makes little sense as an example of inter-Seleukid conflict, and is much better understood as cooperation. The episode shows clearly enough that one of the Seleukid brothers needed to be present in the city to maintain control. A better interpretation would be that Milesios guarded the city until Philip arrived, and was left in command when Philip also left, having presumably seen that all was well.

Antiochos' first war with the Nabataeans, which took place soon after his arrival in Damascus, and so probably in 86, was unsuccessful. Two years later Antiochos struck out in a new attack, which Josephos says was a march against Judaea. This is inaccurate; instead it was a new attack on the Nabataeans. Antiochos aimed to attack the southern regions of Nabataea, the Petra area, which he clearly identified as the main centre of Nabataean power. Since he had been blocked in the north in his first war, and anyway an attack in the Hauran area would hardly dent the Nabataean strength, a less direct approach made sense. To do this he had to march through Judaea's territory, first passing west of the Sea of Galilee, then south along the ancient routeway called the Way of the Sea, along the lowlands between the Judaean hills and the coast. It was here that the Judaean kingdom claimed he was trespassing, and this was the basis for Josephos' charge that Antiochos was attacking Judaea.

Alexander Iannai is said to have constructed a fortified line of blockhouses, with a palisade and a ditch, across this route, stretching from the foothills to the sea. This is called, by moderns, the 'Yarkon line' as though it was something formidable. In fact it is probably only a modern invention, though it may well mark the boundary of Alexander's kingdom in the lowlands, which therefore leaves the small cities north of Joppa – Apollonia, Dor, Strato's Tower – independent. The 'line' if it ever existed, was wholly useless, for, as anyone with any military sense would know, Antiochos simply had to concentrate his forces at one point, break through, and march on.[13] Alexander made no further attempt to interfere, probably because it was clear that Antiochos was determined to fight the Nabataeans. When he marched to attack Petra, however, he was beaten by the Nabataean forces. They retired before his advance until his army was in the desert south of the Dead Sea, then surrounded it with horsemen – '10,000 horsemen', according to Josephos, who clearly did not have any actual figures. The Seleukid army was destroyed by these classic nomad tactics, and Antiochos died in the fighting.[14]

The city of Damascus was left bereft of its protection – its Seleukid garrison and probably a proportion of its citizen-soldiers had been destroyed. The city council took over control and, faced with the choice of an Ituraean or a Nabataean takeover, they chose to submit to the victorious and more distant Nabataeans, who were perhaps already their trading partners.[15]

Perhaps because events at Damascus moved too quickly – for the city council it was an emergency – Philip could not regain control of the city. Once a Nabataean garrison was in Damascus it would be logistically very difficult for Philip even to reach the city along the dry and resourceless route east of the Antilebanon, shadowed on his mountain flank by the no doubt hostile Ituraeans, who could also block access to the Damascus oasis along the Bekaa Valley and the Barada River route; the mobile desert cavalry which the Nabataeans had used to defeat Antiochos could deter any attack along the desert side. The Seleukid kingdom was thus reduced still further. Also it was now very difficult for Philip to reach Palestine, even if he wanted to. The unintended result was that in the next years the Palestinian cities were no longer able to turn to the Seleukids for protection. They then came under Judaean control, which was acceptable, if uncomfortable, once the cities understood that Alexander Iannai had adopted a less brutal policy of expansion than his predecessors – though a return to the old unpleasantness was always possible.

The kingdom ruled by Philip I was now quite compact, being formed of Kilikia and the territories of the North Syrian cities, stretching from the Mediterranean to the Euphrates and from the border of Kommagene to the valley of the Eleutheros River. But in this area some parts were independent, such as the Beroian principality of the sons of Herakleon, and some were autonomous, such as the great cities, but at least there were now no detached fragments of Seleukid territory, as Damascus had been. The area was populous, wealthy, and well-fortified, and had been under a single king since 88. It may be counted as the articulation of another Seleukid kingdom, replacing that which Antiochos VII had reconstituted.

And yet Philip's kingdom was small, and his authority was reduced by the autonomy granted to several of the cities, by the independence taken by others, and by the defeats he had suffered. Kommagene and Beroia were independent states: Seleukeia-in-Pieria had its charter of autonomy; Antioch had the right to mint its own civic coins, and this presupposes a much more active and perhaps more disobedient, city council than before. In 81, Laodikeia-ad-Mare began a new dating era, probably implying a grant of autonomy from Philip I.[16] In Kilikia the cities had long had some coining rights, and so some autonomy which is likely to have expanded as the royal authority weakened. Philip was ruling a state which now consisted of a collection of semi-independent cities, and this will have much reduced his powers of action.

The new calculations based on coin production suggest that Philip's reign extended to about 75 BC.[17] The volume of Philip's coinage has long been noted as very great, and compressing it into the two years he was usually allotted has always been anomalous and difficult to accept. Either he was intending some great military expedition which the coins would finance, or he reigned much longer than the two years he was given in the ancient sources.[18] Even at twelve years his coin production was at a rate still more suitable for the payment of a considerable army, which was always one of the main purposes of coin production in this period.[19] It seems likely he really was arming, for he was under threat from all sides. At the same time the collapse of Parthia after the death of Mithradates II might have seemed to provide a prospect of recovering territory to the east. Perhaps also he concentrated all this coining into the single Antioch mint, which therefore had to be more productive than normal – not to mention that there was a probable shortage of coin after the closure of many mints during the various wars of the past generation. Against the idea that he was building an armament is the total absence of any record that he did any campaigning during his reign, except for his brief expedition to Damascus.

In the absence of any specific data on Philip I the interpretation of what happened in his reign depends partly on the interpretation of these coins, and on the record of events in the lands round about. The coin problem implies a reign of ten or more years; the terminus has been suggested as 75 BC. This is an interpretation, of course, dependent on accepting the assumption of a more or less regular production of coins, but even so it assumes an unusually high coining rate, but it may be accepted provisionally and other events examined on the assumption of a united North Syrian/Kilikian kingdom which lasted until 75.

The events in the surrounding lands have been similarly subjected to a great deal of interpretation and re-interpretation. The two areas where datable events seem relevant are Kilikia and Judaea. In Judaea the ruler from 76 onwards was the widow of Alexander Iannai, Salome Alexandra. She had been instrumental in making him king in the first place by marrying him, and at his death she assumed the rule of the kingdom by right. She was not necessarily acceptable to all, but was certainly in general politically skilful enough to hold on to power until her own death in 67. The particular item which is relevant to North Syria is the notice in Josephos that Salome submitted to Tigranes in 70.[20] Therefore Tigranes had already gained control of North and Central Syria by that year.

Tigranes remained allied with Mithradates VI of Pontos after the latter's defeat by Rome in 81. He was more or less safe from attack from Parthia, since the issue of the succession there was not resolved until about 70. Sheltered by other states from east and west, and so not threatened by either of the Great Powers, in 78 Tigranes turned his attention southwards. In Rome Sulla had died, and Mithradates, who had already survived defeat in two Roman wars with undimmed ambitions, was aiming to flex his muscles again. He persuaded Tigranes that Kappadokia and Kilikia could be useful sources of manpower for his newly founded royal city of Tigranocerta (thereby implicating Tigranes in his own schemes, so he hoped). Tigranes combed through both regions and carried off '300,000' people, so it is said, to his new capital, which was situated somewhere on the borderlands of Mesopotamia and Armenia. Kilikia was still technically part of Philip's kingdom, but there appears to have been nothing Philip could do about it, any more than the Kappadokian king could.[21] We must assume that this mass kidnapping was preceded by Tigranes' conquest of the region. Whatever purpose the great coin production at Antioch was for, Philip had not apparently recruited a large enough army with it to challenge Tiganes.

Meanwhile the Ptolemaic kingdom was going through its own succession crisis. Ptolemy IX Lathyros had gained control of Egypt in 88, one of the many changes in that year, but when he died in 81 there was no obvious successor. His daughter Kleopatra Berenike III (by Kleopatra IV) took control until the arrival of her stepson Ptolemy XI Alexander II. He then married her, killed her after a marriage of eighteen days, and was then himself murdered in a riot by Alexandrians. One reason for his killing was that Berenike had been popular; another was that Ptolemy XI had in effect been the Roman candidate for the throne, provided by Sulla, who was now dictator at Rome.

The problem in Egypt now was that the various murders had almost eliminated the Ptolemaic royal family. There was Selene, but she was in Syria. She might well have been the best choice, with two sons approaching adulthood, but she was clearly identified with the Seleukids. Ptolemy XII was in exile with

Mithradates of Pontos, and so he was assumed to be anti-Roman. He was thus less than pleasing to the Romans, but their own candidate had proved to be disastrous.

Ptolemy XII and his younger brother were the sons of Ptolemy IX Lathyros by a non-Ptolemaic mother (whose name is not known), and this would normally have pushed them well down the order of succession. But needs must. The Alexandrians – presumably the city council – summoned the brothers, made the younger one king in Cyprus and the elder one king in Egypt. Ptolemy XII swiftly married his sister, Kleopatra VI Tryphaina.[22] This coup dented the Roman influence in Egypt, and more or less aligned the Ptolemaic kingdom with Mithradates.

Internationally, the early 70s were therefore a tense period. Egypt had aligned with Mithradates and Tigranes against Rome, at a time when Rome was distracted by Sulla's dictatorship and its aftermath. In this situation the alignment of the Syrian states became important. Their neutrality could favour their neighbours Egypt and Tigranes; if they aligned with Rome, for fear of Mithradates and Tigranes, they might distract the latter so that Rome was advantaged. As the likelihood of a new war became clear, Philip I and the Seleukid succession, and so the control of Syria became an important issue. When Philip died, about 75, the issue had to be decided with some urgency.

His death, therefore, occasioned a debate in Syria. It is reported by Justin that 'the people' cast about to consider who to submit to – Rome, Mithradates, Ptolemy, Tigranes.[23] Whether this was a real, open debate, or merely Justin's way of bringing out the alternatives as they seemed to him (or his source), is not certain. The absence of a Seleukid 'candidate' in the list rather suggests that the alternatives were Justin's. The various Seleukid sons were surely considered, and when Selene sent her two boys to Rome, they were referred to as 'kings of Syria', as though their installation was only a matter of form.[24] But Rome had little direct influence in Syria, and simply recognizing a candidate as king, as it had with Timarchos, for instance, was ineffectual, because no one in Syria paid any attention, and Rome did nothing more to enforce its opinion. Rome, as in the past, still had no real interest in Syrian affairs.

If the choice was made by anyone, it fell on Tigranes – though Tigranes was also in fact the only local ruler with the capability of taking control in Syria. Exactly who is implied by Justin's term 'the people' is difficult to discern, but the obvious authorities in Syria after Philip's death were the city councils, of which the most important was that of Antioch. So, it is most likely, if an invitation to Tigranes was in fact ever made, that it came from the Antioch city council – copying in this the action of the Alexandrian city council a few years before, possibly quite deliberately. However, if the choice to submit to Tigranes was Antioch's it is clear that it was only made on behalf of the city itself. Tigranes must persuade, in one way or another, the other communities in Syria to submit.

The choice of Tigranes is curious but not illogical. Given that any Ptolemy was automatically disliked and excluded, and that Rome and Parthia were both involved in internal troubles, and both distant, and that Mithradates of Pontos was suspect because of his quarrels with Rome – and he was soon to be at war with Rome again – Tigranes was the only substantial ruler left, so long as a king was required. The history of Selene may have brought her public dislike. The Seleukid children were also rejected no doubt because to choose either Philip's son or Selene's would be to reignite the dynastic war which had been dormant for the past decade and a half.

An alternative might have been to dispense with kingship altogether, but this does not seem to have been considered. In strategic terms it was obviously necessary for the cities of Syria to work together, and that would mean some sort of military commander, which is what a king essentially was.

The invitation probably applied only to Antioch, and not to the rest of the former Seleukid state, just as Damascus' invitation to Aretas of Nabataea had not affected other parts of Syria. On the other hand, the treatment of Kappadokia and Kilikia by Tigranes had been brutal, and Tigranes had surely taken note of the indefensibility of Syria once Philip was dead. It seems likely that by its decision to choose him, Antioch just pre-empted Tigranes' own attack; Tigranes helped the process by making it clear from the start that he had no interest in heavy-handed changes; he would succeed the Seleukids not just as king and would leave their governing practices in place. This would be quite convincing to anyone who had watched his progress in the past years as he simply imposed his suzerainty and left kings and others in place, an imperial method probably learnt from Mithradates II. He was not a governing and ruling king, but a collector of other kingdoms. It would also be clear to those who were watching that his empire was liable to collapse at an adverse blow. The Syrians would have to do this work again.

The 'choice' of Tigranes therefore involved the deliberate rejection of the surviving Seleukid candidates. Probably Philip's son Philip II was too young. Similarly Selene's eldest son (by her marriage with Antiochos X) was still a teenager, though she promoted him as a candidate for the kingship after Philip I's death, just as she may have done when Antiochos X himself died.[25] No doubt her intention was that she would rule as regent in his name. But this prospect or that of a minor as king – either Philip or Antiochos – was not one at all pleasing to anyone in Syria. Nevertheless these three children all had claims to the Seleukid kingship, and both the international situation and the process of Armenian conquest held out some hope for them of a Seleukid restoration.

The activities of Selene can provide a possible confirmation of the date of Philip's death and thus of the start of Tigranes' Syrian campaign. Her two sons are known to have gone to Rome in 75, where they stayed for two years. Selene is credited by Josephos with ruling in 'Syria', an obvious exaggeration perhaps assumed by Selene herself.[26] She certainly had a claim of sorts to succeed Philip, though Tigranes beat her to it, in the north at least. Josephos was thus probably only retailing Selene's claim. She is not mentioned as a contender in Justin's list of candidates in 75, but it would seem that she had a foothold somewhere. Bevan suggested that she had been in Seleukeia-in-Pieria, but without evidence, and she was certainly in Ptolemais-Ake later.

She sent her sons to Rome as actual 'kings of Syria', as Cicero puts it, which only means that Selene and her sons claimed to be the rightful rulers, and that she assumed that they would take actual possession.[27] But they went on to lay a claim to be kings also of Egypt. The removal of Rome's candidate, Ptolemy XI, had sharply reduced Roman influence in Egypt, and this was Selene's opportunity. A new war with Mithradates was developing during 74, but did not break out until 73. The possibility of Ptolemaic assistance to Mithradates was present, but if one of Selene's sons became king as a Roman protégé, this would cease. At that time also, the Senate finally set in motion the full annexation of Cyrenaica, which had been bequeathed to Rome in the will of its last Ptolemaic king, who had died in 96.[28] This brought directly-ruled Roman territory to the western border of Egypt. The threat was obvious, and Rome might have a new candidate for the kingship. Any enmity Ptolemy XII might have felt or displayed towards Rome now rapidly faded away.

Selene and her sons were recognized by the Senate as 'kings of Syria', though, as ever, the Senate was not prepared to do anything else. Indeed, it may be that nothing more was done than to refer to them casually as such kings. The fact that they turned up in Rome in 75, though, does rather suggest that they were angling for an alliance against Mithradates and Tigranes, and that they might be able to open up a second front in the new Mithradatic war, and that their activities and claims in Rome may have been the spur to Tigranes' move into Syria. Selene had made two elementary mistakes: she failed to secure the Seleukid kingship before grabbing for a second prize, and she relied on Rome.

By the time the Senate considered their position Tigranes was on the march southwards.

When Selene and her sons were rebuffed at Rome in all their ambitions it was in part in order not to antagonize Tigranes. But then Antiochos XIII went off to Kilikia and began an insurrection against Tigranes, though with little success.[29] He did so at the same time as the new Mithradatic war began, so presumably he was again laying claim to some form of gratitude in the event of Syria becoming 'available'. The Roman rejection of his claims was successful in that Tigranes stayed neutral in the new war.

The dating of Tigranes' conquest of North Syria is generally put at 83 BC, based on a comment by Appian that Tigranes' governor Magadates was in command of 'all these conquests' for 'fourteen years', and that Tigranes' forces withdrew in 69 – a firm date.[30] This is actually much less clear than it seems, since he appears to refer to all Syria as far south as 'Egypt', plus various other areas, including Kilikia. But Tigranes did not reach Palestine until 70, and did not conquer Kilikia until 78 or later. The figure 'fourteen', whatever it refers to, cannot be used for Tigranes' occupation of Syria, and must therefore be discarded; the Armenian acquisition of Syria can be dated to sometime between 78 and 72.

The process of the occupation of Syria by Armenian forces took several years, and it seems unlikely that it was accomplished without a good deal of negotiation, first between the king and the representatives of Antioch, and then with other cities, probably conducted by Magadates. Having occupied Antioch and installed Magadates as his viceroy, Tigranes permitted the continuation of the autonomy which the city had developed in the previous decade or so, and the autonomous coinage of the city continued to be minted alongside Tigranes' own.[31] All this implies a preliminary agreement between the two parties.

This fits in with Tigranes' own empire-building methods, which involved as little disturbance to the local political systems as possible: local kings had been left in place in Osrhoene, Adiabene, and Atropatene. The King of Kommagene, Mithradates I and his Seleukid wife, were left undisturbed. In Syria the application of this system meant leaving the local 'tyrants' in position in some of the cities and regions, as well as leaving cities autonomous; where the cities were run by oligarchies these were also left in place.

From Tigranes' point of view, who ran the local communities was unimportant, but he required their submission, general obedience, and tax contributions, and no interference with his larger plans. This may be how Tigranes understood the Seleukid system, as it had developed in the last generation; it had always accepted some sub-kings and had allowed some civic local government, which had evidently expanded recently, but what he was doing was simply accepting conditions as he found them in a pragmatic way. It was not the glorious conquests of Mithradates II or Mithradates VI or Alexander; nor was it, in the event, lasting; but it was easy.

It is this curious process which lies behind the divergent traditions of Tigranes' 'conquest': one version, in Justin, claims that it was all peaceful;[32] the other, represented by Strabo and Appian, insists on its violent nature.[33] These are, of course, partial views of the same process; examples can be discovered of both methods being used, but they are interpretations of the events which may provide clues to what really happened. Given the variety of states which had emerged in the recent past in Syria it is in fact surprising that a more violent conquest did not take place. It is a tribute to Tigranes' overwhelming strength that so much was indeed achieved peacefully. But in the end it did not promote loyalty, nor did it instil fear, and his power evaporated even more rapidly than it had been imposed.

The expansion of Tigranes' control, therefore, at the expense of the Seleukid kingdom in Syria, began in Kilikia in 78 or 77 BC. He took away a substantial part of the urban population, Soloi being especially hard hit, but whether he took control of the region as well at that time is not certain; it seems unlikely that a man like Tigranes, who had been hungry for the empire since he first achieved power in Armenia, would give up a conquest.[34] He does seem to have given up Kappadokia, where King Ariobarzanes ruled until 63 – though it is clear that Mithradates of Pontos had the real power in that kingdom.

Controlling Kilikia, it is probable that Tigranes dominated Kommagene as well. He had taken control of Sophene long before, so Kommagene was now surrounded on east, north, and west. King Mithradates I, whose wife was the Seleukid Laodike, kept the throne, just as the kings of other annexed kingdoms did. But with Tigranes dominating or having annexed Osrhoene, Sophene, Kommagene, and Kilikia, the chances of the North Syrian cities retaining a peaceful independence for long were minimal. Perhaps it was only the survival of Philip I until 75 which delayed Tigranes' next expansion. Antioch's submission must have occurred not long after Philip's death, that is, in 75 or shortly after. The city's internal affairs were left undisturbed, but Tigranes did appoint Magadates as his viceroy for Syria, though what powers he had are never stated, and Tigranes was also frequently present in Syria himself.[35]

Domination of Kommagene and control of Antioch presumes that Tigranes was also in control of the northern cities of Kyrrhos, Doliche, and Nikopolis, which lay between Antioch and his kingdom, and above all of Seleukeia-Zeugma, which was an essential link between his provinces of Syria and Osrhoene and further east. All of these lay between Antioch and Kommagene, and Seleukeia-Zeugma was one of the vital strategic points of the whole region, control of which was essential to anyone who aspired to power in Syria. It was the main crossing point of the Euphrates, the one bridge (*zeugma*) over the river, a well-fortified city situated mainly on the west bank, but with a fortified suburb across the river. This suburb was called Apamaea, and it became regarded as a separate city, probably taken over by Osrhoene at some point.[36] In 88 Seleukeia-plus-Apamaea must have permitted the passage of the Parthian army of Mithradates Sinakes in his way to relieve the siege of Beroia, possibly because by then Osrhoene was a Parthian sub-kingdom. When Tigranes took control of Mesopotamia in 87 or 86, he took Parthia's place in Osrhoene and so gained access to Seleukeia and its bridge. For Tigranes this was a vital link in his empire, and one must assume that he controlled the city with a substantial garrison; he used it later as a prison.[37]

Doliche and Kyrrhos, between Zeugma and Antioch, may be presumed to have come into Tigranes' control along with, or even before, Antioch's submission. The principality which Straton had controlled in 88, Beroia and Hierapolis and the unlocated Herakleia, lay south-west of Zeugma and east of Antioch; the ruler after Straton was Dionysios son of Herakleon, though when Dionysios took over is not known – he was in power in 69.[38] It may be presumed that the dynasty was left undisturbed – it had already submitted to Parthia. Tigranes did not disturb other monarchies, so one may assume that this one also continued in existence, so long as the rulers signified their submission. This is all the clearer since men related to each other were in power in Beroia before and after his presence in Syria. A principality of that size, containing two towns and a rural temple, was not a serious threat. But with Antioch, Seleukeia-Zeugma, and Herakleon's principality under his control, Tigranes had acquired a good half of Philip's former kingdom.

Far more important than any of these minor cities, or even than the northern kingdoms, were the other three great cities of Syria, Seleukeia-in-Pieria, Apamaea, and Laodikeia-ad-Mare, all of them large, populous, and wealthy. Each of them requires to be discussed separately, because the evidence for each is different.

Seleukeia was never part of Tigranes' kingdom, and it acquired a reputation, according to Pompeius later, for good fortifications and a determined defence of its independence.[39] The implication was that the city had stood up for itself under attack, though there is no indication other than Pompeius' reported comment that Tigranes ever actually tried to take the place. It had, of course, resisted Tryphon in the past, but earlier it had fallen easily to Ptolemy III and was taken fairly easily by Antiochos III, so its martial reputation was a good deal older and less impressive than Tigranes' time. The city was already autonomous under the charter granted in 109, and it would seem that Tigranes respected that; by doing so he enhanced that autonomy to a recognition of the city's effective independence. This would fit with his acceptance of autonomy at Antioch and other cities, and with the continuation in office of the various kings.

Laodikeia–ad-Mare had begun a new dating era in 82–81 BC, according to its coins. This presumably marked a formal grant of autonomy by Philip I, and its coins were now inscribed 'holy and autonomous'. The date is calculated from the fact that the highest date on these autonomous coins is 'year 34', and that another new era was begun in 48 BC; the actual date of the older era's beginning may, of course, given the mode of calculation, be a year or so earlier, but here was another city whose independence Tigranes found existing and respected.[40]

For Apamaea the evidence is less precise. The city was never a major minting centre, but a new set of coins began to be produced in the city in 76–75, proclaiming that the city was 'holy and *asylos*'.[41] This was a status which is somewhat less than autonomy, but one which was highly prized. It may be presumed that the city's new condition was commemorated and advertised – by the coins – as soon as it was acquired. In the Syrian context, this was a status granted only by the king. It may have been granted by Philip I – whose reign ended about that time – but it may just as likely have been granted by Tigranes – or even, in the emergency of 75, spontaneously adopted by the city itself as a defence mechanism. Tigranes certainly accepted that the city was autonomous – but then he accepted that at most cities.

The absence of a clear grant of autonomy in this particular case is worth pursuing, since Apamaea was, after 81, the only one of the four great Syrian cities which did not – so far as we know – have such a status. The city was a major Seleukid military centre, well-fortified and with a powerful acropolis, which had been recently refurbished by Antiochos IX.[42] Tigranes would need to keep a firm grip on this city, for if he decided to restrict himself to Philip's former kingdom, this would be his southern frontier fortress. It was also a major route centre, with good route connections towards Antioch and the north, to the coast at Arados and Tripolis, and south into the Bekaa Valley, and it was well suited to dominate the nearby steppe and desert to the east. That is, Apamaea was not only a military centre and a powerful city, it occupied a vital strategic geographical position, which it was necessary to control if Syria as a whole was to be controlled and dominated. It may thus have been Tigranes' decision to restrict the autonomy of the city, simply because he needed to maintain a firm grip on it, and he may not have been able to wholly trust the population.

The nearest parallel for the treatment of Apamaea may well be Seleukeia-Zeugma, similarly militarily vital in an imperial context. Any consideration of the strategic factors involved in Tigranes' takeover of Syria shows that a major city and a military centre such as Apamaea should have been one of Tigranes' early priorities. We may therefore take it that, whoever made the grant of 'holy and *asylos*' to Apamaea, Tigranes came to control the city, and was thus the ruler of North Syria. His power was based primarily in Antioch, Apamaea, and Seleukeia-Zeugma, and he had gained control by the end of 65. He had moved very quickly to ensure this extension of his empire. This, in fact, was the 'peaceful' conquest recognized by Justin.

The outbreak of the Third Romano-Mithradatic war in 73 was a dangerous time for Tigranes, who was Mithradates' son-in-law. He kept out of the fighting, no doubt hoping that Mithradates would win, or that if he lost he would not entangle Tigranes in his fall. Meanwhile he continued to expand his control of Syria, somewhat ostentatiously; a process which made it clear to all that he was not fighting on Mithradates' side. By 72 he had gained control of Damascus, which in turn meant that he had reduced the Ituraeans to submission, for Ptolemaios son of Mennaeas controlled access to the Damascus oasis from the Bekaa Valley, and dominated it from the hills.[43]

Damascus had been under Nabataean control since the death of Antiochos XII in 84. In the year or so preceding Tigranes' arrival, the city changed hands. It seems that the Nabataeans voluntarily withdrew. The city then apparently at last fell into Ituraean hands, a change which was disputed by the Judaeans, whose Queen Salome Alexandra sent her military son Aristoboulos to the city, to contest its control with Ptolemaios.[44] Aristoboulos was unable to change the situation, but Tigranes was. Ptolemaios began issuing his own coins at about this time, perhaps to celebrate his brief success at Damascus, but also to emphasize his independence in the face of the looming threat of Tigranes.[45] However, like every other king in the region, he submitted to, but was not dislodged by, Tigranes.

Tigranes took over the North Syrian cities during the immediate aftermath of the death of Philip I, and he probably completed that first phase during 75. He moved on from there much more slowly. He was in control of Damascus in 72, and then moved on against Selene in Ptolemais-Ake in 70. Of course, we do not know what fighting he had to indulge in during his advance, and no doubt the Romano-Mithradatic war gave him pause. Perhaps he hoped that he could be satisfied with North Syria alone at first, which would mean he had acquired the rule of the last part of the Seleukid kingdom, but the return of Antiochos XIII to stimulate a rising in maltreated Kilikia and Selene's control of Ptolemais-Ake posed the threat that between them they might revive Seleukid fortunes in the north. Since Selene had the more powerful base, her elimination would be the first priority. He was now conquering with violence – the interpretation of Strabo and Appian.

How far Selene's authority reached out from Ptolemais-Ake is not known, but the city's territory later stretched from the Tyrian border to Mount Carmel along the coast and inland over the coastal plain to the foothills of Galilee. It was a considerable geographical area, but it was only of concern to Tigranes because it was the last Seleukid remnant in Syria. Selene's son Antiochos XIII had been a candidate for the kingship since his father's death in 95, and had maintained his claim ever since, both at Rome and in action in Kilikia. Rome's lack of concrete support for his claims surely encouraged Tigranes to attack Selene in her city.[46]

He laid siege to Ptolemais, a slow process, but the presence of his army in Palestine spread alarm among the other cities and states in the region. If Ptolemais fell, Tigranes would have a local base from which to spread his power further, should he wish to. The Nabataeans had already abandoned Damascus at his approach, and the Ituraeans had quickly succumbed; given Tigranes' apparent partiality for Greek cities, the Judaean kingdom's control of the Greek cities it had gained was clearly a vulnerable point. Hence the immediate and swift – even, one may say, eager and precipitate – submission of Salome Alexandra of Judaea. She was ruling Judaea in the face of constant internal disputes, so when Tigranes laid siege to Ptolemais, Salome was, as described by Josephos, 'naturally frightened'.[47] Josephos had, of course, the usual misogynist assumption that being a woman meant that she was therefore ruled by her emotions, but the real problem for her was that if she resisted Tigranes he could easily contact a dissident Jewish faction and disrupt the kingdom – it was only a few years since one such faction had called in Demetrios III to fight their battles for them. It is therefore not surprising that there seems to have been no argument from other (male) Judaeans that Tigranes was a threat and must be conciliated. Salome sent envoys to the Armenian king at the siege, laden with valuable gifts – that is, she was placing her kingdom in a posture of submission.

The embassy was well timed, at a moment when Tigranes was still involved in the siege, but before he had conquered. The envoys were sent to tender the submission of Judaea to the new Great King.[48] Salome and her advisers had clearly taken due note of the methods used by Tigranes in his advance southwards, and Judaea therefore entered Tigranes' political system as another sub-kingdom. Josephos makes it clear that the alternative to this submission was thought to be invasion, and that the Judaean rulers fully appreciated that this would be very unpleasant, and that the internal divisions of Judaea may not have been proof against such an invasion. (The other alternative, joining with Selene in joint resistance, does not seem to have been considered; an alliance in any way with any Seleukid was clearly an even worse prospect.)

When Tigranes conquered Ptolemais-Ake, therefore, which he succeeded in doing during 69, he had established his rule over, as Appian puts it, 'all the Syrian peoples this side of Euphrates as far as the borders of Egypt'.[49] The few remaining independent states and cities – Ashkelon, Philadelphia, Tyre, Sidon, and others – may or may not have submitted as well. One would expect them to have been even quicker off the mark than Salome, given their powerlessness after the conquest of Ptolemais. The Nabataean kingdom may thus have been the only really independent state left in all Syria.

The moment of Tigranes' victory at Ptolemais-Ake was also the moment when he suffered his mortal blow. Mithradates of Pontos was defeated by the Roman general L. Licinius Lucullus in 71, and he fled from the battlefield to take refuge in Armenia: Tigranes was his son-in-law and therefore Mithradates was given shelter, though he was not received personally by Tigranes, who was clearly attempting to evade a Roman attack.[50] Tigranes then began his campaign into Palestine, no doubt hoping the Romans would accept that Mithradates was finished, and making clear his disassociation from the defeated king. But Rome, vengeful as ever in the face of obstinate resistance, wanted Mithradates, alive or dead. While he was engaged in the campaign for Ptolemais-Ake, Tigranes was informed of the arrival of a Roman envoy, Ap. Claudius Pulcher, at Antioch.

Tigranes did not hurry; he had, after all, already sheltered Mithradates for twenty months. He completed the siege, captured Selene, and then travelled to Antioch, where Pulcher had been kept waiting at his insistence.[51] In the subsequent interview, Pulcher demanded the surrender of Mithradates, which Tigranes could not agree to, and which Pulcher knew in advance would be the reply. So far the formalities of diplomacy. Pulcher is described as speaking arrogantly to the king, who is characterized as an over-confident oriental, unaccustomed to 'free speech'. Pulcher is further assumed to have distorted or misunderstood his instructions from Lucullus.[52] Neither interpretation is convincing. Pulcher's message, rudely delivered or not, was uncompromising, and there was no point in hiding it: he was sent to demand the surrender of Mithradates, and he was not allowed any leeway for negotiation. Lucullus' victory was incomplete without the capture of the person of the Pontic king, nor would peace in Asia be secure until he was imprisoned or dead. After three wars, Rome required nothing less.

Tigranes was unable to comply, for Mithradates was not only a fugitive to whom he had given shelter, but he was Tigranes' own father-in-law. This was known to the Romans, and Tigranes' reply was no surprise, either to Pulcher or to Lucullus. Pulcher's rudeness was irrelevant, and was probably an invention, either of the historians or of Pulcher himself, excusing his failure, as is Tigranes' lack of appreciation of 'free speech'. But what is not irrelevant was Pulcher's preceding stay in Antioch, an episode normally downplayed or ignored.

Plutarch describes Pulcher as intriguing with 'many chiefs' who were dissatisfied with Tigranes, particularly with King Zarbienos of Gordyene, and corresponding with many cities.[53] These 'cities' were, of course, the cities of Syria, starting no doubt with the city of Antioch, where he was staying, and with whose 'chiefs' he discussed Tigranes. Antioch was the centre of a wide communications network, with links to a dozen cities in North Syria: communication would be easy, particularly if he contacted disaffected Antiochenes first. The city was the greatest in Syria, would obviously be influential in political matters, and its example in submitting to Tigranes had been followed by many other cities. The 'many chiefs' may be important men from these other cities, but Plutarch's words clearly separate them from the men of the cities. They are therefore men who are 'chiefs' of communities other than the cities. That is, the structure of Tigranes' empire had left many local rulers in place, and these were being subverted by Pulcher. The 'many chiefs' were partly the kings (such as Zarbienos), and partly other local rulers, including no doubt the city oligarchs, whose continued existence and local power had been accepted by Tigranes. It was clear to Pulcher when he investigated that Tigranes' empire-building had very shallow foundations, and that it would be easy to overthrow it. Plutarch's brief record of what happened notes that Pulcher assured the discontented groups he had contacted that they would receive 'relief from Lucullus, but ordered them to keep quiet for the present'.[54]

Pulcher did not have instructions from Lucullus to scheme the overthrow of Tigranes' conquests. His mission was to ask for the surrender of Mithradates only. This he did, in a way which guaranteed wide publicity, and which evoked the expected refusal. Pulcher could return to Lucullus with this reply – Lucullus cannot have been surprised – but with the further information that it would not take much effort to knock down Tigranes' empire. And this is what Lucullus proceeded to do, by invading his home kingdom of Armenia, and striking straight for his new capital Tigranocerta. Tigranes only then ordered Magadates to collect his soldiers and remove them from Syria, and no doubt from other areas too.[55] Tigranes' great new city was taken and dismantled, and the Kilikians whom Tigranes had forcibly recruited to help populate it were sent home.[56] In Syria, the evacuation of Armenian troops had signalled the end of the brief time of Armenian rule even earlier.

Tigranes' pathetic empire was clearly unstable and liable to collapse at a blow, as many must have seen at the time. The choices faced by Antioch at the beginning of Tigranes' Syrian career were thus pared away relentlessly. Tigranes had failed, Mithradates had been vanquished, and Ptolemy had knuckled under to Rome at the first sign of Roman pressure. The Seleukids were not yet quite finished, but Tigranes, in a last vengeful act, had Selene executed in her prison at Seleukeia-Zeugma, and Antiochos XIII, his brother, and Philip II were still theoretically in the game. But Lucullus' decisive action had demonstrated quite clearly, however much some Greeks and Macedonians did not like the thought, exactly where power lay: with Rome.

Conclusion – The Seleukid Legacy

Several possible claimants to the Seleukid throne remained after Tigranes' withdrawal. He had killed Selene, but the others pop up in several places in the dozen years or so after Tigranes left. There was never any possibility of any of them securing a throne. None of them had the wealth, the backing, the military forces, or perhaps the ability to gain a position from which to become king. In 64 Pompeius decisively ended all their chances when he annexed North Syria as a Roman province; he was dismissive in his comments, but he must have known that it would be too dangerous to allow any Seleukid to have power in the region – just as it would be too dangerous for any Ptolemy to survive in Egypt or any Antigonid in Macedon.[1] These kingdoms had been centred above all on the royal dynasties, and they had to go. They thus faded away, their pretensions melting away in the heat of Roman expansion, which had no room for the old dynasties.

The Seleukid kingdom may therefore reasonably be said to have ceased to exist in 75, when Philip I died, and Tigranes took over North Syria. Selene's final foothold at Ptolemais-Ake was not a viable base for a Seleukid revival – quite apart from her Ptolemaic origin – any more than the various claimants were viable kings. On the other hand, there were fragments of the Seleukid kingdom surviving all across the Near and Middle East for several centuries, as far east as India.

First, Syria. The North Syrian cities had been the mainstay of the final form of the Seleukid state, from the time of Antiochos VII until the death of Philip I. This was the kingdom Antiochos had fashioned, with appendices in Kilikia and Palestine. The region had held out even after Philip I's death, having survived several civil wars, and Tigranes had taken it over whole. But Tigranes' regime had also involved accepting far too many local groups as autonomous – cities, mountain regions, even stretches of desert – and this finally destroyed North Syrian unity. When the condition of the area is remarked ten years later in Pompeius' progress from north to south, it had broken into many small pieces. The cities were autonomous, of course, but that meant that ten or more were acting independently, and they were interspersed with minor but also independent areas – the Bargylos hills were a principality, the city of Emesa had grown and was the seat of an Arab king, the people of the Ghab marshes were an independent group, the town of Tarutia in the desert was autonomous, and even close to Antioch the town of Gindarus was independent – and so on. Pliny the Elder attempted to list their names in his *Natural History*, but could not cope with all the strange names (in Aramaic, of course) and simply counted 'seventeen tetrarchies with barbarian names' to finish with.[2] When Pompeius arrived he found all these existing, and simply froze the system in place. Then over the next two centuries all these independent units were slowly absorbed into the Roman provincial system. The last to go was the Nabataean kingdom, in AD 106.

Beyond Syria the fragmentation was less detailed, and several major kingdoms had emerged. All of them, inevitably, were strongly affected by their Seleukid past. As an example, take Judaea. This is a state explicitly founded on the rejection of Seleukid authority and Greek culture, a religious-cum-peasant rebellion which denied not just the authority of the Seleukid king, but all the elements of Greco-Macedonian culture. The original rebels had forcibly converted their neighbours in and around Judaea, making them into Jews; and their early conquests of Greek cities had resulted in those cities being razed to the ground, and their populations murdered and enslaved. The Maccabaean revolt was a true revolution, as thorough as any modern version; it aimed to remake humanity. It had, of course, failed, and the Maccabean revolt had been snuffed out by Antiochos IV's and Demetrios I's soldiers. When Judaean power revived, it did so as a state which was a near copy of the Seleukid kingdom it was supposedly rejecting. Its high priest became a king, with a professional army (partly made up of non-Jewish mercenaries) and a royal court; it incorporated Greek cities as going concerns, and produced coins. The names of the kings were both Greek and Aramaic – and it was the Greek version which is most easily recorded. By the time of Alexander Iannai even the forcible proselytism had disappeared, and he was operating as a 'normal' conqueror.

Or take the Parthians, another rejectionist regime, which had signalled its difference by adopting a new dating era of its own – but such a concept was in origin a Seleukid one. The king of the Parthians minted coins with images of Greek gods on them, with the king's titles in Greek, even in many cases calling themselves 'phil-hellenes'. They encouraged and protected the Greek cities they had conquered. They became, in effect, copies of the Seleukid kings they had fought, and even made it a practice to collect Seleukid kings, princes and princesses as prisoners. The Parthian kings might call themselves king of kings in imitation of the Akhaimenids, but they were largely Greek in culture. The sub-kingdoms which they allowed to continue in existence were often originally Seleukid provinces, and the sub-dynasties were often descended from Seleukid governors.

This is a major part of the legacy of Seleukid history, and these kingdoms, spread from North India to Asia Minor, were often still in existence as Seleukid facsimiles for another two or three centuries. Another part of this legacy is the many cities spread from Asia Minor to India which had been founded by the Seleukid kings, and this is even more lasting and important than the kingdoms. Many of the cities, notably in Syria, became autonomous members of the Roman Empire from the 60s BC onwards. Some became the capitals of the kingdoms which had a brief century or so of near-independence before they were finally incorporated into the Roman system. In the Parthian Empire, they similarly survived as autonomous urban centres. The cities which were destroyed, by rebels or enemies or in the Roman civil wars, were invariably refounded and rebuilt by Roman magistrates and governors and emperors.

Further, many of the cities survived the collapse of the empires which succeeded the Seleukid kingdom. They became the repositories of the culture of the future, carrying forward the Seleukid idea of urban autonomy into other societies. In the Greco-Roman world it was the cities which incubated new ideas and which were the generators of wealth, and this continued through to the Roman, Sassanid, Byzantine, and Arab empires. So also, of course, did the very Seleukid idea of founding cities – Baghdad of the Abbasids and Cairo of the Fatimids were very typical Seleukid actions.

Politically, therefore the Seleukid legacy was a whole series of cities of a particular type, self-governing in internal matters, but unlike the cities of Greece on which they were theoretically modelled, largely uninterested in full independence; in Syria and Palestine they settled down comfortably enough in the Roman Empire. The other part of the political legacy was a series of relatively small kingdoms which were approximate copies of the Seleukid state. Many of these had developed out of loyalty to a local god, so that the kings were also high priests, and had usually been high priests before they became kings, and, like the cities, most of them were absorbed into the Roman and Parthian empires.

The final decade of the Seleukid kingdom, say from 100 BC, had seen a steady increase in these minor kingdoms, both in their number and in their independence. Judaea and Nabataea, Kommagene and Osrhoene, had existed by that date for some decades, but by 69, when Tigranes pulled out there were also two Ituraean states, the main one centred on Chalkis and Baalbek, and another in the north Lebanese mountains centred on Arqa, and a kingdom at Emesa, and the active commercial city of Palmyra dominating the surrounding desert roads, a principality in the Bargylos hills behind Laodikeia, and several small, barely known even more minor states in the interstices between these kingdoms and the cities. There were also a number of 'tyrannies', independent cities under personal rulers – Philadelphia was a longstanding example, Byblos and Berytos were ruled by a man called Dionysios in the 60s – Pompeius executed him and 'freed the cities;[3] Herakleon's son, another Dionysios, ruled at Beroia and its neighbours. The other Phoenician cities were also independent, as were those in Palestine which had escaped the Judaean grasp.

So the final political legacy of the Seleukid kingdom was, paradoxically, the extreme fragmentation of the land from Gaza to Kommagene, paradoxical because one of the main aims of the Seleukids had always been to maintain the unity of the kingdom, though their means had been limited. Yet this extreme fragmentation proved to be to the advantage of the Syrians, at least in the short-term, for when Pompeius arrived to take over and eliminate the remaining Seleukids, he was able to move through the country dealing out his decisions with little difficulty. It was only when he reached Judaea that he encountered a polity which felt itself powerful enough to object to his decisions. A unified North Syria which took umbrage at his pretensions may well have forced him into a major campaign, probably of sieges. So Syria's disunity was a protection.

The Seleukid kings had certainly found it difficult to hold on to their entire kingdom because of its great size. It stretched from Asia Minor to the Hindu Kush, and they had very limited manpower resources for what was essentially a military problem. That they held on to most of it for a century and a half is a tribute to the energies of the kings. In the end one of the ways they had tried to do so was by granting part-independence to rebellious or discontented sections of the population. This would not necessarily lead on to full independence, but that was often the aim of the recipients, and they went on working towards it. The Judaean state took nearly forty years to pass through such a process, the Parthian state perhaps even longer – though in many ways it was the Parthians who took the message most clearly, for this was the pattern of state organization they seem to have adopted from the start.

The cities were generally not among those hankering for freedom, but the country areas, inhabited by people who were overwhelmingly not Greek, became steadily keener on the idea, and as the kings weakened, more were able to achieve it.

In this case it does not seem that the success of the Jews in detaching Judaea from the kingdom was particularly contagious. The experience of the people of Judaea had been very unpleasant, but mainly at the hands of fellow Jews, and after their initial rebellion they had been thoroughly suppressed by Seleukid armies largely because of their internal divisions. When they did gain independence (not until 129 BC) they turned on their neighbours in Idumaea and across the Jordan and in Samaria. The result was constant warfare. This was hardly a compelling example for others to follow. More convincing was Arados, which had made its claim for independence clear for centuries before achieving it. Having done so Arados settled down as a city state, independent, self-sufficient, commercial. It was a model which was followed by the neighbouring Phoenician cities without the need for the initial violence of Arados' conquest of its *peraia*.

This Seleukid disintegration, it must be noted, was unique among the fates of the Hellenistic kingdoms. Only Macedon was broken up, by the Romans in 167, and this was reversed within twenty years, first by the rebellion of the Macedonians and then by Roman annexation of the whole and its conversion into a single Roman province. The Attalid kingdom's main regions were taken over complete by Rome, with minor regions being awarded to allies, and Egypt fell as a complete unit to Rome in 30 BC. Even the Carthaginian republic was eventually taken over whole, as was its old enemy Syracuse. Only the Seleukid kingdom was sliced up by its external and internal enemies into fractions of its great size. The fragments in Syria were then taken over slowly, piece by piece, by Rome over a period of a century and a half.

Rome, it seems clear, had no part in this disintegration. Occasional Roman visitors arrived for over a century and more, inspected the kingdom, and then went away. Occasional Seleukid claimants or enemies turned up in Rome, were heard, and received no help. At no time did any Roman interfere in Seleukid affairs with any effect – not with Timarchos, not with Alexander Balas, not with the last stirrings in the 60s BC – only Octavius could be said to have had some effect, but his murder no doubt convinced any other Romans to keep clear. When the Roman army finally arrived in Syria, as did that of Pompeius in 66, it was merely to mop up the fragments, leaving the cities autonomous, and the kingdoms and principalities largely intact and in existence. This was the tradition in which Tigranes had left the communities alone, and Pompeius made no more than a few minor changes – at least until he reached Judaea.

Partly the disintegration which the Romans found was due to the sheer size of the original kingdom, so that breaking off fragments – Baktria, Parthia, Asia

Minor – did not seriously damage the essential heartlands of Syria, Babylonia and Iran. And partly it was due to the inability of the Seleukid kings to maintain control over the more distant parts of a kingdom which was 2,000km long and more, and which could only be crossed at the speed of a marching soldier. Or to put it the other way around: it was due to the ambitions of governors installed by these Seleukid kings, who were able to develop a local interest network which enabled them to strike for independence and make themselves into kings at a time of central government weakness.

And so we come to the ultimate cause of the progressive disintegration of the kingdom: the steadily expanding weakness of the royal government. Even as early as the second decade of the state's existence, Seleukos I had in effect divided the kingdom with his eldest son, who went off to govern the eastern provinces (taking his father's second wife with him). Asia Minor and Baktria both broke away in the mid-third century, and both had been removed definitively, and without hope of recovery, by 190 BC.

The initial collapse, in 246–241 BC, was due to a dispute between the two sons of Antiochos II, but once solved, there were no more drastic problems of that sort for a century. But then the civil wars between 152 and 138 brought the loss of Iran and Babylonia to Parthia, the potential loss of Koele Syria, the separation of Kommagene and Judaea, the foundation of the Nabataean kingdom, and the effective abandonment of Philadelphia. And this civil war originated from the usurpation of Antiochos IV twenty years before. Antiochos VII reconstructed a new kingdom based on control of North Syria, and while it suffered civil wars in the 120s and from 113 onwards the central part, North Syria, remained very largely intact until 75, even though each bout of warfare brought the separation of more peripheral fragments.

Until 175 the royal succession had been reasonably clear: the king nominated his successor, who was always his eldest surviving son, a practice which, having been followed for a century, might be considered to be a rule. Antiochos IV's ambition broke that sequence when he murdered his nephew and stepson; it then became clear that the kingship was available to whoever could seize it. The resulting turbulence at the top might not have mattered had there been a robust government system which could have functioned by itself for a time. But lightness of government was an essential Seleukid government characteristic, and without a firm control at the top that lightness of touch could become an absence of rule. But the kings were in charge, and it was they and their decisions which controlled it and moved it. Only exceptionally was a man like Antiochos V's regent Lysias able to substitute for the king for a time, and even he had to refer major decisions to the king, and when the king died he faced rebellion and (by Demetrios I) usurpation.

The lack of a robust government machine was largely due to the size of the kingdom and to its racial basis. The personnel of the government system were invariably Greeks or Macedonians, quite often recruited from outside the kingdom. There was no place in the ruling group for Iranians or Babylonians, Jews or Phoenicians or Syrians, except in local positions like high priesthoods or village chiefs, or specialists in local affairs, such as the Babylonian temples. This was a legacy of the original Macedonian conquest and of Alexander the Great's failure to insist on widening the basis of the recruitment of his forces beyond his Macedonians and his Greek mercenaries. Seleukos used Iranian horsemen and Indian mahouts to win his war of conquest, but later kings only recruited small specialist forces to supplement the main army of Greco-Macedonian settlers who formed the phalanx infantry. Only in the army were such non-Greeks welcome, and even then only in these more specialist roles; this moderate openness did not translate into the use of such groups in administration or command.

This was too narrow a population basis for the kingdom's well-being, and the Greco-Macedonian settlers and their descendants insisted on a degree of self-government in their cities, which seemed to be a good substitute for a more rigorously bureaucratic government such as that instituted by the Ptolemies in Egypt. But when these settlers and their descendants divided amongst themselves, as they did in the succession disputes, their subjects and enemies could take advantage. United, the king and the Greco-Macedonians could hold what they had won; divided, they slowly fell.

Which is all to say that the kingdom was doomed from the start. By basing his power on a very narrow population base, Seleukos I had made it certain that the first succession dispute – and there was bound to be one – would begin the process of collapse. And yet unless he had based his power on the Greek and Macedonian settlers he would not have survived and there would have been no kingdom. Without the promise of land and cities to live in, the settlers would not have come; and without the settlers Seleukos and his successors would not have a kingdom to rule. The essential basis in the kingdom, the unifying element, was the king. When disputes about the occupation of the throne arose, disintegration happened. The kings made the kingdom, held it, and let it fall. In its origins was the kingdom's ending.

The kingdom failed – but all kingdoms, all empires, fail. Its legacy was, however, extraordinary. Its successor kingdoms dominated the Middle and

Near East for the next three centuries, in the form of the phil-Hellenic Parthian kingdom in Iran, the phil-Hellenic Kushans in Central Asia and Northeast India, and for even longer in the phil-Hellenic Roman Empire. The Roman system of government was very similar to the Seleukid, though more open to promoting talent from outside the Roman group, the wealth exhibited in the first two centuries of the empire was largely based on the trade and production generated in former Seleukid provinces, and the position of the Roman emperor very largely came to resemble that of the Seleukid king, more so at least than that of any other Hellenistic king. The Roman Empire was a Hellenistic state, at least until its collapse in the third century (the same period when the Parthians and the Kushans vanished). And below the summit of the empire, the Seleukid cities from the Hellespont to Baktria continued to exist and provide shelter, employment, intellectual nourishment, and security to their people, some of them right down to the present day. The cities were the essential legacy of the kingdom.

Notes and References

Introduction

1. E. R. Bevan, *The House of Seleucus*, 2 vols, (London, 1902).
2. A. Bouche-Leclerq, *Histoire des Seleucides*, 2 vols, (Paris, 1913).
3. Bellinger, 'End.'
4. Houghton, et al., *Seleucid Coins*.
5. Nathanael J. Andrade, *Syrian Identity in the Greco-Roman World*, (Cambridge, 2013); Rolf Strootman, *Courts and Elites in the Hellenistic Empires*, (Edinburgh, 2014); Paul J. Kosmin, *The Land of the Elephant Kings*, (Cambridge MA, 2014).
6. Susan Sherwin-White and Amelie Kuhrt, *Sardis to Samarkhand*, (London, 1993); Amelie Kuhrt and S. Sherwin-White (eds), *Hellenism in the East*, (London, 1987).

Chapter 1

1. He is recorded as king with his father in 187 (*Astronomical Diaries*, '-189') and he commanded independently in the Roman war.
2. Polybios 27.17.3–7; Holbl, *Ptolemaic Empire*, pp. 156–157.
3. Dates in these eastern kingdoms are uncertain, though G. E. Assar, 'Genealogy and Coinage of the Early Parthian Kings, I', *Parthia* 6, (2004), pp. 69–93, with revisions in *Parthia* 7, seems reasonably convincing.
4. *Astronomical Diaries*, '-183'.
5. Polybios 22.9.13; Diodoros 29.17.
6. W. K. Pritchett and B. D. Merritt, *The Chronology of Hellenistic Athens*, (Cambridge MA ,1940), pp. 117–118; also *IG* II (2) 1236.
7. Polybios 23.9.1–3; 24.1.1–3. 5, 8 and 14.10–15.10; Diodoros 29.22.
8. Polybios 24.15.11–13.
9. Diodoros 29.24; Polybios frag. 96.
10. Bevan, *House*, 2.125; 'weak': Holbl, *Ptolemaic Empire*, p. 141.
11. Diodoros 29.29; Porphyry, *FGrH* 260 F 48.
12. Livy 43.12.3–4; Polybios 25.4.8–10.
13. Appian, *Mithradatic Wars* 2.
14. H. R. R. Broughton, *The Magistrates of the Roman Republic*, (New York, 1951–1952), vol 1, 380.
15. Polybios 23.5.1.
16. Appian, *Syrian Wars* 45; Otto Morkholm, *Antiochos IV of Syria*, (Copenhagen, 1966), pp. 35–56.
17. Bevan, *House*, 2.124–125; J. M. Helliesen, 'Demetrios I Soter: a Seleucid King with an Antigonid Name', in H. J. Dell (ed.) *Ancient Macedonian Studies in honour of Charles F. Edson*, (Thessalonike, 1981).

18. Holbl, *Ptolemaic Empire*, p. 143.
19. Appian, *Syrian Wars* 45; R. Parker and W. Dubberstein, *Babylonian Chronology 626*BC–AD *75*, (Providence RI, 1956), p. 23; A. J. Sachs and D. J. Wiseman, 'A Babylonian King List of the Hellenistic Period', *Iraq* 16, (1954), pp. 202–211.
20. *OGIS* 247; *IG* XI, 4, 1112 and 1113.
21. Morkholm, *Antiochos IV*, p. 36.
22. Ogden, *Polygamy*, p. 141.
23. Morkholm, *Antiochos IV*, p. 20.
24. J. D. Grainger, *Hellenistic Phoenicia*, (Oxford, 1991), pp. 202–215.
25. Appian, *Syrian Wars* 45; *OGIS* 248 (= Austin 208); Sachs and Wiseman, 'Babylonian King List', p. 208, Morkholm, *Antiochos IV* pp. 42–43.
26. *Astronomical Diaries*, '-181', '-178'.
27. Diodoros 30.72; John of Antioch, frag. 58.

Chapter 2
1. Sachs and Wiseman, 'Babylonian King List'.
2. Daniel 11.40–45.
3. Appian, *Syrian Wars*, 45.
4. Ibid.
5. Livy 42.6.12.
6. Polybios 31.13.2–3; II Maccabees 3.5.
7. II Maccabees 8.10–11.
8. Livy 42.6.6–11.
9. For references to all this see Morkholm, *Antiochos IV*, pp. 56–63.
10. II Maccabees 4.21.
11. Ibid, 4.22.
12. Ibid, 4.2–10.
13. Ibid 4.23–25.
14. Ibid, 4.30–34.
15. Ibid, 5.4–5.
16. Livy 42.19.7–8 and 26.7–8.
17. Polybios 28.1.7; Diodoros 30.2.
18. Diodoros 30.16.
19. Porphyry, *FGrH* 260 F 49a; Polybios 28.18; Diodoros 30.18; for a full account of the war see my *The Syrian Wars*, (Leiden, 2009), ch. 13.
20. Polybios 28.21; Diodoros 30.17.
21. Polybios 28.19–20.
22. Porphyry *FGrH* 260 F 49 a–b; Livy 44.19.1–9.
23. Polybios 28.17.13, 21–23; Livy 45.11.8.
24. Polybios 29.23.4; Livy 45.11.2–7.
25. Josephos *AJ*, 12.246; I Maccabees 2.20–28; II Maccabees 5.11–16.
26. Livy 45.12.7.
27. Livy 45.11.9–11.
28. Livy 45.12.1–3.
29. Polybios 29.25.3–4.

30. I Maccabees 1.42–50; II Maccabees 6.1–2.
31. This may or may not be the same man who was previously the local governor and envoy to Rome and Egypt.
32. Polybios 30.25–26.
33. Polybios 26.1.1a and 1–14; Diodoros 19.30; Athenaios 45c and 438d–439e.
34. II Maccabees 4.30; Ogden, *Polygamy*, p. 143.
35. Getzel M. Cohen, *The Hellenistic Settlements in Syria, the Red Sea Basin and North Africa*, (California, 2006), pp. 277–286, 288–289, provides a wealth of authorities and commentary.
36. Ibid, 286–288.
37. Ibid, 205–209, 106–108; Josephos *AJ* 13.393, and *BJ* 1.103.
38. Ibid, 213–221, 226–228.
39. Ibid, 151–152; Strabo 11.14.15.
40. Cohen, *Hellenistic Settlements/Syria*, pp. 79–80.
41. Otto Morkholm, *Studies in the Coinage of Antiochos IV of Syria.*
42. Otto Morkholm, summarized in his *Antiochos IV*, (Copenhagen, 1963), pp. 122–130.
43. Josephos, *AJ* 12, 294–297; I Maccabees 3.31–37; II Maccabees 9.23–25.
44. Diodoros 31.17a; Appian, *Syrian Wars* 45–46; Porphyry *FGrH* 260 F 38 and 56.
45. Pliny, *Natural History* 139, 147, 152.
46. Getzel M. Cohen, *The Hellenistic Settlements in the East from Armenia and Mesopotamia to Bactria and India*, (California, 2013), pp, 109–117; Otto Morkholm, 'The Seleucid Mint at Antiochia on the Persian Gulf, *American Numismatic Society Museum Notes*, 16, (1976), pp. 31–44.
47. Cohen, *Hellenistic Settlements/East*, pp. 206–208.
48. Polybios 31.9; Appian, *Syrian Wars* 66; Josephos *AJ* 12.358–359; Porphyry *FGrH* 260 F 53 and 56; II Maccabees 1.13; Strabo 16.1.18.
49. Appian, *Syrian Wars* 66; Sachs and Wiseman; Polybios 31.9.4; I Maccabees 1.6.1–17; II Maccabees 1.13 and 9.2–3 (both inaccurate).

Chapter 3
1. I Maccabees 1.42–56; II Maccabees 6.1–2.
2. I Maccabees 1.52.
3. I Maccabees 2.15–25.
4. I Maccabees 2.27–28.
5. John D. Grainger, *The Wars of the Maccabees*, (Barnsley, 2012), pp. 11–12, for a summary.
6. I Maccabees 3.21–11; Josephos, *AJ* 12.257; B. Bar-Kochva, *Judas Maccabaeus*, (Cambridge, 1989), pp. 199–206.
7. I Maccabees 3.13–25; Josephos, *AJ* 12.288–292; Bar-Kochva, *Judas*, pp. 207–218.
8. I Maccabees 3.46–66.
9. I Maccabees 3.31–34 and 47–54.
10. I Maccabees 4.1–22; Josephos, *AJ* 12.305–306 and 310–311.
11. II Maccabees 11.16–33.
12. I Maccabees 4.34–35; Bar-Kochva, *Judas*, pp. 279–281, and 289–290.
13. I Maccabees 4.36–61.

14. I Maccabees 5.10–14, 5.3–68.
15. I Maccabees 6.21–47; Josephos, *AJ* 12.366–372.
16. Josephos, *AJ* 12.378–380, 386; I Maccabees 6.55–63.
17. II Maccabees 14.3.
18. Getzel M. Cohen, *The Hellenistic Settlements in Syria, the Red Sea Basin and North Africa*, (California, 2006), pp. 263–264.
19. II Maccabees 10.13.
20. Diodoros 31.17.1; Polybios 30.27.1–4.
21. Polybios 31.2.8–11; Diodoros 31.29; Appian, *Syrian Wars* 46; Pliny, *Natural History* 34.24.
22. Polybios 31.7.1–8.8.
23. Polybios 31.2.1–7.
24. Polybios 31.11.1–15.13; Polybios was deeply involved in the plot, but seems not to have been blamed by the Senate; it is quite possible that some senators were also involved.
25. Josephos, *AJ* 12.389–390; Appian, *Syrian Wars* 47; Livy, *Epitome* 46; Eusebios, *Chronographia* 1.40.15.
26. Diodoros 31.18
27. I Maccabees 7.5–18.
28. I Maccabees 7.19–26.
29. I Maccabees 7.26–30; II Maccabees 34.12–30.
30. I Maccabees 7.39–50; Josephos *AJ* 12.408–412.
31. Appian, *Syrian Wars* 45.
32. Diodoros 31.27a; Appian, *Syrian Wars* 47; A. Houghton, 'Timarchos as King in Babylonia', *Revue Numismatique* 21, (1976), pp. 212–217; P. Herrmann, 'Milesier an Seleukidenreich, Prosopographische Beitrage zur Geschichte Milets in 2 Jhdt v. Chr.', *Chiron* 17, (1987), pp. 171–173.
33. I Maccabees 9.1–22; Josephos, *AJ* 12.420–430; Bar-Kochva, *Judas* pp. 282–399.
34. I Maccabees 9.23–35, 56–72.
35. Josephos, *AJ* 12.387–388.

Chapter 4

1. So argued, reasonably convincingly, by Ogden, *Polygamy*.
2. Justin 35.1.2; Diodoros 31.28.
3. Arthur Houghton, 'Timarchos as King in Babylonia', *Revue Numismatique* 21, (1976), pp. 212–217.
4. Georges Le Rider, *Suse sous les Seleucides et les Parthes*, (Paris, 1965), pp. 346–347.
5. Justin 41.6.1–2.
6. *Inscriptions de Delos* 442; A. R. Bellinger, 'Hyspaosines of Charax', *Yale Classical Studies* 8, (1942), pp. 53–67.
7. Diodoros 31.19a; R. D. Sullivan, 'The Dynasty of Commagene', *Aufstieg und Niedergang der romischen Welt*, II.8, (Berlin, 1977), pp. 732–798, 742–748.
8. H. Hommel, 'Ein Konig aus Milet', *Chiron* 6, (1976), pp. 319–327.
9. Appian, *Syrian Wars*, 47.
10. Polybios 33.15.

11. Diodoros 31.29a.
12. Diodoros 31.32a.
13. Polybios 32.10.1–8 and 33.6.2; Justin 35.1,2–4.
14. Diodoros 31.19a.
15. Diodoros 33.15, 18.6–14.
16. Polybios 33.5.1–4.
17. Josephos, *AJ* 13.35.
18. Polybios 33.15 and 18.4; see also Ogden, *Polygamy*.
19. Erich S. Gruen, *The Hellenistic Monarchies and the Coming of Rome*, (California, 1984), ch. 16, interprets events to suggest that Attalos was largely a free agent, but he carefully remained within bounds originally set by Rome.
20. Ibid, 695–698.
21. Josephos, *AJ* 13.35; I Maccabees 10.1.
22. I Maccabees 10.1.
23. Josephos, *AJ* 13.37; I Maccabees 10.2.
24. Josephos *AJ* 13.37–42; I Maccabees 10.6–14.
25. Josephos, *AJ* 13.42; I Maccabees 10.14 (mentioning only Beth Zur).
26. Josephos *AJ* 13. 43–46; I Maccabees 10.15–21.
27. Josephos, *AJ* 13.46–57; I Maccabees 10.22–47.
28. I Maccabees 10.21.
29. Diodoros 31.40a.
30. Josephos, *AJ* 13.58.
31. See note 7.
32. Oliver D. Hoover, 'Notes on some Imitation Drachms of Demetrios I Soter from Commagene', *American Journal of Numismatics* 10, (1998), pp. 71–94.
33. Diodoros 31.19a.
34. Josephos, *AJ* 13.58; I Maccabees 10.48–50.
35. Appian, *Syrian Wars* 67; Justin 35.1.9–11.
36. *Astronomical Diaries*, vol. 2, '-149' (June 150).
37. Alexander was a more prolific coiner than Demetrios, presumably because he needed to publicize his name quickly. His coins were also more consistently dated. Only at Antioch is there an overlap in the coins of the two kings; Alexander seems to have secured control of many other areas fairly easily. However, he did not coin, even at Ptolemais-Ake, until 162 SE (= 151/150 BC).

Chapter 5
1. I Maccabees 10.51–54; Josephos, *AJ* 13.82.
2. Livy, *Epitome* 50.
3. Justin 35.2.1.
4. Porphyry, *FGrH* 260 F 32.16 – hence his later nickname of 'Sidetes'.
5. Josephos, *AJ* 13.86.
6. Livy, *Epitome* 50; Justin 35.2.2.
7. Houghton et al., *Seleucid Coins*.
8. D. B. Weiskopf, 'Late Babylonian Texts in the Oriental Institute', *Biblioteca Mesopotamia* 24, no 12.

9. A. R. Bellinger, 'Hyspaosines of Charax', *Yale Classical Studies* 8, (1942), pp. 53–67; S. A. Nodelman, 'A Preliminary History of Charakene', *Berytus* (1960), pp. 83–121.

10. Josephos, *AJ* 13.88.

11. L. Robert, 'Encore une Inscription grecque d'Iran', *CRAI* (1967), pp. 283 and 291; also quoted in A. H. D. Bivar, *Iran under the Arsacids, Cambridge History of Iran*, vol. 3.1, 33.

12. Le Rider, *Suse sous les Seleucides et les Parthes*, (Paris, 1965).

13. Josephos, *AJ* 13.86.

14. Diodoros 33.3; Hierax was probably Egyptian, and his career is outlined in *Prosopographia Ptolemaica* I, 264, II 2163, VI 17012; Diodotos was from near Apameia in Syria; Ammonios, from his name if nothing else, was probably also Egyptian. Ptolemy VI had placed these with Alexander from the beginning and, together with Alexander's Ptolemaic wife, they ensured Ptolemaic influence over him.

15. Josephos, *AJ* 13.88.

16. Justin 35.2.3.

17. Josephos, *AJ* 13.88–102; I Maccabees 10.69–89.

18. Polybios 8.15.1–20.7, describing another plot involving Cretans.

19. Justin 35.2.3.

20. Josephos, *AJ* 13.105; I Maccabees 11.7.

21. Josephos, *AJ* 13.106–107; I Maccabees 11.8; Diodoros 32.9a.

22. Josephos, *AJ* 13.108.

23. Ibid.

24. Diodoros 32.9c.

25. Josephos, *AJ* 13.109–110; I Maccabees 11.9–12.

26. Josephos *AJ* 13.112.

27. Diodoros 32.9c; Josephos, *AJ* 13.113–115.

28. Josephos, *AJ* 13.116–119; Justin 35.2.4; Appian, *Syrian Wars* 67; Diodoros 32.9c, 9d, 10.1.

Chapter 6

1. Josephos, *AJ* 13.120.

2. N. C. Debevoise, *A Political History of Parthia*, (Chicago, 1938).

3. J. Harmatta, 'The Second Elymaean Inscription from Bard e-Neshandeh', *Acta Antiqua Academiensis Scientiarum Hungaricae* 32, (1989), pp. 161–1871.

4. *Astronomical Diaries*, vol 2, '-144'.

5. Justin 41.7.

6. Houghton et al., *Seleucid Coins*, p. 313.

7. I Maccabees 11.38, 44–50; Josephos, *AJ* 3.129–130, 135–144; Diodoros 33.4a.

8. Diodoros 33.4a; A. Houghton, 'The Revolt of Tryphon and the Accession of Antiochos VI at Apamea', *Schweizer Numismatische Rundschau* 72, (1992), pp. 119–141.

9. Diodoros 33.9.

10. Houghton et al., *Seleucid Coins*, pp. 330–332.

11. *Astronomical Diaries*, vol 2, '-144'.

12. I Maccabees 11.59–60; Josephos, *AJ* 13.156–159.

13. Josephos, *BJ* 1.4.2.

14. I Maccabees 11.63–67, 12.24–30; Josephos, *AJ* 13.154–162; see my *Wars of the Maccabees*, (Barnsley, 2012), for a more detailed examination of these events.
15. Josephos, *AJ* 13.187; Justin 36.1.7; Livy, *Epitome* 55; I Maccabees 13.31; Appian, *Syrian Wars* 68; Diodoros 33.28.
16. K. Liampi, 'Der Makedonische schild als propagandisches mittel in der Hellenistischen Zeit', *Meletemata* 10, (1950), pp. 157–175; Houghton et al., *Seleucid Coins*, 'revolt of Tryphon'.
17. Diodoros 33.28.
18. I Maccabees 12.41–53, 13.11–24; Josephos, *AJ* 13.188–192, 196–212.
19. I Maccabees 13.31–42.
20. H. A. Ormerod, *Piracy in the Ancient World*, (Liverpool, 1924).
21. *Astronomical Diaries*, vol 2, '-140'.
22. Ibid.
23. Justin 36.1.4.
24. *Astronomical Diaries*, vol 2, '-140'.
25. W. Moore, 'The Divine Couple of Demetrios II Nicator and his coinage at Nisibis', *American Numismatic Society Museum Notes* 31, (1986), pp. 129–143.
26. *Astronomical Diaries*, vol 2, '-140'.
27. J. Harmatta, 'Parthia and Elymais in the 2nd Century BC', *Acta Antiqua Academiae Scientarum Hungaricae* 29, (1991), pp. 189–217.
28. Cohen, *Hellenistic Settlements/East*, pp. 97–98.
29. Houghton et al., *Seleucid Coins*, pp. 311–312.
30. Justin 36.1.4.
31. *Astronomical Diaries*, vol 2, '-138' (July 138); Justin 36.1.5.
32. Appian, *Syrian Wars* 68; Josephos, *AJ* 13.222; Houghton et al., *Seleucid Coins*, pp. 311–312.

Chapter 7
1. Houghton et al., *Seleucid Coins*, pp. 362–369.
2. Ibid, Reign of Antiochos VII.
3. Josephos, *AJ* 13.226.
4. I Maccabees 15.37.
5. Houghton et al., *Seleucid Coins*, 'coins of Tryphon'.
6. I Maccabees 15.14.
7. Dov Gera, 'Tryphon's Sling Bullet from Dor', *Israel Exploration Journal* 35, (1985), pp. 153–163.
8. I Maccabees 15.23.
9. I Maccabees 15.1 says Antiochos 'sent a letter from overseas to Simon'. This was presumably by sea from Tyre or Seleukeia, rather than from Rhodes before he arrived in Syria.
10. I Maccabees 15.25–36.
11. Josephos, *AJ* 13.223–224.
12. I Maccabees 15.37; Josephos, *AJ* 13.224.
13. Josephos *AJ* 13.225–227.

14. I Maccabees 15.40–16.10.
15. The placing of cavalry in the centre with infantry flanking it is unknown in any other ancient campaign. If it was successful, it seems very odd that no other commander ever used it. The battle would involve the cavalry charging an unbroken phalanx of spearmen, which very rarely happened. I conclude that the author was inventing, or misunderstanding.
16. Josephos, *AJ* 13.227 – but 'peaceful' clearly excludes being murdered.
17. Justin 36.1.9.
18. Diodoros 31.19a; *OGIS* 396.
19. Oliver D. Hoover, 'Notes on some Imitation Drachms of Demetrius I Soter from Commagene', *American Journal of Numismatics*, 10, (1998), pp. 71–94.
20. J. B. Segal, *Edessa, the Blessed City*, (Oxford, 1970).
21. So Gera argues, in 'Tryphon's Sling Bullet' (note 7).
22. I Maccabees 16.11–22; Josephos, *AJ* 13.228–229.
23. I Maccabees 16.18; this detail is not in Josephos.
24. I Maccabees 13.2–9; assembly: I Maccabees 14.27–47; *ethnarchos*: Josephos, *AJ* 12.214; *hegemon*: I Maccabees 13.42.
25. I Maccabees 14.41.
26. I Maccabees 13.49–51; Josephos, *AJ* 13.215.
27. I Maccabees 12.33–34, 13.11, and 14.5 (Joppa), 13.43–48 (Gazara); Josephos, *AJ* 13.215.
28. I Maccabees 16.18 – 22; Josephos, *AJ* 13.228–229.
29. Josephos, *AJ* 13.230–234.
30. I Maccabees 16.14.
31. H. Eshel, *The Dead Sea Scrolls and the Hasmonaean State*, (Jerusalem, 2008).
32. Every high priest in the Persian and Hellenistic period had been confirmed in office, on payment of the required tribute, by the king. This ceased when Judaea became independent after 128. The king usually did no more than confirm the succession from within the high priestly family.
33. Josephos, *AJ* 13.236–248.
34. Echoes of Thucydides have been detected: R. Marcus in the Loeb edition, vol. VIII, p. 349, Note a, though this in itself does not invalidate Josephos' account – it is the overall descriptive tone which is unconvincing.
35. Josephos, *AJ* 13.237 and 242.
36. The dating of this is confused. Josephos dates Antiochos' invasion to Antiochos' fourth year, Hyrkanos' first, and the Olympic year 162 (*AJ* 13.238); the first two of these may be reconciled, but Ol. 162 did not begin until July 132. Eusebios, *Chronographia*, I, 255, is even worse, putting it in the third year of Ol. 162, which would be 130. Various interpretations can be made – that Eusebios should be Ol. 161, for instance, or that the siege lasted into Ol. 162 – but on political grounds the siege must have happened fairly soon after Hyrkanos' accession, and is tied to the fleeing of Ptolemaios. Much more surprising than the muddle over the dating is Antiochos' forbearance in not invading until the civil war was finished.
37. Josephos, *AJ* 13.245–247; a brief comment is in Josephos, *BJ* 1.2.5; Diodoros 34/35.1–5; Eusebios, *Chronographia* I, p. 255.

38. This was in a complaint to Rome: Josephos, *AJ* 13.261; I doubt the theory of T. Rayak, 'Roman Intervention in a Seleucid Siege of Jerusalem', *Greek, Roman and Byzantine Studies* 22, (1981), pp. 65–81.

39. Josephos, *AJ* 13.250–251.

40. Josephos, *AJ* 13.247.

41. Y. Meshorer, *Ancient Jewish Coinage*, vol. I, *Persian Period through the Hasmonaeans*, (Dix Hills NY, 1982), pp. 39–40.

42. George Adam Smith, *The Historical Geography of the Holy Land*, (London, 1931), p. 126 note.

43. Josephos, *AJ* 13.356; *BJ* 1.4.2, dated c. 100 BC.

44. II Maccabees 5.8.

45. Josephos, *AJ* 13.360.

46. Glen Bowersock, *Roman Arabia*, (Cambridge MA, 1983), pp. 18–19.

47. J. Cantineau, *Le Nabataeen*, II, (Paris, 1932), 44; cf. Bowersock, *Roman Arabia*, 18 and note 22.

48. Diodoros 19.94.1; C. C. Edgar, *Zenon Papyri* I, (1925).

49. F. B. Peters, 'The Nabataeans in the Hauran', *Journal of the American Oriental Society*, 97, (1977), pp. 263–277.

50. J. D. Grainger, *The Cities of Seleukid Syria*, (Oxford, 1990).

51. Three articles by Arthur Houghton cover this matter: 'The Royal Seleucid Mint of Soli', *Numismatic Chronicle* 149, (1898), pp. 15–22, 'The Seleukid Mint at Seleuceia-on-the-Calycadnus', *Kraay–Morkholm Essays*, (ed.) G. Le Rider et al., (Louvain, 1989), pp. 77–98, and 'The Seleucid Mint of Mallus and the Cult Figure of Athene Magarsis', *Festschrift fur Leo Mildenburg*, (Wettern, 1984), pp. 91 – 110.

52. Houghton, 'Soli' (previous note), 31.

53. Paul J. Kosmin, *The Land of the Elephant Kings*, (Cambridge, MA 2014), pp. 201–202.

54. B. V. Head, *Historia Numorum*, (Oxford, 1911), p. 732.

55. Grainger, *Cities*, ch. 6.

56. John D. Grainger, *Hellenistic Phoenicia*, (Oxford, 1991), pp. 113–115.

57. Ernest Will, 'Un vieux problem de la topographie de la Beqa antique: Chalcis du Liban', *Zeitschrift fur Deutsche Palasteins-verein*, 99, (1983), pp. 141–146.

58. II Maccabees 5.8 and 5.25–26.

59. H. Seyrig, Le Monnayage de Hierapolis de Syrie a l'epoque d'Alexandre', *Revue Numismatique*, (1971), pp. 11–21; Grainger, *Cities*, p. 26.

Chapter 8

1. A. R. Bellinger, 'Hyspaosines of Charax', *Yale Classical Studies* 8, (1942), pp. 53–67; S. A. Nodelman, 'A Preliminary History of Charakene', *Berytus* (1960), pp. 83–121; for the site and plan of Charax, see J. Hansman, 'Charax and the Kharkeh', *Iranica Antiqua* 7, (1967), pp. 21–567.

2. Strabo 16.1.19.

3. Josephos, *AJ* 20.35.

4. Strabo 16.1.4; Head, *Historia Numorum*, (Oxford 1911), p. 817; M.-L. Chaumont, 'Recherches sur quelques villes helleniques de l'Iran occidental', *Iranica Antiqua* 17, (1982), pp. 153–155; Cohen, *Hellenistic Settlements / East*, pp. 97–98.

5. *Astronomical Diaries*, vol. 3, '-137'.
6. N. C. Debevoise, *The Political History of Parthia*, (Chicago, 1938), p. 29; the name is possibly Babylonian – but it is written in cuneiform, hence the syllables.
7. Noted first in 138 as 'the general who is above the four generals' (*Astronomical Diaries*, '-138').
8. Justin 38.9.3; Appian, *Syrian Wars* 67.
9. Justin 38.9.3 and 10.
10. Justin 38.9.4.
11. *Astronomical Diaries*, '-133'.
12. Strabo 16.1.18.
13. *Astronomical Diaries*, '-133'.
14. The most detailed discussion of the expedition is by T. Fischer, *Untersuchungen zur Partherkrieg Antiochos' VII*, (Tubingen dissertation, 1970), who lists the sources on pp. 5–35, though he did not have the use of the full text of the *Astronomical Diaries*.
15. This is the lowest claim (Justin 38.10.2). Others climb to 300,000. These higher extravagances cast doubt on the lower. The largest Seleukid force taken to the east, by Antiochos III, was about 35,000; this may be about the size of Antiochos VII's army, but we do not know. It was clearly large enough to beat the Parthians.
16. Josephos, *AJ* 13.250.
17. Josephos, *AJ* 13.251–252, quoting Nikolaos of Damascus, *FGrH* 90 F 92.
18. Justin 38.10.6.
19. Fischer, *Untersuchungen*, ch. 1.
20. Houghton et al., *Seleucid Coins*, pp. 394–395.
21. Diodoros 34/35.19.1.
22. Suggested by Bellinger, 'Hyspaosines', pp. 66–67.
23. Justin 38.10.5–6.
24. G. Le Rider, *Suse sous les Seleucides et les Parthes*, (Paris, 1965).
25. Diodoros 34/35.19.1.
26. Justin 38.10.8.
27. This is Justin's interpretation (previous note) followed, for instance, by Bevan, *House*, 2.244–245. Fischer, *Untersuchungen*, puts the occupiers' camp in Parthia itself, but Justin is clear that the soldiers were in 'the cities', which implies Media rather than Parthia, and Hyrkanos' detachment was in Babylonia. And, had Antiochos actually occupied the centre of Parthian power, why did no ancient source say so? It is an obvious setting for implications of hubris.
28. Justin 42.1.2.
29. Justin 38.10.7; Appian, *Syrian Wars* 68; Josephos, *AJ* 13.253.
30. Justin 38.10.8 – the risings took place simultaneously, 'on a prearranged day'.
31. Bevan, *House*, 2.244, suggested he was at Ekbatana.
32. Debevoise, *Parthia*, pp. 31–34; Bevan, *House*, 2.243–245; Bouche-LeClercq, *Seleucides*, pp. 381–384; Fischer, *Untersuchungen*, pp. 29–48.
33. Justin 38.10.2.
34. *Astronomical Diaries*, '-130', an isolated fragment: 'That month, the Arabs ...', which in the context means they were raiding somewhere in the neighbourhood of Babylon.
35. Justin 38.10.7 and 11.

36. Diodoros 34/35.17.1.
37. Justin 42.1.4–6 – in 128, the year after the death of Antiochos.
38. Josephos, *AJ* 13.254.
39. Josephos, *AJ* 13.249.
40. Diodoros 34/35.17.2.
41. Justin 38.10.10; Athenaios 153a (from Poseidonios); cf. Fischer, *Untersuchungen*, pp. 49–56.
42. Justin 38.10.10; Porphyry, *FGrH* 260 F 32.19–20; Eusebios, *Chronographia* 1.40.18.
43. Justin 42.1.1–2.
44. A. K. Narain, *The Indo-Greeks*, (Cambridge, 1957 and 1980), p. 134.
45. Justin 38.10.11.
46. See the table in Fischer, *Untersuchungen*, pp. 91–92.
47. Justin 42.1.4–5.
48. Diodoros 34/35.21; Justin 42.1.3.
49. Justin 42.2.3–4.

Chapter 9
1. Justin 38.10.9; Diodoros 34/35.15.1.
2. Houghton et al., *Seleucid Coins*, pp. 394–395.
3. Houghton et al., *Seleucid Coins*, second reign of Demetrios II.
4. Justin 38.9.4–9.
5. A. Houghton and G. Le Rider, 'Un premier regne d'Antiochos VIII Epiphane a Antioch en 128', *Bulletin de Correspondence Hellenique 112*, (1988).
6. Appian, *Syrian Wars* 69; Porphyry *FGrH* 260 F 32.20; *Inscriptions de Delos* p. 1546, 1548; Eusebios, *Chronographia* 1.40.19.
7. Justin 39.1.6.
8. Justin 38.10.10.
9. J. Neusner, 'Parthian Political Ideology', *Acta Iranica* 3, (1963), pp. 40–59.
10. For accounts of this Egyptian dispute see Holbl, *Ptolemaic Empire*, pp. 197–200 and J. Whitehorne, *Cleopatras*, (London, 1994), pp. 116–119.
11. Justin 38.9.1; 39.1.2 and 4.
12. For the crisis in the Attalid state cf. R. H. Kallet-Marx, *Hegemony to Empire, the Development of Roman Imperium in the East from 148 to 62 BC*, (California, 1995), pp. 99–111; the terminus of the via Aquillia at Side is noted by R. H. French, 'Sites and Monuments from Phrygia, Pisidia and Pamphylia', *Epigraphica Anatolica* 17, (1991), pp. 53–54.r
13. A. E. Viesse, 'Les "Revoltes Egyptiennes". Recherches sur les Troubles interieures en Egypte du Regne de Ptolemee II a la conquete romaine', *Studia Hellenistica* 41, (Louvain, 2004).
14. Justin 39.1.3.
15. Josephos, *AJ* 13.263.
16. Justin 39.1.4–5.
17. Josephos, *AJ* 13.267–269; Justin 39.1.14; Eusebios, *Chronographia* 1.40.20; E. Ehling, 'Alexander II Zabeinas-ein angeblicher (Adoptiv) Sohn des Antiochos VII oder Alexander I Balas', *Schweitzer Munzblatter* 45, (1995), pp. 2–7.

18. Justin 39.1.6.
19. Justin 39.1.3.
20. Josephos, *AJ* 13.267.
21. Appian, *Syrian Wars* 68.
22. Porphyry, *FGrH* 260 F 32.20.
23. Justin 39.1.3.
24. Bellinger, 'End', p. 63.
25. Houghton et al., *Seleucid Coins*, pp. 421–422.
26. Bellinger, 'End', p. 63.
27. Diodoros 34/35.22' Bevan, *House*, pp. 248–249; K. Ehling, 'Seleukidische Geschichte zwischen 130 und 121 v. Chr.', *Historia* 47, (1998), pp. 141–151.
28. Josephos, *AJ* 13.267.
29. Josephos, *AJ* 13.254.
30. Josephos, *AJ* 13.254–255.
31. Josephos, *AJ* 13.255–256.
32. Josephos, *AJ* 13.257–258.
33. Strabo 16.2.12; J. D. Grainger, *Hellenistic Phoenicia*, (Oxford 1991), pp. 129–132.
34. Eusebios, *Chronographia* 257 F (= Porphyry *FGrH* 260 F 32.21); E. T. Newell, 'Late Seleucid Mints in Ace-Ptolemais and Damascus', *Numismatic Notes and Monographs* 34, (1939), p. 56.
35. Justin 39.1.7–8; Josephos, *AJ* 13.268; Appian, *Syrian Wars* 68.
36. E. T. Newell, 'The Seleucid Coinage of Tyre: a Supplement', *Numismatic Notes and Monographs* 78, (1938); G. MacDonald, *Catalogue of the Greek Coins in the Hunterian Collection*, vol. 2, (Glasgow, 1905).
37. Appian, *Syrian Wars* 68; Livy, *Epitome* 60.
38. *British Museum Catalogue, Phoenicia*, Tyre 44; Grainger, *Hellenistic Phoenicia*, pp. 136–137.
39. Holbl, *Ptolemaic Empire*, p. 200.
40. Appian, *Syrian Wars* 69; Justin 39.1.9; Livy, *Epitome* 60.
41. *British Museum Catalogue, Seleucid Kings* 85; Bellinger, 'End', p. 65.
42. Appian, *Syrian Wars* 69; Porphyry, *FGrH* 260 F 32.20.
43. Houghton et al., *Seleucid Coins*, Reign of Alexander II.
44. Holbl, *Ptolemaic Empire*, pp. 200–201.
45. The names of these three daughters were Tryphaina, Kleopatra, and Selene, though the modern habit has been to add 'Kleopatra' in front of Tryphaina and Selene; this is apparently wrong (Holbl, *Ptolemaic Empire*, p. 203). With some relief I can use their shorter and 'correct' names.
46. Justin 39.2.3.
47. Justin 39.2.3–4.
48. Justin 39.2.5–6; Diodoros 34/35.28, 28a; Josephos, *AJ* 13.269; Eusebios, *Chronographia* 1.257–258.
49. Josephos, *AJ* 13.269–270.
50. Josephos, *AJ* 13.259–266.
51. Gruen, *Hellenistic Monarchies*, vol. 2, 750–751, seems decisive; cf. also T. R. S. Broughton, *Magistrates of the Roman Republic*, vol. 2, p. 509, note 2.

52. J. Rouvier, 'Numismatique des villes de Phenicie', *Journal Internationale d'Archeologie Numismatique*, 3, 4 and 5, pp. 1271–1280 and 1293; *British Museum Catalogue, Seleucid Kings*, coins of 197 SE; A. Houghton, *Coins of the Seleucid Empire from the Collection of Arthur Houghton*, (New York, 1983), pp. 723–725; Grainger, *Hellenistic Phoenicia*, pp. 138–140.
53. H. Seyrig, 'Sue quelques eres Syrienne: I. L'ere des rois de Commagene', *Revue Numismatique* 6, (1964), pp. 51–56.
54. Sullivan, 'Commagene', pp. 753–763.
55. Oliver D. Hoover, 'Notes'.
56. Houghton et al., *Seleucid Coins*, Reign of Antiochos VIII.
57. Justin 39.2.7; Appian, *Syrian Wars* 69.

Chapter 10
1. So stated as a fact by M.-L. Chaumont, 'Recherches sur quelques villes helleniques de l'Iran occidental', *Iranica Antiqua* 17, (1982), but without references.
2. Athenaios 210a (from Poseidonios).
3. Athenaios 210f (from Poseidonios).
4. Athenaios, 210 and 450a–b; the same reputation was fastened on his rival: Diodoros 34/35.34; rival propagandizing may be detected.
5. Appian, *Syrian Wars* 69.
6. Josephos, *AJ* 13.270.
7. Livy, *Epitome* 62.
8. For modern reconstructions of this contest see E. Will, *Histoire Politique de la Monde Hellenistique*, vol 2, (Nancy, 1982), pp. 455–457; Bevan, *House*, vol. 2, pp. 253–259; Bellinger, 'End'.
9. Bellinger, 'End', pp. 66–67.
10. Josephos, *AJ* 13.327.
11. O. Hoover, 'A Revised Chronology for the late Seleucids at Antioch (121/0–64 BC), *Historia* 56, (2007), pp. 280–301.
12. Hoover (previous note) is clear about the problems of using these methods.
13. Houghton et al., *Seleucid Coins*, Reigns of Antiochos VIII and Antiochos IX; Bellinger, 'End', pp. 71–72.
14. Bellinger, 'End', p. 67, referring to his own study of the coins from the Dura excavations.
15. Holbl, *Ptolemaic Empire*, pp. 204–206.
16. Justin 39.3.3.
17. Justin 39.3.5–11.
18. Justin 39.3.12.
19. Eusebios, *Chronographia*, 1.259.
20. B. V. Head, *Historia Numorum*, (Oxford, 1911), pp. 797–798.
21. Josephos, *AJ* 13.318.
22. E. A. Myers, *The Ituraeans and the Roman Near East*, (Cambridge, 2010); A. H. M. Jones, 'The Urbanisation of the Ituraean Principality', *Journal of Roman Studies* 21, (1931), p. 266; Damascus: Josephos, *AJ* 13.392 and *BJ* 1.4.8.
23. A. H. M. Jones, *Cities of the Eastern Roman Provinces*, (Oxford, 1971), pp. 256–257 and note 37.

24. Z. Ma'oz, N. Goren-Inbar , and C. Epstein, 'Golan', in E. Stern (ed.), *New Encyclopedia of Archaeological Excavations in the Holy Land*, vol. 2, (Jerusalem, 1994), pp. 525–546.

25. S. Dov, *Settlements and Cult Sites on Mount Hermon, Israel. Ituraean Studies in the Hellenistic and Roman Periods*, British Archaeological Reports, International Series, S 589, (Oxford, 1993).

26. Head, *Historia Numorum*, (Oxford, 1911), p. 783.

27. Ibid, 783, 784.

28. J. Teixidor, *The Pagan God, Popular Religion in the Greco-Roman Near East*, (Princeton NJ, 1977).

29. J. C. Balty, 'Le Belus de Chalcis et les Fleuves de Ba'al de Syrie-Palestine', *Archeologie de Levant, Receuil R. Saideh*, (Lyon, 1982), pp. 287–298.

30. Lucian of Samosata, *The Syrian God*.

31. *British Museum Catalogue, Phoenicia*, Tripolis no 41; H. Seyrig, 'Eres' 39; Houghton et al., *Seleucid Coins*, pp. 540–541.

32. Josephos, *AJ* 13.279; Rouvier, no 1299.

33. Bellinger, 'End', p. 68; Hoover, 'Revised Chronology', pp. 285–288.

34. *British Museum Catalogue, Phoenicia* p. lxx; Houghton et al., *Seleucid Coins*, pp. 540–541.

35. Seyrig, 'Eres', 39–41.

36. C. B. Welles, *Royal Correspondence of the Hellenistic Period*, (New Haven, 1934), pp. 71–72; Austin, p. 173.

37. Most authorities plump for Grypos: Jones, *Cities*, p. 255 – 'Antiochos VIII probably'; Bevan, *House*, vol. 2, p. 256 and Austin, p. 173 without qualification; Welles (previous note) is 'inclined to feel that the evidence points rather to Grypos as author'; the one dissident is Bouche-LeClercq, *Seleucides*, p. 603, who inclines towards Antiochos IX Kyzikenos; but none of this is definitive.

38. *British Museum Catalogue, Syria*, p. 269.

Chapter 11

1. Josephos, *AJ* 13.270.

2. Josephos, *AJ* 13.288–300; I. Shatzman, *The Armies of the Hasmonaeans and Herod*, (Tubingen, 1991), greatly exaggerates the Hasmonaean army's military competence.

3. Josephos, *AJ* 13.275.

4. Holbl, *Ptolemaic Empire*, p. 207.

5. Diodoros 34/35.39a; Justin 39.4.1–2.

6. Josephos, *AJ* 13.276–278.

7. Josephos, *AJ* 13.280.

8. Josephos, *AJ* 13.281.

9. J. W. Crowfoot et al., *The Buildings of Samaria*, (London, 1942); Y. Meshorer, *Ancient Jewish Coinage*, vol. I, *Persian Period through the Hasmonaeans*, (Dix Hills NY, 1982), p. 44.

10. Josephos *AJ* 13.280; *BJ* 1.65; most historians assume the city's capture: Jones, *Cities*, p. 255; E. Mary Smallwood, *The Jews under Roman Rule*, (Leiden, 1981), p. 13; B. Lifshitz, 'Scythopolis: l'histoire, les institutions, et les cultes de la ville a l'epoque hellenistique et imperial', *Aufstieg und Niedergang des Romischen Welt* II.8, pp. 262–294, are examples.

11. Josephos, *AJ* 13.335.
12. Josephos, *AJ* 13.249.
13. Josephos, *AJ* 13.247–252.
14. E. T. Newell, 'Late Seleucid Mints in Ake-Ptolemais and Damascus', *American Numismatic Society Notes and Monographs* 84, (1939); Bellinger, 'End', pp. 70–71.
15. A. B. Brett, 'The Mint of Ascalon under the Seleucids', *American Numismatic Society Notes and Monographs* 4, (1950), pp. 43–54.
16. Newell, 'Late Seleucid Mints', (note 14).
17. Josephos, *AJ* 14.247–255; this appears in a collection of documents, with no clear date other than Hyrkanos' reign. It includes an 'order' to expel the garrison of Joppa, but not the means to do so; it is no doubt a fake.
18. Meshorer, *Ancient Jewish Coinage*, vol. 40–41.
19. Josephos, *AJ* 13.322.
20. Assumed, reasonably, by S. Freyne, *Galilee from Alexander the Great to Hadrian, 323 BC to 135 CE*, (Edinburgh, 1980), p. 29.
21. J. D. Grainger, *The Cities of Seleukid Syria*, (Oxford, 1990), pp. 122–123.
22. The exception is the War of the Brothers, 241–227, in which Asia Minor was separated from Syria and the rest of the kingdom for much of the time; it proves the rule, in a sense, in that Asia Minor ever afterwards was always semi-detached from the rest.
23. Josephos, *AJ* 13.324–326.
24. Josephos, *AJ* 13.318–319; Freyne, *Galilee*, pp. 43–44; E. Schurer, *The History of the Jews in the age of Jesus Christ*, revised ed., 3 vols, (Edinburgh, 1983–1980), vol. I, p. 217.
25. Schurer, (previous note), vol. I. p. 142; Freyne, *Galilee*, pp. 35–41.
26. Meshorer, *Ancient Jewish Coinage*, vol. I, pp. 35–81 and 118–134.
27. E. van't Dack et al., *The Judaean-Syrian-Ptolemaic Conflict of 101 BC. A Multilingual Dossier concerning a 'War of Sceptres'*, Collecteanea Hellenistica 1, (Brussels, 1989); J. E. G. Whitehorne, 'A Reassessment of Cleopatra III's Syrian Campaign', *Chronique d'Egypte* 70, (1996), pp. 197–205.
28. Josephos, *AJ* 13.324 merely says that Alexander thought it 'advantageous to himself'; no other reason is even suggested in Schurer vol. I, p. 220.
29. L. Kadman, *Corpus Nummorum Palaestiniensium*, Series 1, vol. V; *The Coins of Akko-Ptolemais*, (Jerusalem, 1961).
30. Josephos, *AJ* 13.324.
31. Ibid.
32. Josephos, *AJ* 13.337; *BJ* 1.86.
33. Josephos, *AJ* 13.338–344.
34. Josephos, *AJ* 13.355.
35. Justin 39.4.4.
36. Josephos, *AJ* 13.356–357; *BJ* 1.86.
37. Josephos, *AJ* 13.335.
38. Josephos, *AJ* 13.353; Van't Dack et al., 'War of Sceptres', pp. 39–49; S. Applebaum, 'Hellenistic Cities of Judaea and its Vicinity – some new Aspects', in B. Levick (ed.), *The Ancient Historian and his Materials, Essays in Honour of C. E. Stevens*, (Farnborough, 1975), pp. 59–65.

39. Josephos, *AJ* 13.352, 357.
40. Josephos, *AJ* 13.357–364; *BJ* 1.87–88.
41. Josephos, *AJ* 13.330.
42. Josephos, *AJ* 13.357–364.
43. Van't Dack et al., 'War of Sceptres', 'papyrus 3'.

Chapter 12
1. Bellinger, 'End', pp. 71–72.
2. Justin 39.4.4.
3. H. A. Ormerod, *Piracy in the Ancient World*, (Liverpool, 1924), pp. 200–209.
4. J. D. Grainger, *The Cities of Pamphylia*, (Oxford, 2009), pp. 141–142; R. Kallet-Marx, *Hegemony to Empire*, (California, 1995), pp. 229–230.
5. Josephos, *AJ* 13.385; Trogus, *Prologue* p. 39; Poseidonios, frag 36.
6. Bevan, *House*, vol. 2, p. 259, for example, and Bellinger, 'End', p. 72.
7. Holbl, *Ptolemaic Empire*, p. 210.
8. Josephos, *AJ* 13.365–366.
9. Houghton et al., *Seleucid Coins*, Reign of Seleukos VI.
10. Appian, *Syrian Wars* 69; Josephos, *AJ* 13.366; Plutarch, *Moralia* 486 E.
11. Houghton et al., *Seleucid Coins*, Reign of Demetrios III.
12. Strabo 16.2.7.
13. E. Badian, 'Sulla's Cilician Command', reprinted in *Studies in Greek and Roman History*, (Oxford, 1968), pp. 157–178. Badian's dating is disputed, but still seems the best calculation; against it, cf A. E. Sherwin-White, 'Ariobarzanes, Mithradates and Sulla', *Classical Quarterly* 27, (1977), pp. 173–193; in support, see Kallet-Marx, *Hegemony to Empire*, pp. 355–361, amongst others.
14. Debevoise, *Parthia*, pp. 35–42.
15. Reproduced in M. A. R. Colledge, *Parthian Art*, (London, 1977), p. 89 and plate 15.
16. A. R. Bellinger, 'Seleucid Dura: the Evidence of the Coins', *Berytus* 8, (1948), pp. 51–67.
17. The theory is based entirely on the name: J. B. Segal, *Edessa, 'The Blessed City'*, (Oxford, 1970), ch. 1.
18. Strabo 11.14.15.
19. *OGIS* 431, from Delos; Artaxerxes II had been the last really strong and effective Akhaimenid king, and ruled for nearly half a century (404–359), like Mithradates himself (124–87).
20. Plutarch, *Sulla*, 5; Livy, *Epitome* 70; J. Dobias, 'Les premiers rapports des Romains avec les Parthes', *Archiv Orientalni* 3, (1931), pp. 215–256.
21. Plutarch, *Crassus* 28.
22. Plutarch, *Sulla* 5.
23. Strabo 11.14.15; Justin 38.3.1.
24. Strabo 11.14.15.
25. Ogden, *Polygamy*, pp. 157–158.
26. R. D. Sullivan, 'The Dynasty of Commagene', *Aufstieg und Niedergang des Romische Welt* II.8, pp. 732–798.

27. Ogden, *Polygamy*, p. 158.
28. Josephos, *AJ* 13.369.
29. Appian, *Syrian Wars* 69.
30. Hoover, 'A Revised Chronology', pp. 288–289; Bellinger, 'End', p. 73, suggested two years.
31. Josephos, *AJ* 13.368.
32. Ibid; Eusebios, *Chronographia* I.259–262; Appian, *Syrian Wars* 69.
33. Bevan, *House*, p. 259; Bellinger, 'End', pp. 73–74.
34. Appian, *Syrian Wars* 69; for doubts, see Bevan, *House*, vol. 2, appendix W, p. 304.
35. Noted by Bellinger, 'End', p. 74, from the fact that Antiochos' portrait is 'in front of' Philip's on their joint coins.
36. Eusebios, *Chronographia* 1.262.
37. Josephos, *AJ* 13.369.
38. Josephos, *AJ* 13.371.
39. Hoover, 'A Revised Chronology', p. 290.
40. Eusebios, *Chronographia* 1.261.
41. Appian, *Syrian Wars*, 47, 70; comment by Hoover, 'A Revised Chronology', pp. 291–292.
42. Josephos, *AJ* 13.376–378.
43. Josephos, *AJ* 13.379.
44. Houghton et al., *Seleucid Coins*, Reign of Demetrios III.
45. Josephos, *AJ* 13.384.
46. Josephos, *AJ* 13.384–386.
47. Josephos, *AJ* 13.386.
48. Newell, 'Late Seleukid Mints', pp. 86–92.

Chapter 13

1. M. L. Chaumont, 'Etudes d'histoire parthe I: Documents royaux a Nisa', *Syria* 48, (1971), pp. 143–164; K. W. Dobbins, 'The Successors of Mithradates II of Parthia', *Numismatic Chronicle* 15, (1975), pp. 19–45.
2. Josephos, *AJ* 13.385.
3. There is much confusion over the Parthian kingship in the 80s: Dobbins (note 1) has made a serious attempt to sort it out.
4. Strabo 11.14.15; Dio Cassius 37.5.3–5; Plutarch, *Lucullus* 31.8.
5. Justin 38.3.2 and 5.
6. B. C. McGing, *The Foreign Policy of Mithradates VI Eupator, King of Pontus*, (Leiden, 1986), p. 108 ff.
7. Josephos, *AJ* 13.387. It is my interpretation that Philip 'sent' Antiochos to Damascus. Antiochos was the youngest of the brothers, not heard of earlier, and he had no independent power or authority, unlike Philip. Josephos assumes enmity between all the brothers. I assume the opposite.
8. Josephos, *AJ* 13.375–376.

9. The basis for this assumption is that Alexander's defence line against Antiochos XII in 84 was south of these towns but north of Joppa. This was the ineffective 'Yarkon line', which was set, we must assume, to protect Alexander's lands.

10. A. R. Bellinger, 'Notes on some Coins for Antioch-in-Syria', *American Numismatic Society Museum Notes* 5, (1952).

11. Josephos, *AJ* 13.386.

12. Josephos, *AJ* 13.386–389.

13. There must be strong doubts as to this story, in particular because no credible remains have been located of what of what must have been a major construction.

14. Josephos, *AJ* 13.389–391; G. W. Bowersock, *Roman Arabia*, (Cambridge MA, 1985), p. 24.

15. Josephos, *AJ* 13.392.

16. Seyrig, 'Eres', pp. 26–32.

17. Hoover, 'A Revised Chronology', p. 297; see also Bellinger, 'End', pp. 95–97.

18. This is calculated on the assumption that the Armenian conquest by Tigranes began in 83, since Appian, *Syrian Wars* 48, gives him a fourteen-year reign in Syria; this also therefore alters the period of Armenian domination.

19. In Hoover's calculations ('A Revised Chronology', pp. 296–298) only Demetrios I in 152–151, Alexander Balas in 147–146, and Antiochos VIII in 113–112, produced coined at the same rate as Philip, and these were all years when they came under attack.

20. Josephos, *AJ* 13.419.

21. Appian, *Mithradatic Wars* 67; the '300,000' figure is, of course, a great exaggeration.

22. Holbl, *Ptolemaic Empire*, pp. 213–214, 222.

23. Justin 40.1.1–2.

24. Cicero, *In Verram* IV.27–30.

25. As is shown by calling him king of Syria in Rome.

26. Josephos, *AJ* 13.420.

27. Cicero, *In Verram* IV.27–30; Bellinger, 'End', pp. 81–82.

28. Livy, *Epitome* 70, Cicero, *de Lege Agraria*, 2.51; Holbl, *Ptolemaic Empire*, p. 210.

29. Justin 40.2.2.

30. Appian, *Syrian Wars* 48 and 69.

31. E. T. Newell, 'The Seleucid Mint of Antioch', *American Journal of Numismatics* 51, (1917), p. 1–152.

32. Justin 40.1.4.

33. Appian, *Syrian Wars* 48 and 69; Strabo 11.14.15.

34. It had to be completely refounded by Pompeius: Strabo 14.3.1 and 5.9.

35. Appian, *Syrian Wars* 48.

36. J. Wagner, *Seleukeia am Euphrat/Zeugma*, (Wiesbaden, 1976); J. L. Kennedy et al., *The Twin Towns of Zeugma on the Euphrates, Journal of Roman Archaeology*, Supplement (though this is mainly about the Roman town); Grainger, *Cities*, passim.

37. Strabo 16.2.3.

38. Strabo 16.2.7.

39. Strabo 16.2.8.

40. Seyrig, 'Eres', p. 31.

41. Seyrig, 'Eres', pp. 15–18.
42. Josephos, *AJ* 14.38.
43. Newell, *Late Seleucid Mints*, p. 95.
44. Josephos, *AJ* 13.418.
45. A. Kindler, 'On the Coins of the Ituraeans', in M. Hoc (ed.), *Proceedings of the XIth International Numismatic Congress*, (Louvain-la–Neuve, 1993).
46. He may also have been a candidate in 95, if the coin identification by A. R. Bellinger in 'Notes on some Coins from Antioch-in-Syria', *American Numismatic Society Museum Notes*, is accepted.
47. Josephos, *AJ* 13.399–432; *BJ* 1.107–119; Schurer, 1.229–232.
48. Josephos, *AJ* 13.419–420.
49. Appian, *Syrian Wars* 48.
50. Plutarch, *Lucullus* 22.1; Appian, *Mithradatic Wars* 82; Memnon 38.1; McGing, *Foreign Policy*, p. 152.
51. Plutarch, *Lucullus* 199.1 and 21.1–2; Appian, *Mithradatic Wars* 83; Memnon 31.2.
52. Plutarch, *Lucullus* 21.2 and 6; A. R. Sherwin-White, *Roman Foreign Policy in the East*, (Norman OK, 1984), pp. 174–175.
53. Plutarch, *Lucullus* 21.2.
54. Ibid.
55. Appian, *Syrian Wars* 49.
56. Plutarch, *Lucullus*, 29.4; Strabo 12.2.9.

Conclusion

1. Justin 40.2.2–5.
2. Pliny, *Natural History*, 5.81–82.
3. Josephos, *AJ* 14.37–40; Appian, *Mithradatic Wars* 106, *Syrian Wars* 70; Diodoros 40.2–4; Porphyry, *FGrH* 260 F 32.27.

Abbreviations

Astronomical Diaries – A. J. Sachs and H. Hunger, Astronomical Diaries and other texts from Babylonia, (Vienna, 1988).

Austin – Michel Austin, *The Hellenistic World from Alexander to the Roman Conquest*, 2nd ed., (Cambridge, 2006).

Bellinger, 'End' – A. R. Bellinger, 'The End of the Seleucids', Transactions of the Connecticut Academy of Arts and Sciences, (1949).

Bevan, *House* – E. R. Bevan, *The House of Seleucus*, 2 vols, (London, 1902).

FGrH – F. Jacoby, Fragmente der Greichische Historiker.

Holbl, *Ptolemaic Empire* – Gunther Holbl, *A History of the Ptolemaic Empire*, (London, 2000).

Houghton, et al., *Seleucid Coins* – A. Houghton, C. Lorber, O. D. Hoover, *Seleucid Coins, a Comprehensive Catalogue*, vol 2, (Lancaster PA, 2006).

IG – *Inscriptiones Graecae*.

Josephos, *AJ, BJ* – Josephos, *Antiquitates Judaicae, Bellum Judaicum*.

Ogden, *Polygamy* – D. Ogden, *Prostitutes, Polygamy, and Death*, (London, 1999).

Bibliography

Andrade, Nathanael J, *Syrian Identity in the Greco-Roman World*, (Cambridge, 2013).

Applebaum, S, 'Hellenistic Cities of Judaea and its Vicinity – some new Aspects', in B Levick (ed.), *The Ancient Historian and his Materials, Essays in Honour of C. E. Stevens*, (Farnborough, 1975).

Assar, GE, 'Genealogy and Coinage of the Early Parthian Kings, I', *Parthia* 6, (2004) and *Parthia* 7, (2005).

Austin, Michel, *The Hellenistic World from Alexander to the Roman Conquest*, 2nd ed., (Cambridge, 2006).

Balty, JC, 'Le Belus de Chalcis et les Fleuves de Ba'al de Syrie-Palestine', *Archeologie de Levant, Receuil R. Saideh*, (Lyon, 1982).

Bar-Kochva, B, *Judas Maccabaeus*, (Cambridge, 1989).

Bellinger, AR, 'Hyspaosines of Charax', *Yale Classical Studies* 8, (1942).

Bellinger, AR, 'Notes on some Coins for Antioch-in-Syria', *American Numismatic Society Museum Notes* 5, (1952).

Bellinger, AR, 'The End of the Seleucids', Transactions of the Connecticut Academy of Arts and Sciences, 8, 1948, 51–108.

Bevan, ER, *The House of Seleucus*, 2 vols, (London, 1902).

Bivar, AHD, *Iran under the Arsacids, Cambridge History of Iran*, vol. 3.1.

Bouche-Leclerq, A, *Histoire des Seleucides*, 2 vols, (Paris, 1913).

Bowersock, Glen, *Roman Arabia*, (Cambridge MA, 1983).

Brett, AB, 'The Mint of Ascalon under the Seleucids', *American Numismatic Society Notes and Monographs* 4, (1950).

British Museum Catalogue, Seleukid Kings.

Broughton, HRR, *The Magistrates of the Roman Republic*, (New York, 1951–1952).

Cantineau, J, *Le Nabataeen*, II, (Paris, 1932).

Chaumont, ML, 'Etudes d'histoire parthe I: Documents royaux a Nisa', *Syria* 48, (1971).

Chaumont, ML, 'Recherches sur quelques villes helleniques de l'Iran occidental', *Iranica Antiqua* 17, (1982).

Cohen, Getzel M, *The Hellenistic Settlements in Syria, the Red Sea Basin and North Africa*, (California, 2006).

Cohen, Getzel M, *The Hellenistic Settlements in the East from Armenia and Mesopotamia to Bactria and India*, (California, 2013).

Colledge, MAR, *Parthian Art*, (London, 1977).

Crowfoot, JW, et al., *The Buildings at Samaria*, (London, 1942).

Dack, E. van't, et al., *The Judaean-Syrian-Egyptian Conflict of 103–101* BC. *A Multilingual Dossier concerning a 'War of Sceptres'*, Collecteanea Hellenistica 1, (Brussels, 1989).

Debevoise, NC, *The Political History of Parthia*, (Chicago, 1938).

Dobbins, KW, 'The Successors of Mithradates II of Parthia', *Numismatic Chronicle* 15, (1975).

Dobias, J, 'Les premiers rapports des Romains avec les Parthes', *Archiv Orientalni* 3, (1931).

Dov, S, *Settlements and Cult Sites on Mount Hermon, Israel. Ituraean Studies in the Hellenistic and Roman Periods*, British Archaeological Reports, International Series, S 589, (Oxford, 1993).

Ehling, E, 'Alexander II Zabeinas – ein angeblicher (Adoptiv) Sohn des Antiochos VII oder Alexander I Balas', *Schweitzer Munzblatter* 45, (1995).

Ehling, K, 'Seleukidische Geschichte zwischen 130 und 121 v. Chr.', *Historia* 47, (1998).

Eshel, H, *The Dead Sea Scrolls and the Hasmonaean State*, (Jerusalem, 2008).

Fischer, T, *Untersuchungen zur Partherkrieg Antiochos' VII*, (Tubingen dissertation, 1970).

Jacoby, F, Fragmente der Greichische Historiker.

French, RH, 'Sites and Monuments from Phrygia, Pisidia and Pamphylia', *Epigraphica Anatolica* 17, (1991).

Freyne, S, *Galilee from Alexander the Great to Hadrian, 323 BC to 135 CE*, (Edinburgh, 1980).

Gera, Dov, 'Tryphon's Sling Bullet from Dor', *Israel Exploration Journal* 35, (1985).

Grainger, JD, *The Cities of Seleukid Syria*, (Oxford, 1990).

Grainger, JD, *Hellenistic Phoenicia*, (Oxford, 1991).

Grainger, JD, *The Cities of Pamphylia*, (Oxford, 2009).

Grainger, JD, *The Syrian Wars*, (Leiden, 2009).

Grainger, JD, *The Wars of the Maccabees*, (Barnsley, 2012).

Gruen, Erich S, *The Hellenistic Monarchies and the Coming of Rome*, (California, 1984).

Harmatta, J, 'The Second Elymaean Inscription from Bard e-Neshandeh', *Acta Antiqua Academiae Scientiarum Hungaricae* 32, (1989).

Harmatta, J, 'Parthia and Elymais in the 2nd Century BC', *Acta Antiqua Academiae Scientiarum Hungaricae* 29, (1991).

Hansman, J, 'Charax and the Kharkeh', *Iranica Antiqua* 7, (1967).

Head, BV, *Historia Numorum*, (Oxford, 1911).

Helliesen, JM, 'Demetrios I Soter: a Seleucid King with an Antigonid Name', in H. J. Dell (ed.) *Ancient Macedonian Studies in honour of Charles F. Edson*, (Thessalonike, 1981).

Herrmann, P, 'Milesier an Seleukidenreich, Prosopographische Beitrage zur Geschichte Milets in 2 Jhdt v. Chr.', *Chiron* 17, (1987).

Holbl, Gunther, *A History of the Ptolemaic Empire*, (London, 2000).

Hommell, H, 'Ein Konig aus Milet', *Chiron* 6, (1976).

Hoover, Oliver D, 'Notes on some Imitation Drachms of Demetrios I Soter from Commagene', *American Journal of Numismatics* 10, (1998).

Hoover, O, 'A Revised Chronology for the late Seleucids at Antioch (121/0–64 BC)', *Historia* 56, (2007).

Houghton, Arthur, 'The Royal Seleucid Mint of Soli', *Numismatic Chronicle* 149, (1898).

Houghton, Arthur, 'Timarchos as King in Babylonia', *Revue Numismatique* 21, (1976).

Houghton, Arhthur, *Coins of the Seleucid Empire from the Collection of Arthur Houghton*, (New York, 1983).

Houghton, Arthur, 'The Seleucid Mint of Mallus and the Cult Figure of Athene Magarsis', *Festschrift fur Leo Mildenburg*, (Wettern, 1984),.

Houghton, Arthur, and G Le Rider, 'Un premier regne d'Antiochos VIII Epiphane a Antioch en 128', *Bulletin de Correspondence Hellenique 112*, (1988).

Houghton, Arthur, 'The Seleukid Mint at Seleuceia-on-the-Calycadnus', *Kraay–Morkholm Essays*, (ed.) G Le Rider et al., (Louvain, 1989).

Houghton, Arthur, 'The Revolt of Tryphon and the Accession of Antiochos VI at Apamea', *Schweizer Nimismatische Rundschau* 72, (1992).

Houghton, Arthur, C Lorber, OD Hoover, *Seleucid Coins, a Comprehensive Catalogue*, vol 2, (Lancaster PA, 2006).

Inscriptiones Graecae.

Jones, AHM, 'The Urbanisation of the Ituraean Principalty', *Journal of Roman Studies* 21, (1931).

Jones, AHM, *Cities of the Eastern Roman Provinces*, (Oxford, 1971).

Josephos, *Antiquitates Judaicae, Bellum Judaicum.*

Kadman, L, *Corpus Nummorum Palaestiniensium*, Series 1, vol. V, *The Coins of Akko-Ptolemais*, (Jerusalem, 1961).

Kallet-Marx, RH, *Hegemony to Empire, the Development of Roman Imperium in the East from 148 to 62 BC*, (California, 1995).

Kennedy, JL, et al., *The Twin Towns of Zeugma on the Euphrates, Journal of Roman Archaeology*, Supplement, (Portsmouth, 1998).

Kindler, A, 'On the Coins of the Ituraeans', in M Hoc (ed.), *Proceedings of the XIth International Numismatic Congress*, (Louvain-la–Neuve, 1993).

Kosmin, Paul J, *The Land of the Elephant Kings*, (Cambridge MA, 2014).

Kuhrt, Amelie, and S Sherwin-White (eds), *Hellenism in the East*, (London, 1987).

Liampi, K, 'Der Makedonische schild als propagandisches mittel in der Hellenistischen Zeit', *Meletemata* 10, (1950); Otto Morkholm, *Antiochos IV of Syria*, (Copenhagen, 1966).

Lifshitz, B, 'Scythopolis: l'histoire, les institutions, et les cultes de la ville a l'epoque hellenistique et imperial', *Aufstieund Niedergang des Romischen Welt* II.8.

MacDonald, G, *Catalogue of the Greek Coins in the Hunterian Collection*, vol. 2, (Glasgow, 1905).

McGing, BC, *The Foreign Policy of Mithradates VI Eupator, King of Pontus*, (Leiden, 1986).

Ma'oz, Z, N Goren-Inbar, and C Epstein, 'Golan', in E Stern (ed.), *New Encyclopedia of Archaeological Excavations in the Holy Land*, vol. 2, (Jerusalem, 1994).

Meshorer, Y, *Ancient Jewish Coinage*, vol. I, *Persian Period through the Hasmonaeans*, (Dix Hills NY, 1982).

Moore, W, 'The Divine Couple of Demetrios II Nicator and his coinage at Nisibis', *American Numismatic Society Museum Notes* 31, (1986).

Morkholm, Otto, *Studies in the Coinage of Antiochus VI*, (Copenhagen, 1963).

Morkholm, Otto, *Antiochos IV of Syria*, (Copenhagen, 1966).

Morkholm, Otto, 'The Seleucid Mint at Antiochia on the Persian Gulf, *American Numismatic Society Museum Notes* 16, (1976).

Myers, EA, *The Ituraeans and the Roman Near East*, (Cambridge, 2010).

Narain, AK, *The Indo-Greeks*, (Cambridge, 1957 and 1980).

Neusner, J, 'Parthian Political Ideology', *Acta Iranica* 3, (1963).

Newell, ET, 'The Seleucid Mint of Antioch', *American Journal of Numismatics* 51, (1917).

Newell, ET, 'The Seleucid Coinage of Tyre: a Supplement', *Numismatic Notes and Monographs* 78, (1938).

Newell, ET, 'Late Seleucid Mints in Ace-Ptolemais and Damascus', *Numismatic Notes and Monographs* 84, (1939).

Nodelman, SA, 'A Preliminary History of Charakene', *Berytus* (1960).

Ogden, D, *Prostitutes, Polygamy, and Death*, (London, 1999).

Ormerod, HA, *Piracy in the Ancient World*, (Liverpool, 1924).

Parker, R and W Dubberstein, *Babylonian Chronology 626 BC–AD 75*, (Providence RI, 1956).

Peters, FB, 'The Nabataeans in the Hauran', *Journal of the American Oriental Society* 97, (1977).

Pritchett, WK, and BD Merritt, *The Chronology of Hellenistic Athens*, (Cambridge MA, 1940).

Rajak, T, 'Roman Intervention in a Seleucid Siege of Jerusalem', *Greek, Roman and Byzantine Studies* 22, (1981).

Rider, Georges Le, *Suse sous les Seleucides et les Parthes*, (Paris, 1965).

Robert, L, 'Encore une Inscription grecque d'Iran', *Comptes-Rendus de l'Academie des Inscriptions et de Belles-Lettres*, (1967)

Rouvier, J, 'Numismatique des villes de Phenicie', *Journal Internationale d'Archeologie Numismatique* 3, 4 and 5.

Sachs, AJ, and H Hunger, *Astronomical Diaries and other texts from Babylonia*, (Vienna, 1988).

Sachs, AJ, and DJ Wiseman, 'A Babylonian King List of the Hellenistic Period', *Iraq* 16, (1954).

Segal, JB, *Edessa, the Blessed City*, (Oxford, 1970).

Seyrig, H, 'Sue quelques eres Syrienne: I. L'ere des rois de Commagene', *Revue Numismatique* 6, (1964).

Shatzman, I, *The Armies of the Hasmonaeans and Herod*, (Tubingen, 1991).

Sherwin-White, AR, *Roman Foreign Policy in the East*, (Norman OK, 1984).

Smallwood, Mary E, *The Jews under Roman Rule*, (Leiden, 1981).

Smith, George Adam, *A Historical Geography of the Holy Land*, (London, 1931).

Strootman, Rolf, *Courts and Elites in the Hellenistic Empires*, (Edinburgh, 2014).

Sullivan, RD, 'The Dynasty of Commagene', *Aufstieg und Niedergang der romische Welt*, II.8, (Berlin, 1977).

Teixidor, J, *The Pagan God, Popular Religion in the Greco-Roman Near East*, (Princeton NJ, 1977).

Viesse, AE, 'Les "Revoltes Egyptiennes". Recherches sur les Troubles interieures en Egypte du Regne de Ptolemee II a la conquete romaine', *Studia Hellenistica* 41, (Louvain, 2004).

Wagner, J, *Seleukeia am Euphrat/Zeugma*, (Wiesbaden, 1976).

Weiskopf, DB, 'Late Babylonian Texts in the Oriental Institute', *Biblioteca Mesopotamia* 24.

Welles, B, *Royal Correspondence of the Hellenistic Period*, (New Haven, 1934).

Whitehorne, JEG, *Cleopatras*, (London, 1994).

Whitehorne, JEG, 'A Reassessment of Cleopatra III's Syrian Campaign', *Chronique d'Egypte* 70, (1996).

Will, E, *Histoire Politique de la Monde Hellenistique*, vol 2, (Nancy, 1982).

Will, Ernest, 'Un vieux problem de la topographie de la Beqa antique: Chalcis du Liban', *Zeitschrift fur Deutsche Palasteins-verein* 99, (1983).

Index

Abila, trans-Jordan, 30

Absalom, Judaean prince, 161

Achaian League, 5, 8, 19, 23

Adana, Kilikia, 101

Adiabene, 82–3, 85, 106, 110, 137, 141, 171, 179, 181, 191

Adora, Idumaea, 127

Adriatic Sea, 2

Aegean Sea, 77

Aemilius Paullus, M., 25, 27

Agathokles, Ptolemaic regent, 13

Aigai, Kilikia, 101

Aischrion, Seleukid commander, 81, 83

Aitolian League, 5

Akra, Jerusalem, 27, 39, 47, 60

Alexander I Balas, Seleukid king, 28, 54–65, 66–76, 77, 123–4, 204

Alexander II Zabeinas, Seleukid king, 123–5, 129–30
  death, 131

Alexander Iannai, Judaean king, 154, 157, 161–5, 182, 184–5, 187, 201

Alexandria, Egypt, 20, 22–5, 119, 122, 125, 153, 167, 177

Alexandria-ad-Issum, Kilikia, 101

Alexandria-on-the-Erythraean Sea, 33
  see also Antioch

Alkimos, Jerusalem high priest, 40, 45, 49

Amanus Mountains, 32

Amathos, trans-Jordan, 163, 165

Amman/Philadelphia, 30

Ammaus, Palestine, 38

Ammonios, Seleukid minister, 66, 68, 72–5

Andriskos, Macedonian pretender, 62

Andronikos, murderer, 15–16

Anthedon, Palestine, 163

Antigonos III Doson, Macedonian king, 13

Antigonos, Judaean king, 160

Antilebanon Mountains, 102

Antioch, Syria, 14, 16–17, 21, 28, 32, 39–40, 58, 62, 64, 66, 71–4, 79, 86, 88, 100, 102, 113, 116–18, 122–3, 125, 130–1, 134, 140, 142, 147, 153, 158, 160, 162, 166, 169, 174–7, 180, 182, 186, 188–9, 191, 193, 198, 201

Antioch-by-Hippos, trans-Jordan, 31

Antioch-on-the Erythraean Sea, 53, 68, 106
  see also Alexandria

Antioch-on-the-Euphrates, Mesopotamia 31

Antioch-in-Pieria, Syria 31–2

Antiochis, concubine of Antiochos IV, 28, 35, 54, 61

Antiochis, wife of Ariarathes IV, 42, 50, 55

Antiochos III, 1–6, 12, 18, 26

Antiochos IV;
  hostage in Rome, 3, 8–9
  conducts *coup d'etat*, 11–16, 205
  and Rome, 16–19, 25, 47
  and Greece, 19–20
  and Judaea, 20–1
  and Sixth Syrian War, 22–6, 41, 121
  and eastern expedition, 25–27, 32–5, 51–2
  Daphne procession, 27, 34
  internal policies, 28–9, 31–2
  death, 35, 38, 43

Antiochos V, 24, 33, 36, 40, 54, 205

Antiochos VI, son of Alexander Balas, 78
  proclaimed king, 79–81
  death, 81

Antiochos VII, 51, 66–7, 103
  king, 86, 88
  Syrian campaign, 88–92, 104
  and Judaea, 93, 98
  and Kilikia, 101–102
  and Parthian War, 97, 105–106, 108–12, 135

marriage, 86, 106, 116
death, 112, 116, 123, 151
Antiochos VIII Grypos, 116–18, 124
marriage, 130–1, 174, 200
ruling king, 134, 136–43, 148–51, 156–9,
166–9
death, 169
Antiochos IX Kyzikenos, 116, 118, 138–43,
147, 150, 151–9, 162–3, 166–9, 174, 194
Antiochos X, 174–8, 183, 189
Antiochos XI, 174, 176–7
Antiochos XII, 174, 182–5
Antiochos XIII, 183, 191, 196, 199
Antiochos the Young King, son of
Antiochos III, 12, 51
Antiochos, son of Seleukos IV, 10–12
death, 15–16, 22
Antiochos, son of Antiochos VII, 116
Antiochos, son of king Ar'abuzu, Parthian
governor, 82, 85, 86
Antonius, M., against pirates, 167–8, 170
Apameia, Treaty of, 2, 5, 41, 167
Apameia, Syria, 21, 78–9, 88, 90, 100, 123,
125, 130, 160, 166, 193–5
Apameia-on-Euphrates, 193
Apameia-on-the-Silhu River, 84
Apollodotos, 164
Apollonia, Palestine, 156, 181
Apollonios, envoy to Rome, 17–18
to Alexandria, 20
Apollonios, commander in Judaea, 27,
36–7, 39
Apollonios, sons of, 43–4
Apollonios Taos, governor of Koile Syria,
68, 72–3, 75
Arabia, Arabs, vii, 99, 145, 158, 178
Arados, 89, 92, 100, 109, 128, 129, 132–4,
137–8, 143, 149, 151, 158, 174, 194, 204
Arbela, Mesopotamia, 25, 109
Ardaya, Seleukid governor, 78, 82
Aretas I, Nabataean king, 98
Aretas II, Nabataean king, 98, 189
Ariarathes V, Kappadokian king, 42, 44, 50,
55
Ariobarzanes, Kappadokian king, 172, 192
Aristoboulos, Judaean king, 195
Armenia, vii, 31, 33, 47, 53, 170–1, 181,
197, 199

Arqa, Phoenicia, 203
Arsakes II Parthian king, 1
Artabanus I, Parthian king, 115, 137
Artavasdes, Armenian king, 171
Artaxias, Armenian king, 33, 47
Artemidoros, royal Friend, 11
Ashdod, Palestine, 73
Ashkelon, Palestine, 80, 88, 125, 130, 134,
140, 156, 158–9, 166, 197
Asia Minor, vii, 1, 4, 6, 40, 109, 120, 131,
170–3, 202
Asophos, trans-Jordan, 163
Aspendos, Pamphylia, 142
Athenaios, Attalid prince, 13
Athenaios, Seleukid commander, 113
Athenobios, Seleukid envoy, 89–90, 94, 96
Athens, 5, 12–14, 19, 124, 130
Attaleia, Pamphylia, 59
Attalid kingdom, ix, 1–2, 4, 8, 53, 55, 67,
204
Attalos II, Attalid king, 11, 13, 55–6, 58, 75
Attalos III, Attalid king, 109
Auranitis (Hauran), 183
Azizos, Arab chief, 178

Baalbek, Phoenicia, 144–5
Babylon, 14, 33, 51, 63–4, 78, 82, 85, 110,
114, 137
Babylonia, 28, 32–4, 46, 51, 53, 63, 68, 70,
78, 82–7, 100, 105–108, 113–14, 122,
171, 181, 205
Bagasis, Parthian governor, 78, 84, 107–108
Bakchides, Seleukid commander, 45, 47–8
Baktria, vii, 1, 10, 17, 35, 52–3, 78, 82, 84,
120, 204
Balanaia, Syria, 103
Bambyke, Syria, 145
see also Hierapolis
Barada River, Damascus, 103
Bargylos Hills, Syria, 201, 203
Batanaea, trans-Jordan, 144, 183
Bathbasi, Judaea, 48
Bekaa Valley, 31, 102, 143–4, 185, 194
Beroia, Syria, 40, 100, 169, 175, 177–81,
185–6, 193, 203
Berytos, Phoenicia, 19, 64, 102, 125, 130,
132, 203
Beth Horon, Judaea, 37

Beth Zakaria, Judaea, 39
Beth Zur, Judaea, 38–9, 60–2, 80
Bisitun Pass, 34, 52, 69, 82, 171
Bithynia, ix, 1, 6, 8
Byblos, Phoenicia, 64, 88, 102, 132, 203
Byzantion, 19

Caecilius Metellus, Q., Roman envoy, 8
Carthage, ix, 2, 204
Caspian Gates, 69
Caspian Sea, 69
Central Asia, 83
Chalkis, Phoenicia, 79, 102, 203
Chalkis, Syria, 100
Charakene, 83, 106, 110, 115, 132, 137, 179
Charax, Charakene, 83
Claudius Pulcher, Ap., Roman envoy, 8
Claudius Pulcher, Ap., Roman envoy, 197–9
Cornelius Sulla, L., Roman praetor and
    dictator, 170, 173, 187
Crete, 67, 71
Cyprus, ix, 24, 26, 41, 56, 59, 119, 141, 148,
    153, 163, 167, 188
Cyrenaica, ix, 190

Damascus, Syria, 29–31, 88, 103, 117, 125,
    129–30, 140, 143–4, 146, 156, 158–60,
    164, 166, 169, 175–7, 182, 183–5, 189,
    195
Daphne, sacred grove, Syria, 21–2, 27, 32,
    34, 36, 41, 137
Dead Sea, 99, 185
Delos, 11, 13, 19
Demainetos, politician, 164
Demavar, Iran 69
Demetrias-on-the-Tigris, 85, 106
Demetrios I;
    hostage at Rome, 8–10, 12, 15, 26, 43
    escape, 43–4
    assumes kingship, 44–5, 206
    internal policies, 45, 51, 67
    and Judaea, 45, 50
    marriage, 50–1
    and war with Alexander Balas, 54–65, 75
Demetrios II, 51
    war for kingship, 66–8, 70–1
    king, 72–6
    and Lasthenes 77, 79

and Diodotos/Tryphon, 79–80, 151
and Judaea 78, 80
and Parthian War, 83–6, 106
capture, 87
prisoner, 107–108, 111–12, 114, 154
second reign, 116–18
Egyptian expedition, 119–25, 135
death, 129
Demetrios III, 169–70, 174–5, 179, 181,
    183, 196
Demetrios I, Baktrian king, 3, 10
Demetrios, son of Philip V, 8
Diodoros, foster father of Demetrios I, 43–4
Diodotos, Seleukid official, 71, 74
    rebels, 78–80
    Baktrian king, 81
    see also Tryphon
Dion, trans-Jordan, 182
Dionysios the Mede, Seleukid commander,
    81
Dionysios, lord of Beroia, 193, 203
Dok, Palestine, 93–5
Doliche, Syria, 100, 192, 193n
Dor, Palestine, 88–90, 94, 156, 159, 162,
    183, 184
Drangiana (also Sakastene), 114
Dura-Europos, Mesopotamia, 141, 150–1,
    171, 173, 176, 179

Edessa, Mesopotamia, 92–3, 99, 145, 158,
    171
Egypt, vii, 1, 3–4, 7, 9–10, 13, 22–6, 32, 43,
    57, 78, 131, 187–8, 204
Ekbatana, Iran, 29, 34, 52, 68, 69, 110
Elaeussa, Syria, 169
Elburz Mountains, Iran 69
Eleazar Maccabee, 39
Eleusis, Egypt 25
Eleutheros River, Syria, 73
Elymais, 1, 4, 34–5, 78, 80, 82–5, 87, 108,
    110
Emesa, Syria, 145, 201
Enius, Parthian officer, 110
Ephesos, 54
Epikrates, Seleukid commander, 154, 156
Epiphaneia, Kilikia, 101
Epiphaneia-Hamath, Syria, 31
Epiphaneia-on-the-Euphrates, 31

Eudemos of Seleukeia-on-the-Kalykadnos, 19
Eukratides I, Baktrian king, 52, 69, 78
Eulaios, Ptolemaic regent, 10, 20, 23
Eumenes II, Attalid king, 1–2, 5–8, 13–14, 16, 19, 44
Euphrates River, 51, 53, 83, 92, 100, 109, 134, 170, 193
  as Roman-Parthian boundary, 172–3
Europos, Mesopotamia, 100
Euthydemos I, Baktrian king, 1

Fannius, C., Roman praetor, 132
Fradhasht, Edessan king, 121

Gabala, Syria, 128
Gadara, Palestine, 30, 182
Gadora, trans-Jordan, 163
Galilee, 39, 144, 158–61, 196
Galilee, Sea of, 30, 80, 157, 182, 184
Gaulan, Gaulanitis, 30, 99, 144
Gaza, Palestine, 30, 61, 77, 80, 99, 103, 162–5, 182, 203
Gazara, Palestine, 89–91, 94, 96–7, 126, 132, 156, 160
Gerasa, trans-Jordan, 31, 99, 127, 165, 182
Gindarus, Syria, 201
Gophna Hills, Judaea, 36, 45
Gordyene, 181, 198
Gorgias, Seleukid commander, 38
Gotarzes, Parthian governor, 171, 181–2
Greece, 2, 5, 22

Hamath Tiberias, Palestine, 80
Hannibal, 8
Hauran, trans-Jordan, 99, 103, 144, 183
Hekatompylos, Parthia, 52, 69
Heliodoros, minister of Seleukos IV, 10–14, 40
Heliokles, Baktrian king, 83–4
Heliopolis/Baalbek, Phoenicia, 102–103
Heraklea, Syria, 169, 193
Herakleides, Seleukid treasurer, 16–17, 46
  conspirator, 49, 54–6, 59, 75
Herakleon, Seleukid commander and assassin, 168–70, 175, 178, 185
Hierapolis-Bambyke, Syria, 29, 100, 103, 145–6, 169, 175, 193, 203
Hierapolis-Kastabala, Kilikia, 104

Hierax, Seleukid official, 66, 71, 74, 78
Himeros (Euhemeros), Parthian governor, 114–15
Hippos, trans-Jordan, 182
Hyknapses, Iranian ruler, 52, 70
Hyrkanos, of Iraq al-Amir, 20–1, 23–4
Hyrkanos, Judaean ruler, 91, 93–4, 97, 109–10, 113–14, 126–7, 132, 146
  and Samaria, 152–4
  and Seleukid civil war, 155–7, 160, 162
  death, 160
Hyrkania, 69, 82, 107
Hyspaosines, Seleukid governor, 53, 68, 83, 87
  king, 106, 108, 110, 114–15, 132, 137

Idumaea, 127, 151, 157, 204
Ilion, 19
Indates, Parthian commander, 109
India, 3–4, 52, 170, 202
Iran, ix, 32, 34, 38, 51–2, 63
  Parthian conquest, 69–71, 105–106, 120, 182, 205
Iraq al-Amir, trans-Jordan, 20–1
Isokrates, rhetorician, 42
Italy, 2, 50, 167
Ituraeans, 144, 146, 159–60, 180, 182, 185, 195–6, 204

Jericho, Palestine, 93
Jerusalem, 20–2, 27, 29, 32, 60–2, 80, 93–4, 97, 99, 145–6, 150, 152, 155, 157–8, 162
  temple, 36, 39, 104, 145–6
  siege of, 95–6, 98
Jesus/Jason, Jerusalem high priest, 21, 23, 27
Jews viii, 18, 27, 29, 36–7, 60, 100–101, 103, 145
Jonathan Maccabee, 48
  governor of Judaea, 60
  high priest, 60–1, 72–3, 75, 78–80, 91
  capture and death, 81–2
Joppa, Palestine, 20, 81, 89–91, 94, 96–7, 132, 151, 155, 160, 183–4
Jordan River, 20–1, 30, 39, 62, 126, 163, 204
Judaea, and Antiochos IV, 20–1, 23–4, 27–8, 32
  and Lysias, 36–9

and Demetrios I, 44, 47–9, 68, 71
and Demetrios II, 78
and Antiochos VII, 89–92, 94–7
and Rome, 132, 155–6, 203–204
independence, 136–7, 144, 151, 158, 160,
    165, 180, 201
army, 150, 152, 155, 162
and Samaria, 152–5, 157
invasion of, 153, 184
civil war, 182
Judah Maccabee, 37, 39, 45–9
Judas-Aristoboulos, Judaean ruler, 160–1
Judas, son of Simon, 90

Kabneskir II, Elymaean ruler, 78, 80, 83–4
Kabneskir III, Elymaean ruler, 85, 87
Kalchedon, 19
Kallimandros, friend of Demetrios II, 117
Kallimandros, Seleukid commander, 153–4
Kamniskires, Elymaean ruler, 70, 73
    see also Kabneskir
Kangavar, Iran, 69
Kappadokia, 1, 8, 42, 53, 55, 67, 170, 173,
    188–9, 192
Karia, 66
Karmania, 35
Karrhai, Mesopotamia, 99
Kasiana, Syria, 74, 78–9
Kendebaios, Seleukid commander, 90–1, 94
Kidron, Palestine, 90
Kilikia, 5, 28, 32, 36, 55, 61–2, 71, 74, 80,
    82, 89, 101, 104, 121, 130, 134, 137,
    166–7, 169, 175, 185, 186–9, 191–2, 200
Kineas, Ptolemaic regent, 23
Kleomenes, Seleukid governor, 69–70, 171
Kleopatra Syra, wife of Ptolemy V, 1, 7,
    9–20, 66
Kleopatra Thea, daughter of Ptolemy VI
    wife of Alexander Balas, 66
    wife of Demetrios II, 74, 83, 86, 116–19,
        121–5, 129–30, 134–5
    wife of Antiochos VII, 86, 107, 111
    death, 134, 136
    legacy, 134, 138, 141
Kleopatra II, 10, 20, 23, 50, 119–22, 130
Kleopatra III, 119, 121–2, 141–2, 153–4,
    161, 163, 166
    death, 167

Kleopatra IV, 131, 141
    wife of Antiohcos IX, 141, 153, 174
    death, 142
Kleopatra VI Tryphaina, 188
Kleopatra Berenike III, daughter of
    Ptolemy IX, wife of Ptolemy X, 168–9,
    187
Kleopatra, daughter of Mithradates VI,
    wife of Tigranes, 182
Knidos, Karia, 66–7
Koele Syria, 2, 17, 20, 22–3, 27, 29–30,
    36–7, 59, 68, 72–3, 75, 77–8, 90
Komanos, Ptolemaic regent, 23
Kommagene, 31, 53, 62, 68, 92, 98–100,
    106, 109, 127, 133, 136–7, 144, 158, 173,
    180, 185–6, 192, 202–203
Krateros, eunuch, 118
Kyrrhos, Syria, 100, 192–3
Kyzikos, 19, 118, 130, 138

Laodike, daughter of Antiochos III, 51
    wife of Seleukos IV, 10–11
    wife of Antiochos IV, 14, 16 28
Laodike, daughter of Seleukos IV, wife of
    Perseus, 8, 10
    wife of Demetrios I, 50, 66
Laodike, daughter of Antiochos IV, 28, 56,
    58, 67
Laodike, two daughters of Antiochos VII,
    116
Laodike, daughter of Demetrios II, 116
Laodike, daughter of Antiochos VIII, wife
    of Mithradates I of Kommagene, 174,
    192
Laodike, queen of the Samenians, 176, 178
Laodikeia-ad-Mare, 42, 79, 100, 125, 160,
    166, 186, 193–4, 203
Laodikeia (Nehavand), Iran, 69
Larissa, Syria, 79
Lasthenes, Cretan mercenary commander,
    67, 71–2, 75
    minister of Demetrios II, 77–8, 120
Lebanon Mountains, 102, 144
Lenaios, Ptolemaic regent, 10, 20, 23
Leptines, assassin, 42
Licinius Lucullus, L., 197–8
Lower Zab River, Babylonia, 85
Lykos River, Babylonia, 110

Lysias, Seleukid regent, 33, 35–6, 40, 50, 205
  and Judaea, 36–9
  and Philip, 38–9
  and Rome, 41–2
  and Ariarathes V, 42
  death, 44
Lysias (city), 40
Lysias (fort), 40
Lysimachos, Gazan politician, 164

Macedon, ix, 2, 8, 13, 17–18, 22, 25, 27, 204
Magadates, Armenian governor, 191–2, 199
Mallos, Kilikia, 28, 80, 101
Marathos, Syria, 128
Marisa, Idumaea, 127
Mattathias, Jewish rebel, 36–7
Medaba, trans-Jordan, 126, 151
Media, 16, 28–9, 46, 69–70, 84–5, 100, 108, 110–11, 113–14
Media Atropatene, 52, 69, 82–3, 110, 191
Melitene, Kappadokia, 53, 55
Memphis, Egypt, 23–4
Menelaos, Jerusalem high priest, 21–4, 27, 36–7, 39–40, 49
Menneas, Ituraean ruler, 144
Menyllos, Ptolemaic envoy, 43–4
Mesene (also Charakene), 106
Mesopotamia, 36, 47, 81, 84, 92, 109, 137, 176, 181–2
Michmash, Judaea, 48
Milesios, Seleukid commander, 184
Miletos, 54
Mithradates I, Parthian king, 69–70, 73, 77, 82, 84, 107
Mithradates II, Parthian king, 115, 137, 170–3, 179, 181–2, 189
Mithradates I, Kommagenean king, 133, 174, 191–2
Mithradates V, Pontic king, 58, 67
Mithradates VI, Pontic king, 170, 182, 187–90, 195–8
Mithradates Sinakes, Parthian satrap, 178–9, 181, 193
Mizpah, Judaea, 37–8
Modiin, Judaea, 36
Mopsuhestia, Kilikia, 101, 175–6

Mount Gerizim, Palestine, 126, 151
Mount Hermon, Palestine, 144

Nabataeans, 98–100, 103, 127, 135, 165, 177, 180, 182–5, 195–6
Nikanor, Seleukid commander, 38
Nikanor, Seleukid commander, 45–6
Nikanor, Parthian governor, 82, 85
Nikopolis, Syria, 100, 192
Nisibis, Mesopotamia, 47, 84, 92, 137
Noumenios, Seleukid fleet commander, 33
Numisius, T., Roman envoy, 25

Obodas I, Nabataean king, 183
Octavius, Cn., Roman envoy, 41–3, 47, 204
Oenoparos River, Syria, 75, 78
Olba, Kilikia, 104
Olympia, 19
Onias III, Jerusalem high priest, 21–2
Onias IV, priest of temple in Egypt, 49
Orobazos, Parthian envoy, 172–3, 203
Orophernes, Kappadokian king, 55
Orthosia, Syria, 88, 90, 132
Osrhoene, 92, 99, 102, 106, 109, 127, 134, 136–7, 144, 158, 173, 181, 191–3, 202
Ostia, Italy, 43

Palamedes, Seleukid commander, 81
Palestine, 2, 22, 30, 57, 60–1, 63, 68, 73, 80–1, 91–2, 100, 103, 144, 160, 162–4, 166, 191, 196, 200
Palmyra, Syria, 203
Paropamisadai, 3
Parthia, vii, 1–2, 10, 17, 35, 52–3, 204
  expansion, 68, 77, 82–3, 116–20, 131, 137, 141, 170–4, 178–9, 201–202
  and Antiochos VII, 97, 105
  and Rome, 170
Pegai, Palestine, 96–7, 126, 132
Pelusion, Egypt, 22–3, 122, 124–6
Pergamon, 13
Persepolis, Iran, 52
Perseus, Macedonian king, 8, 17–18, 50
Persian Gulf, 33, 53
Persis, 52, 83–5, 110, 137
Petra, Nabataea, 99, 184–5
Pharnakes I, Pontic king, 6–7

Philadelphia (Amman), trans-Jordan, 93, 95, 98–9, 126–7, 135, 158–9, 163–5, 182, 197, 203
Philetairos, Attalid prince, 13
Philip I, Seleukid king, 174, 176–82, 184–6, 188, 194–5, 200
Philip II Seleukid king, 189, 199
Philip V, Macedonian king, 6, 8, 13, 15, 29
Philip, pretended Seleukid regent, 35, 38, 40–1, 52–3
Philomelion, 40
Philotera, Palestine, 157
Phoenicia, Phoenicians, 2, 13, 20, 79, 100–102, 125, 143, 145, 148, 158
Phraates II, Parthian king, 107–108, 110–18, 126
Phriapatios, Parthian king, 3–4, 10
Pilinissu of Akkad, Parthian governor, 107–108
Piracy, 82, 167–8
Pompeius Magnus, Cn., 193–4, 200–203
Popilius Laenas, C., Roman envoy, 25–6
Poseidion, Syria, 131
Prusias I, Bithynian king, 6
Prusias II, Bithynian king, 8
Ptolemaios, Seleukid governor, 38
Ptolemaios, governor of Kommagene, 53–6, 62–3, 68, 92
Ptolemaios Makron, Ptolemaic governor of Cyprus, 24, 56
  Seleukid governor of Koile Syria, 41
Ptolemaios, Judaean pretender, 93–5
Ptolemaios, son of Menneas, Ituraean ruler, 144, 182, 195
Ptolemais-Ake, 20, 31, 34, 38, 57–9, 61, 64, 66, 68, 71, 73, 80–1, 88, 99, 116, 125, 129–30, 133–4, 146, 152, 155–7, 159–60, 161–4, 166, 183, 190, 195–7, 200
Ptolemy V, 1–4
  death, 7, 20, 44
Ptolemy VI, 10, 17, 20, 22–3, 26, 43–4, 47, 78
  and Alexander Balas, 56–7, 66, 68, 72
  offered Seleukid kingship, 73–5, 121
  and Demetrios II, 75
  death, 75, 77
Ptolemy VII Memphites, 121
Ptolemy VIII, 20, 23, 77–8, 109, 119, 122–5, 130, 135

Ptolemy XI Lathyros, 141, 153–4, 161–4, 168–9, 181, 187
Ptolemy X Alexander I, 141, 148, 153, 161, 163, 168, 181
Ptolemy XI Alexander II, 187, 190
Ptolemy XII, 187–8, 190
Pydna, Macedon, 25, 41

Quinctius Flamininus, T., 8

Raphia, Palestine, 163
Rhagai, Iran, 52, 69
Rhodes, 8, 19
Rhodogune, wife of Demetrios II, 107–108, 116, 118
Rhosos, Kilikia, 32
Ri-in-nu, Parthian queen, 107
Rome, vii–viii, 2, 4–5
  and Attalid kingdom, 7–8
  eastern policy, 8–9, 170, 174, 188, 204
  and Antiochos IV, 17–19, 23
  and Macedon 22, 25
  and Demetrios I, 8–10, 13, 15, 26, 43, 46–7
  and Alexander Balas, 56, 58
  in Asia Minor, 109, 120–1, 131, 182, 187, 197
  and Judaea, 132, 155–6
  and piracy, 167–8
  and Syria, 188–90

Saka nomads, 111, 114–15, 126
Sakastene, 114
Salome Alexandra, Judaean queen, 161, 187, 195–7
Samaria, Palestine, 37, 99, 147, 151
  siege and conquest of, 152–9, 204
Samaritans, 151–2, 157
Samoga, trans-Jordan, 128
Samos, Kommagenean king, 92, 133
Samosata, Kommagene, 92, 133
Samothrace, 23
Sarpedon, Seleukid commander, 81
Selene, daughter of Ptolemy VIII, 131
  wife of Ptolemy IX, 142, 153
  wife of Antiochos VIII, 163
  wife of Antiochos IX, 168
  wife of Antiochos X, 175

widow, 183, 187–91, 195–6
death, 199–200
Seleukeia–in–Gaulan, trans-Jordan, 30
Seleukeia-in-Pieria, Syria, 32, 64, 79, 81–2,
    86, 88–9, 100, 125, 130–1, 148–50, 153,
    157–9, 177, 180, 186, 190, 193–4
Seleukeia-on-the-Kalykadnos, Kilikia, 19,
    101, 169
Seleukeia-on-the-Tigris, Babylonia, 33, 51,
    53, 82, 85–8, 110, 115–17, 171
Seleukeia-Zeugma, Syria, 31, 47, 84, 100,
    109, 193, 195, 199
Seleukid kingdom, decline of, vii–ix
    warships of, 5, 41, 89, 167
    war elephants of, 5–6, 27, 41–2, 64
    kings' names, 9
    wealth, 17–19
    army, 27–8, 62, 111–13
    vulnerability, 60
    government of, 102
    disintegration, 136, 205
    end, 200
    legacy, 201–207
Seleukos IV, position after accession, 1–5,
    13, 18
    and Rome, 3, 8–9, 13–14
    and Pontic war, 6–7
    death, 11–14
    and cities, 29–30
Seleukos V, 116, 118, 124, 130, 134–5
Seleukos VI, 169–70, 174–5
Seleukos, son of Antiochos VII, 114, 116
Sempronius Gracchus, Ti., Roman envoy,
    41, 43–4, 46, 50
Seron, Seleukid commander, 37
Shatt al-Arab, 24
Shechem, Palestine, 177
Sicily, 167
Side, Pamphylia, 67, 109, 120, 167
Sidon, Phoenicia, 64, 88–9, 102, 116, 125,
    132–4, 143, 147, 149–51, 158, 164, 197
Simon Maccabee 80, 82, 89–90, 93–4
Simyra, Syria, 128
Sinai, 22, 104, 121
Skythopolis, Palestine, 99, 152, 154, 156,
    163–4, 182
Soloi, Kilikia, 101, 192
Sophagasenos, Indian king, 3

Sophene, 181, 192
Sosibios, Ptolemaic regent, 13
Spain, 2, 170
Sparta, 27
Straton, lord of Beroia, 177–81, 193
Strato's Tower, Palestine, 156, 159, 162,
    183–4
Susa, Elymais, 4, 52, 68, 70, 78, 80, 85, 87,
    108, 110
Susiana, 4, 52, 62
Syracuse, Sicily, ix, 204
Syria, viii–ix, 3, 6–7, 10, 12, 14, 21, 26,
    28, 31–2, 36, 40, 56, 62, 67, 82–3, 88,
    99–104, 107, 113–14, 116–18, 137, 139,
    166, 170–1, 174, 176, 200
    religion, 144–6, 150, 158, 160
Syrian Wars;
    Fifth, 73
    Sixth, 22–6

Tabai, Iran, 35
Tarsos, Kilikia, 28, 80, 88, 101–102, 148,
    160, 166, 169
Tarutia, Syria, 201
Taurus Mountains, 7, 13, 53, 55, 63, 101,
    104, 120, 160
Tell Hazor, Palestine, 80
Te'udissu (Theodosios), Parthian
    Governor, 108, 111
Theodoros, lord of Philadelphia, 98–9, 159,
    163, 165
Tigraios, Elymaean ruler, 87, 110
Tigranes, Armenian king, 171, 173, 176,
    179, 181, 187–97, 200
Tigranocerta, Armenia, 187, 189
Tigris River, 33, 51, 84–5, 106, 109, 120,
    157, 171, 181–2
Timarchos of Miletos, Seleukid governor of
    Media, 16–17
    rebel, 45–9, 51–4, 204
Trachonitis, trans-Jordan, 103, 144, 183
Tripolis, Syria, 44, 132, 147, 149, 151, 153,
    158, 162, 194
Tryphaina, daughter of Ptolemy VIII, wife
    of Antiochos VIII, 130–1, 141–2, 148,
    174
Tryphon king, 81, 120
    programme, 81

and Judaea, 81–2
  and pirates, 82
  and Babylonia, 81–2
  and Syria, 88–90, 151
  see also Diodotos
'Tryphon', Antiochene rebel, 122–3
Tyre, Phoenicia, 64, 86, 88–9, 102–103, 116, 125, 129, 132–4, 136–8, 143, 145, 149–50, 158, 197

Upper Satrapies, 16–17
Uruk, Babylonia, 110

Via Aquillia, 120, 167

Yueh-chih, nomad state, 53

Zagros Mountains, 52, 69, 82, 85, 110
Zarbienas, Gordyenean king, 198
Zenodotos, chieftain, 55–6, 58, 62
Zenon Kotylas, lord of Philadelphia, 93, 98–9, 126, 159
Zoilos, lord of Dor, 159–60, 162–3, 183